MW00808139

FLAMES OF DISCONTENT

FLAMES OF DISCONTENT

THE 1916 MINNESOTA IRON ORE STRIKE

Gary Kaunonen

University of Minnesota Press

MINNEAPOLIS   LONDON

Published by the University of Minnesota Press
111 Third Avenue South, Suite 290
Minneapolis, MN 55401-2520
http://www.upress.umn.edu

ISBN 978-1-5179-0267-4 (hc)
ISBN 978-1-5179-0268-1 (pb)

A Cataloging-in-Publication record for this book is available from the Library of Congress.

Printed in the United States of America on acid-free paper

The University of Minnesota is an equal-opportunity educator and employer.

22 21 20 19 18 17   10 9 8 7 6 5 4 3 2 1

To Grandma V

CONTENTS

Preface Kitchen Table Politics   ix

Introduction Workers' Rights, Immigrant Voices   1

1 A Place Hard as Iron: Mining's Divided Landscapes   15

2 The Seasonal Struggle: 39
   Labor and Politics in Northern Minnesota

3 Wobbly Firebrands: 69
   Organizing the Finnish Working Class

4 From Strikebreakers to Solidarity: 105
   The Slavic Worker Revolt

5 The Rhetoric of Revolution: 137
   Communicating the Strike

6 Flash Point: Dissent and Violence in 1916   169

Conclusion Rising from the Ashes   205

   Acknowledgments   219
   Notes   223
   Bibliography   235
   Index   249

PREFACE

Kitchen Table Politics

AUGUST 2, 2016, WAS MY GRANDMA VIENA'S ONE HUNDREDTH BIRTHDAY. As I began thinking about this milestone, it dawned on me, about halfway through the writing of this book, that she was born in 1916—admittedly, I was never very good at math. Her family lived in the shadows of the Vermilion and Mesabi iron ranges, tucked down into the swampy, subsistence farming–based valley of the Embarrass River in northeastern Minnesota. The family homestead was located within the boundaries of Waasa Township (named for a province in Finland), which was settled by Finnish immigrants, many of whom were refugees from former industrial lives on the Mesabi and Vermilion iron ranges. Embarrass was the closest thing to a town by her home, and it had an auxiliary local of the Industrial Workers of the World (IWW), the union that organized thousands of workers on the ranges to incite the massive 1916 strike. In a way, my Grandma Viena was born into this struggle—into a family eking out an existence on a subsistence farm during one of Minnesota's most contentious labor upheavals, which was occurring less than ten miles from her home.

She went to high school in Aurora during the Great Depression, daily passing the location where the 1916 strike began. Later, on November 23, 1935, she married a Finnish immigrant named Niilo Kaunonen and settled closer to Embarrass proper. She worked on the family farm, for the local cooperative, and at the Cluett-Peabody Arrow Shirt factory in Virginia. But that little farmhouse surrounded by animal barns, a summer kitchen, a warehouse, hay fields, and, of course, a sauna was her home for decades. She and Niilo, who later Americanized his name to Neal, had made a great but arduous life for themselves and their two children. Her husband was a jack-of-all-trades: he labored on the farm and supplemented the family's income by logging, working on area railroads, and eventually by making his way into the mines. Neal worked for twenty years at the Reserve Mining Company, a short drive from the family farm. Although they both worked outside jobs to support the family and farm, that swampy land tucked down into the Embarrass River valley meant the world to them.

As a kid, I began spending time on that homestead during summers, weekends, and holidays. It was a magical place, though I did not understand how significant it was at that time. Under the house's clapboard siding were the original hand-hewn logs of an immigrant homestead. The warehouse contained the clothes and artifacts of immigrant journeys to America from Finland, and the fields I ran through as a boy were cut by hand out of the dense forests of northern Minnesota. On cold, still nights, the clanging of heavy industrial machines run by unionized mine workers could be heard in the distance. The entire homestead was a museum to my grandparents' determined efforts to make a better life for themselves and their children and grandchildren.

I would learn about and come to understand this struggle as I grew older, especially on Saturday nights in the sauna. I can close my eyes now and remember smoke pouring from the sauna's chimney and the smell of birch wood stoking the fires. Oftentimes, relatives and friends would come over and sauna became a multifamily affair. As a young kid, I took sauna with my dad and younger brother. When I was feeling brave, I would jump from my giant metal wash bucket of tepid, soapy water, scurry up the three steps to the top flight of the tiered benches, sit for a second, feel the immense heat wrap around me, and then head for cover in my bucket of lukewarm water, which sat on the sauna's cool concrete floor.

In that sauna, I learned a valuable rudimentary lesson regarding thermodynamics—hot air rises, cold air sinks—but it was after sauna, when I was supposed to be in bed, that I learned a lot about life. For the adults, time after a sauna was spent sitting around the kitchen table telling stories, discussing current events, and talking politics. I desperately wanted to be a part of these discussions. From my bed, I would quietly dig myself out from under the covers and lie down in front of the heat-exchange register, which looked down onto the kitchen table below. There, in secret, I became a part of those conversations, and it was there that I began to understand what it meant to be "working-class."

Although I do not remember specifics, I do remember that these after-sauna political deliberations were not about Marx, the Industrial Workers of the World, or industrial revolution per se—those were conversations had a couple of generations before—but there were conversations about income inequality, the "bosses," and crooked politicians, along with similarly impassioned discussions about the Minnesota Twins, hunting, and fishing. Later, after Grandpa Neal had died, I remember Paul Wellstone's picture hung with pride, attached by magnets, to Grandma's small refrigerator. That immigrant homestead, and the working-class heroes who lived there, were an introduction to class consciousness that was palpable, raw, and unfiltered. It was working-class politics from working-class people. This emerging perspective was authentic, it was real, and it began to shape the way that I saw the world.

After high school, I went to college, played baseball, dropped out, worked several industrial and service industry jobs (I was escorted off company property from one job at a factory in Mankato after I was found to have passed along a pro-labor political cartoon), and then went back to school. My interest in "labor history" was piqued at Minnesota State University–Mankato when I began reading about the generation of Finnish immigrants who had come before Viena and Neal and organized the Finnish Socialist Federation. I read Marx, the anarchist Peter Kropotkin, and works by organizers of the Industrial Workers of the World. In most cases, these readings were not assigned in classes, but I read them to understand the roots of those kitchen-table political discussions in Embarrass.

After reading Marx's *Theses on Feuerbach* and presenting a controversial interpretation of the paradox of Marxist scholars administering very hierarchical (some might argue exploitative) academic programs during a faculty–student meeting, I found myself in the office of a professor who bluntly asked me, "Where did you get your Marx from?" I paused, not too long, and replied, "From my grandparents." (In addition to Viena and Neal's class consciousness, my mother's side of the family had known Gus Hall, longtime former General Secretary of the

Communist Party–USA.) I was about to launch into an explanation of how I became interested in studies of the working class via my relatives when the professor interrupted and said, "You should talk to [the department head]. He has used Marx in his literary analysis and you should begin to understand Marx in terms of the academy." My mind began to drift at that point because I was certain that I had little interest in academic readings of Marx.

It was, instead, the real, concrete events and the people who had lived through them that interested me. British working-class historian E. P. Thompson described this idea as "bottom-up history" or "history from below."[1] In the midst of my research and writing on the 1916 strike, I began to think about what had brought me to this point. Reflecting on the warm memories of those working-class voices talking politics around a kitchen table, I began to understand that the historical project to capture and chronicle the voices of our working-class past began with Grandma Viena and others in Embarrass—in a little immigrant homestead surrounded by an amazing past. Grandma Viena died on December 17, 2016, her one hundred years a testament to an extraordinary life, lived exceptionally well.

INTRODUCTION

Workers' Rights, Immigrant Voices

ON JUNE 2, 1916, FORTY MOSTLY IMMIGRANT MINE WORKERS FROM THE St. James Mine in Aurora, Minnesota, walked off the job. This seemingly small labor disturbance would mushroom into one of the region's, if not the nation's, most contentious and significant battles between organized labor and management in the early twentieth century. By mid-June, the forty disgruntled mine workers had turned into a hundred, then a thousand, and by July, ten to fifteen thousand mine workers on Minnesota's three iron ranges were idled. The strike had been waged against one of the most powerful and wealthiest corporations in the United States—the Oliver Iron Mining Company (OIMC, or "the Oliver"), a subsidiary of the United States Steel Corporation—as well as several independent mining operations. Unskilled, immigrant mine workers had brought billionaire J. P. Morgan's legacy corporation to an unwelcomed reckoning with organized labor. This stark reality was the truly remarkable feat of the strike, and a testament to the developing class consciousness of exploited immigrants, many of whom had been in the United States for less than a decade, working in and around the open pits and underground shafts of Minnesota's iron ranges.

The strikers' grievances—low wages, long hours, and abhorrent working conditions—were the standard complaints of many industrial workers who had previously engaged in labor disputes throughout the United States. More uncommon was the revolutionary industrial union the immigrant mine workers chose to represent them in this contentious clash between labor and management. The Industrial Workers of the World (IWW) rushed to the Minnesota iron ranges to rapidly organize the striking workforce. Agitating, organizing, and unifying the ranges'

1

multiethnic population in this David versus Goliath industrial battle was the anarchist-branded, somewhat infamous revolutionary industrial union known as "The Wobblies" to their members, and the "I.W.W.s" or "I Won't Works" to mining companies and their industrial cohorts. The Oliver's absolute control on the Minnesota iron ranges was all the more notable given the extreme repression meted out by company guards, police, and vigilantes before, during, and after the strike. Although their efforts were widely considered a defeat, when the dust had settled in September 1916, workers returned to the mines with the promise of a 10 percent pay increase and an eight-hour workday.

The strike was the third, and last, of three major industrial disputes in the Upper Midwest's mining industry during the first two decades of the twentieth century. Unlike the 1907 Mesabi Iron Range Strike in Minnesota and the 1913–14 Copper Strike in Michigan's Upper Peninsula—both led by the Western Federation of Miners (WFM)—the 1916 upheaval was administered by the Wobblies and can be understood as a radical extension of the WFM's prior organizing efforts. Previous pitched battles between organized immigrant workers and management had brought labor relations to a tense stalemate, but the disgruntlement of northern Minnesota's immigrant mine workers finally reached critical mass in the summer of 1916. The ranges would never be the same. The efforts of the Wobblies helped to lay the foundation for a sustained class consciousness in northern Minnesota and surrounding environs, especially among the region's Finnish immigrant workers. The strike also saw labor conscious Finns' onetime foil, strikebreaking South Slavic immigrants, joining forces with their immigrant fellow workers to create a wellspring of union sentiment across the ranges.

This immigrant solidarity, fostered before and during the 1916 strike, frustrated many in Minnesota, especially mining company managers. Craft and trades unions, such as those in the fold of the American Federation of Labor (AFL), balked at the IWW's efforts to extend union membership to immigrant radicals and offered little help to such workers. Progressive politicians such as Hibbing, Minnesota, mayor Victor L. Power saw the IWW as an unorganized nuisance and attempted to steer striking workers toward affiliation with the AFL through the United Mine Workers of America. As the strike raged on throughout the ranges, a citizens' committee with support from the mining companies was set up to drive many of the IWW's most prominent organizers from northern Minnesota. To the chagrin of mining company managers, this vigilante-style organization of middle-class businessmen lost its gumption. At the prodding of the company officials, Minnesota governor Joseph A. A. Burnquist contributed to a nefarious plot to deport the IWW's leaders from the iron ranges. After the governor's "law and order" proclamation was issued, striking workers were engaged by mining company thugs in an ill-fated exchange of gunfire. In the melee, two people died and several others were severely wounded. Although it seemed that the strikers were attempting to defend themselves from hired gun thugs in their own home, they were in fact charged with first-degree murder. Astonishingly, so were IWW organizers, who were more than thirty miles away at the time. The organizers, and the striking workers involved in the shootings, were arrested and deported from the ranges and sent to county jail in Duluth.

To many, the 1916 strike was simply a pitched battle between labor and management, but underlying most of the anti-IWW sentiment was a less than subtle distrust of and animosity toward the region's large immigrant population. As cogs in a rapidly industrializing machinery, immigrants from Finland, southeastern Europe, and Italy had little voice in the conditions of their labor. Thus, the mining bosses' issue during the strike was not so much with unions—some skilled trades in area mines were organized—but rather that the IWW was attempting to organize the cheap, unskilled immigrant labor that mines depended on for profits in the booming economic conditions that occurred during World War I. Slavic immigrants from the Austro-Hungarian Empire were also accused of un-American sentiment as the paranoia of World War I exacerbated fears that the IWW was being funded in part by European governments. Mining company management, in particular, chided the prospects of an industrial union that gave immigrant workers and their families a voice of their own.

History as a Human Right
In this book, the struggle to represent the voices of Iron Range immigrants is an attempt to posthumously restore agency to members of

Minnesota's working class. This voice, individual and collective, should be thought of as nothing less than a human right. The denial of such an inalienable right has historically been a common way for American exceptionalists, oligarchs, union busters, and repressive governments to censor the past, control the present, and squelch future dissent. Being a part of the historical record and public memory should be a basic human right. Curiously, while the United Nations includes a "History" in its thirty-article "Universal Declaration of Human Rights," it does not include *having a history* as one of those rights.[1] Having a history bestows a sense of dignity, identity, place, and unity among individuals and groups, and these qualities provide an essential understanding of what it means to be human and, more important, humane. The censorship or silencing of history is no less detrimental than the withholding of dignity, education, equality, justice, or liberty. It could even be argued that having a history and knowing one's place in history is a fundamental component in establishing and identifying many of the United Nations' thirty articles of universal human rights. In this manner, history may in fact be the precursor of all basic and universal human rights.

Extending from this idea, the chapters in this book are an assertion of history as a human right for striking immigrant workers on the Minnesota iron ranges. Oftentimes multiple perspectives on the same event, experience, or person can form a mosaic of understanding that generates a comprehensive depiction of a historical experience. More often, though, class interests, hierarchical rigidity, and power relationships determine the dominant perspectives established in history and disregard perspectives and voices that run counter to customary American themes of patriotism, positive narratives of assimilation, and adherence to capitalist dogma. This book is meant to counteract these traditional narratives with a working-class examination of the 1916 Minnesota Iron Ore Strike. The book's title, taken from the Wobblies' popular *Little Red Songbook,* which held a cherished collection of "Songs to Fan the Flames of Discontent," is a commemoration of the IWW's original intent, which was to poke, prod, and prompt the public to contemplate the plight of those who had been exploited, dislocated, or silenced in the pursuit of their basic human rights. This book's narrative presents a type of critical history that chronicles a pivotal instance of this assertion of fundamental equality. In bringing this history to readers, the work embraces the use of historical sources created by people involved in the 1916 strike to speak for these underrepresented historical figures, while at the same time seeking to engage current and future generations in a dialogue about the struggles of our past.

Striking workers on Minnesota's iron ranges were not, in most cases, afforded the right of having their own history or the opportunity to posthumously be engaged with contemporary dialogue, because their plight and politics fell on the wrong side of celebratory, traditional narratives in American history. As an example, Minnesota's iron ranges bear the stamp of America's great industrialists as buildings, cities, and parks were named for celebrated captains of industry. There is the town of Coleraine in Itasca County, just east of Grand Rapids, named for Oliver Iron Mining Company manager Thomas F. Cole. The high school in Coleraine bears the name of John C. Greenway, manager of the Oliver's Canisteo Iron Mining District. Olcott Park, in Virginia, Minnesota, was named after Oliver Company and Duluth, Missabe, and Iron Range Railway president William J. Olcott. This list of honorary industrialist namesakes goes on. But the number of places named in honor of the mostly immigrant workers who created the area's wealth is remarkably shorter. These sites are often confined to rural roads named for immigrant homesteaders who were refugees from company blacklists or industrial accidents.

This book offers a corrective to the fetishism of American exceptionalism, progress-oriented narratives of industrial development, and the celebration of men who exploited immigrant labor to achieve outlandish personal wealth. Instead, this account of the 1916 strike proposes that the stories of the people who struggled to make a living on Minnesota's Iron Range deserve equal recognition with the men who profited from their lives and labor. In many ways, then, this book is a statement of a fundamental human right—having a history—and its research and writing toward this end offer a critical perspective developed with the singular goal of narrating a history of the 1916 strike through the voices of those working-class immigrants who lived that history.

Several themes contribute to the strike's exceptional story. The book seeks to unfurl the events of the strike in three acts, which provide a

Oliver Iron Mining Company officials from northern Minnesota and Michigan photographed in Duluth in 1903. Included in the photograph are Oliver president Thomas F. Cole (14), vice president William J. Olcott (13), and regional superintendents Pentecost Mitchell of Hibbing (2), J. H. Hearding of Eveleth (4), and Charles Trezona of Ely (7). Photograph by Louis P. Gallagher. Courtesy of Archives and Special Collections, Kathryn A. Martin Library, University of Minnesota–Duluth.

framework for the complex and violent interactions between organized labor and industrial employers. First, the book examines the landscapes, both physical and social, of the early twentieth-century iron ranges. It was in these contested spaces that escalating conflicts between immigrant workers and their industrial overseers occurred. The book then delves into the development of class consciousness on the ranges, as well as the ethnic animosity facing mine workers and their families. One of the most difficult aspects facing those leading the 1916 strike was uniting ethnic groups that had previously been at odds. Earlier labor conflicts had pitted South Slavic strikebreakers against Finnish and Italian strikers, and the acrimony between these ethnicities played a large role in hindering labor solidarity throughout the Great Lakes region. The strike of 1916 marked a pivotal turning point between the ranges' multiethnic populations, which would change the workings of labor solidarity for years to come. Finally, the book offers a thorough examination of the role that politics played in shaping this labor upheaval. Three separate entities competed for the hearts and minds of the ranges' working-class population in the 1910s. While company-hired gun thugs and the IWW battled in the streets of range towns, and as the state governor secretly plotted with mine managers to bring an end to the strike, Progressive politicians orated reformist visions of a more equitable Iron Range. These political maneuverings had a great impact on the strike and began to shape the future of our nation's labor and social justice movements.

Contested Workscapes and Cultural Spaces of Discontent

The first three chapters of the book offer introductions to the land, people, and places involved in setting the historical stage for the labor turmoil that took place during the summer of 1916. This introduction to the ranges' varied landscapes establishes the context for working-class life in northern Minnesota. Exploring several diverse aspects of landscape, including physical settings, labor–management relations, and cultural, social, and work life, the initial chapters provide the historical backdrop for the strike. This examination includes pointed illustrations of the influence and control established by mining companies and the skewed balance of socioeconomic relations that defined the particular experiences of the Iron Range's immigrant populations.

Mining companies dominated the physical landscape of Minnesota's iron ranges. The measure of this control would ebb and flow over time, causing a great deal of conflict between workers and the corporate men who administered their surrounding environs. While this contested landscape is essential to understanding the 1916 strike, the ranges' workscapes—the physical places where employees labored, were injured (sometimes fatally), organized, clashed with the bosses, and went on strike—provide context for the development of class consciousness prior to the strike. Equally significant are cultural spaces of discontent where workers and their families gathered in solidarity off company time and property. During the late nineteenth and early twentieth centuries, Minnesota's Iron Country was a land of immigrants who brought their own traditions and cultural values with them to the United States.

Once on the iron ranges, the reality of being in an industrial, corporate-controlled setting forced these immigrants to reevaluate their cultural, economic, and social circumstances. To better deal with these imposed settings, many sought to re-create familiar physical and social surroundings. The ability of architecture and landscapes to reinvent, sustain, or create new identities in an adopted homeland is especially significant when examining the entirety of the immigrant experience on the iron ranges.

In these contested landscapes, immigrants provided a counterargument to American capital's requirement of assimilation and exploitation to achieve success and prosperity. Immigrant social halls, boardinghouses, cooperatives, and domestic spaces left a significant cultural footprint on Iron Range communities. Interpreting such places as cultural spaces of discontent brings clearer focus to the analysis of labor–management relations. In 1916, imposing industrial displays of power and prestige created by labor bosses established a landscape of deep social and cultural division. For example, the Oliver Iron Mining Company's offices in Hibbing were professionally designed and constructed to display a sense of control, hierarchy, and authority. Conversely, vernacular or "ordinary" cultural landscapes expressed a disregard for prevailing notions of power by presenting buildings and structures made by workers in their own interests. During the 1916 strike, these buildings constituted the physical embodiment of the immigrant working-class community. They hosted labor meetings, set the stage for street parades, and provided a space for the funerals of slain workers. Within this setting, the ranges' physical and social landscapes were primed for upheaval. All that was needed was the unifying force of the IWW.

Labor Solidarity across the Ethnic Divide

Minnesota's iron ranges have a sense of place and an identity that is all their own. Similarly, the people of northern Minnesota have a working-class identity that is tied to the landscape in which they live. During the early twentieth century, this collective identity was severely fragmented. The key disconnect between the development of a more inclusive identity was the segmentation and segregation of the working class through ethnic divides. In many ways, the ethnic strife between immigrants, who were often competing against one another for work, bitterly divided one group from another. This was a major stumbling block in advancing the labor solidarity needed to confront industrial leaders.

More troubling, immigrant workers in northern Minnesota existed on the margins of the American working class, and well-established union organizations such as the American Federation of Labor (AFL) were reluctant to represent them. In fact, few labor organizations sought to engage the iron ranges' divided ethnic groups, much less organize them into one collective group for a massive labor action. As the IWW worked to organize immigrants, it took pains to create effective media, hire organizers, and craft symbolic representations that highlighted industrial solidarity across the ethnic divide. The Wobblies also sought to educate and inform immigrant laborers about what it meant to be an industrial worker in the United States. This important work was conducted across northern Minnesota at innovative institutions, including the Work People's College near Duluth. The melding of immigrant identities with those of an international industrial worker was the IWW's goal as it struggled to cultivate solidarity among immigrant rank and filers.

In this book, the development of labor solidarity across the ethnic divide is situated in an examination of relations among Finnish, Italian, and South Slavic workers on the ranges. These three ethnic groups are highlighted because of their vastly differing experiences in the years leading up to the 1916 strike. Finnish immigrants earned a reputation as "fiery followers of the Red Flag" and were passionate, early supporters of labor radicalism on the ranges. Finns struck early and often against the power of Iron Range capitalists, and their efforts resulted in a massive strike across the Mesabi Range in 1907. This strike was led by Italian immigrant Teofilo Petriella, who represented the discontent of the Italian workforce. But the experiences of the area's South Slavic workers were much different during this time. Mining companies recruited more than one thousand Slovenians, Croatians, and Serbians to break the labor conflict. Intense animosity between these ethnic groups ensued.

What happened in the years between 1907 and 1916 was nothing short of incredible. In less than a decade, the class consciousness among the South Slavic population mushroomed and the 1916 strike saw once-divided ethnicities working together to bring about a major upheaval to

Finnish and Slovenian mine workers pose for a photograph in front of a headframe on the Mesabi Range, circa 1907. Often work gangs were composed of multiple ethnicities who could not communicate well on the job. Mining companies preferred this dynamic because workers were not able to discuss conditions or pay. Courtesy of the Immigration History Research Center, University of Minnesota.

the ranges' status quo. This upwelling of labor solidarity—*solidaarisuus* in Finnish, *solidarietà* in Italian, and *solidarnost* in Slovenian and Croatian— even saw Slavs attending union rallies in Finnish immigrant halls, sites that only nine years earlier would have seemed like an improbable vision of unity. Sadly, while Finnish and Italian immigrants had experienced the blowback from attempts at labor organization prior to 1916, South Slavic immigrants would feel the unfettered wrath of American capital during the strike. Their involvement in the American labor movement was hard fought and, in some cases, deadly.

The Politics of Organized Labor

Throughout the years between 1907 and 1916, a new force entered the ranges' economic and social setting: Progressive politics. A response to the power of "robber barons" such as Carnegie, Vanderbilt, and Rockefeller in the late nineteenth and early twentieth centuries, Progressives sought to provide a check and balance against their economic extremes. Although the Progressive politicians in northern Minnesota seemed like natural allies for organized labor's fight against the mining companies in 1916, they proved to be anything but. While Progressives sought to quell the power of unregulated capitalism, they were also ideologically at odds with the revolutionary fervor advocated by the IWW. This break in perspective and intended outcomes fractured the working-class movements and created an insurmountable rift between the two entities that could have fundamentally altered labor relations in the area. Later chapters in the book examine the dynamic between the immigrant working-class population and Progressive politicians, as well as the role that communication and rhetorical strategy played prior to and during the strike on the part of the IWW, Progressive politicians such as Hibbing's mayor, Victor Power, and mining companies.

Especially significant and new to scholarship on the 1916 strike was the role played by Minnesota's Republican governor Joseph A. A. Burnquist. The governor's collusion with mining companies and county law enforcement to deport immigrant mine workers and organizers without due process of law demonstrated the unnerving lengths that men in power would go to in seeking to maintain control over other human beings. Burnquist's intervention during the strike was especially problematic because it typified a general response toward immigrants and their attempts to better their laboring and social conditions in the late nineteenth and early twentieth centuries. Other troubling events involving elected officials occurred across the labor movement in the years following the strike.

In July 1917, Bemidji's mayor led a group of vigilantes in their deportation of about twenty-five IWW members from that town. Bemidji's company-influenced newspaper lauded the mayor's efforts. This type of governmentally sanctioned kidnapping was rampant in July of that year as a similar incident occurred in Bisbee, Arizona, though on a much larger scale. On July 12, 1917, Phelps Dodge mining company officials, along with local law enforcement and deputized vigilantes, deported almost 1,300 striking workers and union sympathizers into the southwestern desert. As it had during the 1916 Iron Ore Strike, the IWW led the efforts in Bisbee. Known as the Bisbee Deportation, a multiethnic group including Mexicans, Serbians, Irish, and Finnish strikers were herded onto manure-caked cattle cars at gunpoint and ferried into the sun-soaked, waterless desert. Their deportation ended more than one hundred miles away in Hermanas, New Mexico. Amazingly, only two people died; one deputized vigilante was shot by a striker who refused to be taken captive, while three other deputies shot a striker. Neither state nor federal agencies held any party accountable for what was essentially the kidnapping of more than a thousand people.[2]

Burnquist's actions in 1916 also characterized the response that labor leaders faced for assisting immigrants in their efforts to establish a voice in industrial America. Wobbly organizer Frank Little's short life was reflective of this experience. After joining the IWW in 1906 and becoming an increasingly effective organizer, he came under near-constant surveillance and harassment. Much of this harassment included threats on his life. Little was deported twice while organizing in the Lake Superior basin, once at gunpoint by vigilantes in 1913 during a dockworkers' strike in Superior, Wisconsin, and again in 1916 after Burnquist's decree. A year later, on August 1, 1917, Little was found lynched under a railroad trestle in Butte, Montana. He had been dragged behind a car before being hanged. As with the Bisbee Deportation, no charges were filed.[3] Governor Burnquist's conspiracy with mining company managers to trample the human rights of immigrants and organizers alike had a precedent. He was certainly not the first corrupt elected official to treat organized labor unfairly, but his actions during the 1916 strike epitomized the backroom maneuvering and political intrigue that plagued the struggle to organize the nation's most vulnerable workers.

In total, the political consequences stemming from the strike of 1916 were of national importance. After labor actions on the ranges ended in September, and a continuation strike in northern Minnesota's logging camps began in January 1917, the IWW seemed to be agitating and organizing on borrowed time. The full political and law-enforcement resources of state and federal governments began a national assault on the Wobblies and their allies. IWW offices were raided, literature was burned, organizers were imprisoned, and immigrant members were deported from the country. The assault on the One Big Union, as the IWW referred to itself, was massive, swift, and well orchestrated.

Less than a year after the strike's conclusion, Minnesota became the second state to pass criminal syndicalist legislation, and in September 1917 it was the first state to convict someone under this law. As historian John E. Haynes has argued, "techniques used to suppress the IWW in northern Minnesota were later extended to pacifists, war dissenters, and members of the Nonpartisan League who faced official persecution for their beliefs and activities."[4] Criminal syndicalist legislation, which outlawed actions and groups espousing revolutionary methods of economic, political, or social change, was just one volley in the repressive barrage of World War I–era persecution. Antisedition, anti-immigrant, and antilabor legislation at the state and federal levels stripped citizens and immigrants alike of fundamental human rights, along with the civil liberties guaranteed in the Bill of Rights.

The 1916 strike's legacy was not only of regional or state significance but of national importance as the exacting legislation used to discipline labor on Minnesota's Iron Range laid the foundation for authoritarian actions and legislation used in the repressive World War I years and the subsequent Red Scare era of the late 1910s and early 1920s. These transformations dramatically changed the political and social landscape for organized labor. With this sense of national, regional, and local significance in mind, this book provides a unique interdisciplinary and critical history of the 1916 strike that presents and preserves the perspective and voices of striking workers and their families. The repressive barrage of legal maneuverings, harassment by law enforcement, and violence of hired mining company thugs sought to silence the immigrant workforce in 1916. The following history seeks to restore voice to those silenced by chronicling the fanned flames of discontent through the experiences of those who lived through one of Minnesota's most extraordinary labor upheavals.

1 A PLACE HARD AS IRON

Mining's Divided Landscapes

The camp was located in a mudhole, foul smelling water all about
and refuse everywhere; forty men were housed in a shack 28x16
(roughly estimated), which was almost devoid of ventilation.
—*Hartley Mine inspector, Mesabi Range, 1908*

UNDERSTANDING THE VARIOUS LANDSCAPES THAT DEFINED THE IRON
Range during the late nineteenth and early twentieth centuries provides
important context for the 1916 strike. The study of landscape can help to
explain the interactions between people and place as workers attempted
to find a voice in tightly controlled and corporative physical and social
settings. Understanding landscapes as a backdrop for the historical actors and actions of the 1916 strike demands that we first understand the
physical spaces in which these people lived and worked. Certainly, industrial corporations such as U.S. Steel dominated this landscape, but
perhaps just as demanding was the actual physical setting of Minnesota's
Iron Country. Cold, isolated, and unforgiving are qualifiers that defined
this hardscrabble region. Mining company exploitation of natural and
human resources occasioned a setting that was primed for fiery worker
revolt. Metaphorically speaking, all that was needed was a match. The
IWW provided such a transformative device, but not without the contextual pieces of immigrant communities, the struggle for union representation, and the fight to bring industrial democracy to an almost
completely controlled corporate landscape.

To those outside the state, the ranges' physical landscape was highly
valued because of one thing: reddish-orange iron ore. A raw material in

the production of steel, iron ore drove the United States' economy in the late nineteenth and early twentieth centuries. Perhaps no other material meant so much to a nation that was building an industrial legacy in a time of unprecedented economic growth. The building of this legacy benefited the few while it exploited the many. For those who applied raw labor power to the mining of raw industrial materials, the meager recompense for dangerous and deadly work was increasingly questioned. In many ways, the wealth of Wall Street tycoons and robber barons such as Andrew Carnegie, John D. Rockefeller, and J. P. Morgan was built with the sweat of Minnesota's iron ore mine workers. For such robber barons, immigrant laborers who were good enough to risk their lives in area mines were not good enough to have a say in their own laboring conditions. This contradiction, amplified by repeated calls for industrial democracy, occasioned a tinder-dry cultural, economic, political, and social landscape, waiting for a match to light the fires of worker revolt and revolution. The IWW and its revolutionary industrial unionism provided the much-needed spark in 1916 when northern Minnesota erupted during a workers' insurrection that lasted four months. There was a context to this uprising: the fanned flames of discontent did not originate overnight or with the IWW's first appearance on the iron ranges. Rather, the parched relations between labor and management on the ranges followed a trajectory that arced over time and across immigrant communities, labor, and landscape.

Lives on Minnesota's iron ranges were almost entirely sculpted by the influence and power of million-dollar corporations tasked with the profitable extraction of iron ore at the expense of the environment and the people who gave their sweat, toil, and at times lives to reddish-orange iron ore. Mined Minnesota iron ore provided the base ingredient for the steel that propelled the United States to victory in World Wars I and II, allowed massive structures in expanding megalopolises to be built up, and provided the structure for transportation vessels to haul grain, cargo, and other foodstuffs down the Great Lakes to hungry populations. These were a few aspects of what iron ore provided for the United States, and while absentee industrialists often get most of the credit for the industrial foresight, strength, and wealth that iron ore created, the people who actually did the work to create this wealth get little recognition. In order to establish the historical setting that occasioned the 1916 strike, this chapter provides a contextual examination of the land, communities, cultural activities, and work lives of the historical actors who made up the physical and social landscapes of Minnesota's iron ranges.

Industrial Frontier: Mining the Physical Landscape

Composed of three separate ranges, Minnesota's Iron Country was both home and workplace for tens of thousands of people during the late nineteenth and early twentieth centuries. The northernmost range, the Vermilion, was the first to support a commercial mine, and by 1883 there was full production at the appropriately named Minnesota Mine. Most of the mines on the Vermilion Range operated as underground properties. Mine workers sank deep shafts into the earth, blasted iron ore–bearing rock, and hoisted the hard ore rock to the surface. It was dark, difficult, and often deadly work. Mining boomtowns sprang up on the Vermilion to supply the mines and the mine workers. Tower, Soudan, Winton, and Ely (the Vermilion's largest urban area, approaching five thousand people in 1920) were among the range's fledgling communities, carved from the rocky, undulating, and dense surrounding wilderness.[1]

While the Vermilion Range was the site of Minnesota's first iron ore boom, the Mesabi Range ores were the largest in both size and financial value. Beginning in the summer of 1890, what would become the world's largest iron range was being explored to assess profitability. Over time, the mighty Mesabi (also seen as Mesaba, Mesabe, or Missabe) would stretch in a southwest to northeast line: from Coleraine in Itasca County, then northeast over the St. Louis County line, dipping only four miles southward at Virginia to encompass mines in the Eveleth area, and then regaining course northeast toward Biwabik. In total, the Mesabi Range stretched for more than eighty-seven miles in Minnesota's Arrowhead Region.[2]

The Mesabi differed from the Vermilion in that its iron ore was often close to the surface, soft, and at times located in relatively sandy soil. Thus, the mines of the Mesabi often started as underground ventures and then switched to open-pit mines. In such cases where pit mines developed, the top layers of non-ore-carrying material had to be "stripped" to reach the ore. Stripping crews became common sights all

This panoramic view of the Hull–Rust–Mahoning Mine in Hibbing, Minnesota, in 1929 shows the Grand Canyon–like features of the massive open-pit landscape. During this time, the walls of the pits were terraced so that narrow-gauge tracked trains could haul iron ore from the depths of the mine. Photograph by Peter Schawang. Courtesy of the Library of Congress Prints and Photographs Division.

along the Mesabi. Other mines began as pits and grew to astonishing dimensions—human-made Grand Canyons. One pit mine, the eventual aggregation of three once separate mines, the Hull–Rust–Mahoning, grew to be the largest iron ore pit mine in the world at more than three miles in length, a mile and a half in width, and depths diving to more than six hundred feet.

With mines growing to such sizes, mechanization was inevitable on the Mesabi. Huge steam shovels that swallowed ore-carrying earth, attended to by mostly immigrant crews, liberated the Mesabi's riches. Locomotives steamed out of the massive pits on narrow-gauge rails carrying the precious cargo. At the time of northern Minnesota's mining boom, everything seemed big on the Mesabi, including the municipal areas. Hibbing, the area's largest city, was located at the western end of the Range and grew to almost twenty thousand people (including the surrounding mining locations) by the 1920s. Virginia, approaching a population of ten thousand, was the Range's "Queen City" and the cultural and social hub of the eastern Mesabi.

The last of Minnesota's three iron ranges to be discovered was the Cuyuna Range, located among the hills, shallow lakes, and surrounding farm fields of Crow Wing County. Mined profitably for the first time

A PLACE HARD AS IRON

in 1911, the Cuyuna Range never attained the importance of the Mesabi or held the prestige of the Vermilion but did have deposits of highly valued manganese iron ore—known locally as "bog ore"—and for a time was a leading producer. Located almost a hundred miles southwest of the Mesabi, Cuyuna ore was different from Mesabi and Vermilion ores in that the ore bodies were located deep underground, required a good deal of labor just to reach workable loads, and had to be mined by underground shaft or deep open pits. Some of the iron ore was hard rock as on the Vermilion and some was soft like the Mesabi's. The Cuyuna mining district was also composed of two iron ore ranges, one north and the other south, which were separated by approximately four miles. Owing to the Cuyuna's rather late discovery of ore bodies in 1903, surrounding municipal areas never grew to the size of those on the Mesabi. The Cuyuna's largest urban area was Crosby, which peaked at 3,500 people in 1920. Ironton was the next most populous municipal area with more than a thousand residents, but the rest of the Cuyuna's urban areas (Trommald, Riverton, and Manganese) struggled to reach and sustain populations of more than five hundred.

Perhaps the most unique aspect of the iron ranges' physical landscape was their continual alteration by human labor. From the cutting of vast stands of trees and the building of entire towns, to the digging of massive pits diving hundreds of feet below the Earth's surface, to the piling of mountains of overburden from stripping operations and waste material hundreds of feet into the air, the iron ranges were an industrially sculpted landscape. It was a landscape dependent on raw human power for its survival, but not independent of machines to bring the fruits of human labor to outside markets.

Port cities like Duluth, Superior, and Two Harbors provided convenient water connections to transportation networks on the Great Lakes. They were located some seventy miles from the pits and underground shafts of the Mesabi, Vermilion, and Cuyuna ranges, so a rail-linked infrastructure was key to the early expansion of the area. As environmental historian William Cronon has shown, a "hinterland" such as Minnesota's iron ranges exists in a codependent relationship with an urban metropolis. Recognizing the interconnectedness of city and country, Cronon's work establishes the vital economic and social links between two seemingly independent geographic locations. Just as Chicago became a metropolis for the Midwestern United States' hinterland, Duluth played a similar role in its relationship to the iron ranges.

In examining and understanding the economic and physical landscapes of the Iron Range, the influence of Duluth's maritime connections to the outside world was extremely significant. The iron ore, which brought wealth to capitalists while occasioning the exploitation of thousands of mostly immigrant workers, was insignificant if not for Duluth–Superior and its ports. Likewise, the region's railways or, as Cronon would term them, "artificial corridors," connected the raw commodity of the ranges through a dense wilderness to the docks that shipped the ore to steel mills farther down the Great Lakes. In explaining the relationship between seemingly disconnected physical spaces, Cronon's "metropolis–hinterland model" conveys the importance of industrial landscapes to the development of labor–management relations on the ranges. It does this by providing a way to think about the tangible and intangible ties between mining company officials in Duluth and the everyday struggles of miners working some one hundred miles away.[3]

While the tangible links of Cronon's model are readily apparent, the intangible connections—the economic, political, and social landscapes shared by Duluth and the ranges—had the most profound effect on mine workers. Because much of the ranges' physical location was within the political boundaries of St. Louis County, and because Duluth was the county seat, the city's importance as a center of corporate and governmental power had great implications for labor actions that culmi-

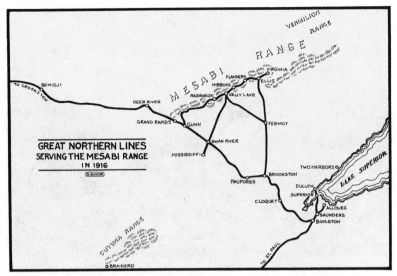

The Great Northern Railway was one of several railroads operating in northern Minnesota at the time of the 1916 strike. Trains carried both iron ore and passengers from the mines of the Mesabi Range to the metropolitan centers of Duluth and Superior. From Ralph W. Hidy et al., *The Great Northern Railway: A History.*

nated in the 1916 strike. Administrative communications by telephone and telegraph between mining company managers in Duluth and their subordinates on the ground in range towns determined strategies to quell worker revolt during the strike. The city's importance to the IWW was significant as well. Early organizers on the scene in Range towns were sent from Duluth. Perhaps most important, when Minnesota's governor, Joseph Burnquist, made a law-and-order proclamation that provided the legal and rhetorical imperatives to facilitate the deportation of the IWW's leaders from the ranges, Duluth was the location of their eventual trials and incarcerations. As an economic and political center in northern Minnesota, Duluth played a major role in strike events that happened in the Iron Range hinterland.

Although links between the Iron Range and Duluth were, of course, physical, as lengthy, steel lines of railroad tracks breeched the vast wilderness, they shared more subtle, emotional connections as well. The

Rail tracks leading to the end of an ore dock in Duluth, circa 1902. Docks like these represented the end of the line for Iron Range ores in Minnesota. From here the ore was shipped down the Great Lakes for processing at huge steel mills. Photograph by Crandall & Fletcher Studio. Courtesy of Archives and Special Collections, Kathryn A. Martin Library, University of Minnesota–Duluth.

transportation corridors etched into the landscape by passenger trains were traversed back and forth by thousands of people as the mines boomed and busted. Travelers, most often immigrants looking to forge a better life, fleeing oppression, or ending a long period of time apart from a loved one, looked to the railway as a connector of landscapes and lives with admiration and affection. One such traveler was Polly Bullard, who was hired to teach at Eveleth's Fayal Mine School. She recalled a November 12, 1908, train trip from Duluth to the Range: "The ride up here was most interesting. The types of people, the configuration of the land, and the arrangement and general appearance of the towns all along the way are entirely different from anything I had seen before." She continued:

> At Duluth the train ran for some time along the lakeshore, and the view was truly wonderful. The sun was rising as we pulled out, and shone through the lake mist and glanced back from the water like a painting

A PLACE HARD AS IRON

of [British landscape painter Joseph Mallord William] Turner. Away out, apparently rising right out of the water, were great high cranes and derricks and a revolving bridge, and up from the shore ran miles and miles of elevated track with hundreds of little ore cars standing on them.[4]

Although distanced some seventy or so miles from Eveleth and the Mesabi, Duluth was both the beginning and the end of Minnesota's iron ranges. As the metropolitan heart to the ranges' hinterlands, the city received the red ore while pumping people, promise, and supplies to the surrounding region's isolated communities.

Boomtowns: Minnesota's Range Communities

For most workers and their families, if they had them, the ranges' social setting was highly controlled by the mining companies. The omnipresent influence of mining company hierarchy, a moral code influenced by corporative industrial mores, and the ownership of vast tracts of land made up a social landscape that was tightly regulated and regimented by an ever-vigilant management class. In most places on the ranges during the late nineteenth and early twentieth centuries, mining companies had, at the very least, some influence on the population, and in many cases exerted great power over the everyday lives of area inhabitants. Essentially, there were two basic social spaces on the iron ranges: company and municipal. Mine workers and their families could live on company property in corporately regulated housing or off company property in one of the ranges' municipal areas. While most municipalities were located off company holdings, there was one well-known company-owned town, Coleraine, which was designed and administered by the Oliver Iron Mining Company (OIMC) for its Canisteo District employees. Although located away from company property, most of the ranges' urban areas, such as Hibbing, Virginia, Chisholm, Mountain Iron, Biwabik, and Aurora, to a name a few, were less corporately regulated but still within the sphere of mining company influence. One such municipality was Eveleth. Describing this town's surrounding landscape, teacher Polly Bullard wrote in the early twentieth century, "From one window of our school we can look nine miles away. I have never seen such a sweep

A bird's-eye view of a typical mining location shows the mix of building types available to mine workers, circa 1910. Housing was often divvied up by a class-based system of hierarchy related to type of work in the mines. Skilled workers tended to live in balloon-framed dwellings, while unskilled workers, often immigrants, lived in log cabins or tar-paper shacks. The large building in the center of the photograph is likely an office or "clubhouse" for employees. Courtesy of the Iron Range Research Center, Minnesota Discovery Center.

of sky anywhere excepting mid-ocean, and ever since I have been here it has been filled with great gray and silver snow clouds rolling and sweeping along. The town itself struggles over the hills. Most of the houses are little yellow and blue things but there are some very comfortable residences."[5]

Because Eveleth was independent of mining company management, it offered a less controlled and structured social setting. Polly's land-lady, Mrs. Samuelson, exercised the full expression of this limited freedom as the schoolteacher remarked: "Mrs. Samuelson is a strange creature. Her Finnish name is Mikki Koukkari. She is a rabid Socialist and all the Socialists who come here to speak stay at her house. One came Saturday night and they had a grand to-do down in the kitchen till two in the morning. Socialism is rampant here among the miners."[6] In spite of socialism's influence among mine workers, the power of the mining companies and their antithetical attitudes toward labor unions

A PLACE HARD AS IRON

and anticorporate political parties was never fully extinguished. Mining company managers were able to exert control and power on the ranges' municipalities by sitting on local governments, school boards, or charity organizations. Company officials also often ran candidates in local elections who were friendly to the interests of the iron ore industry and thus exerted a great deal of influence on local economies and social affairs. Despite Polly's bucolic and freewheeling depiction of Eveleth and its political scene, the ranges' towns and cities were not always so hospitable to workers and alternative politics.

Outside of municipalities, the only other option for living on the ranges was the so-called company "location." Underground mine workers often lived in balloon-framed houses, or workers' cabins. The quality of these dwellings varied depending on work status, native country, or social affiliation. Men working as semiskilled and unskilled laborers in the open-pit mines had it much worse and lived in "camps," which were, in most cases, crudely constructed wood-framed and sawn-timber shanties. In the Mountain Iron District in July 1908, these camps consisted of more than thirty-four rudimentary dwellings at the Mountain Iron, Higgins, Virginia, and Stephens mines. The camps were designed with the intention to fit the most men into the least amount of space. Individual dwellings were intended mostly for single men, because thirty of the thirty-four living spaces did not include quarters for married workers. There were four camps for mine workers with spouses, known as "husband and wife" shacks, which were relatively spacious when compared with the constrained living arrangements for bachelors. All camps were outfitted with "one heater, one cooking range, [and] cooking utensils," except the wife and husband shacks. Bunks (without bedding) were also found in most residences. Living arrangements and roommates were determined by the company as "the customary gangs or crews are assigned to camps by the Superintendent."[7]

According to Samuel Swanson, an open-pit mine worker in the Hibbing area, one of the main tasks when living in the camps was keeping warm. "The fellows who worked as laborers didn't have very good homes," he recalled. "In fact, they were badly built and, unless you were able to steal coal from the locomotives of the company as they went by, you probably had a very cold house. None of them had indoor plumbing

Privies or outhouses lined the back alleys of early range towns. Sanitation in many mining locations was rudimentary at best and related diseases could infect entire populations in quick succession. Photograph by Frances Benjamin Johnston, circa 1903. Courtesy of the Library of Congress Prints and Photographs Division.

and some actually had to walk to the hydrant to get water for cooking."[8] Thankfully, there was no rental charge for living in the camps, though men were charged for fuel and bedding.

In some cases, immigrants were lured to mines with promises of housing and living conditions that the companies had no plan of keeping. Unscrupulous labor recruiters, often paid by the number of heads shipped, guaranteed items that the mining companies had no intention of providing for workers. An October 27, 1906, letter from Canisteo District manager John C. Greenway to William J. Olcott, vice president of the Oliver, recorded a walkout of men because of camp conditions and the promises of a labor recruiter, "with reference to the Hungarian Labor Gang of 23 men, sent to the Holman Mine on October 20th. These men were dissatisfied with everything upon their arrival at that point. They claim they had been promised stoves, both cooking and heating, a house to live in, blankets, mattresses and dishes for table use." Greenway noted that company policy assured only the standard house, stove, and hay for bunks. Ever intractable, the company would not budge regarding living conditions, and after seeing the conditions of the camp, the workers left for Hibbing. Greenway was unconcerned with the loss of unskilled workers, and quipped, "I think this gang was a worthless one so far as work is concerned, but I would again suggest that Mr. Fedders, Labor Agent, be cautioned to exercise care in the promises which are made labor gangs coming to this district."[9]

Upkeep and sanitation in the camps and shantytowns were wholly at the discretion of the mining company. With regard to sanitation, the Mountain Iron mining district superintendent wrote, "The camps are kept in repair by the company. The refuse about the camps is cleaned up from time to time by providing barrels. However, when the occupants of certain camps begin throwing refuse about in a careless manner, the Company then has this cleaned up and carried away, and all of the men occupying the camps are made to pay for it by a prorated payroll deduction." This laissez faire system for handling solid waste paled in comparison to sanitation procedures for bodily human waste: "We provide for the closets [outhouses] by digging a pit, and when this is nearly filled, we have the outhouse moved to another spot, and the pit is then filled with earth."[10]

Conditions were especially dire for the seventy-five workers in the Biwabik district. Beds were not furnished by the company and "one man usually referred to as the 'King' has charge of the camp." As for upkeep of buildings in the Biwabik camps, William Carmichael, the mine's superintendent, once wrote simply, "Not any."[11] Perhaps most egregious, a series of letters in the summer of 1908 detailed the deplorable conditions at the Oliver-owned Hartley Mine where there was "foul smelling water all about and refuse everywhere."[12] The lack of running water, cramped living conditions, backyard privies, and open sewers that ran through the mining camps created a breeding ground for infectious diseases. Mining company managers had to remind petty bosses and mine superintendents, who saw many of the immigrant workers as less than human, that sanitation was, in fact, a part of the company's bottom line.

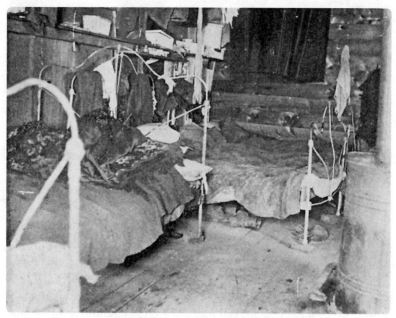

The cramped, unsanitary sleeping quarters available to miners are depicted in this photograph of an "Austrian Bedroom." The image, published in an issue of *Popular Science Monthly* in 1911, is one of several that documented the deplorable living conditions in Virginia and other towns along the Mesabi Range.

Correspondence from 1908 addressed several cases of typhoid—caused either by contaminated water or by a fly epidemic—by instructing camp management to cover the camp's lone privy with a layer of dry clay, and another letter from a local doctor in 1907 informed that mine managers ought to pay more attention to public health concerns because there was a smallpox outbreak in the town of Holman.[13]

Workers in the Adams Mine location were seemingly better off and had balloon-framed houses available for occupancy while working for the mining company. Housing in the Adams location was clearly a class-based system of occupancy. The mine's management class had roomy and well-apportioned houses, many with running water. The living situation was similar for the mine's skilled labor force. Both management and skilled laborers lived in single-family homes with nuclear families mostly intact, living under the same roof.[14] The same cannot be said for

A PLACE HARD AS IRON

Adams's semiskilled and unskilled laborers. There were only twenty-five houses available for the 360 mine workers of this class. This meant that the mostly immigrant-occupied dwellings in this location contained about fourteen people, on average, in each house. This type of a situation often indicated that women married to mine workers were running boarding houses in this location that catered to single men or married immigrant men living away from their families.[15]

Social Ills on the Mesabi Range

With a large population of mine workers living in cramped squalor away from family connections, it was perhaps not unexpected that many sought to drown their sorrows in drink and vice. Mine managers and superintendents endeavored to control and even sometimes cater to this vice, perhaps in an attempt to pacify the labor force. "Blind pigs" or illegal liquor establishments seemed to be open twenty-four hours a day, and "one-armed bandits" (slot machines) were common in private homes. Range towns were rough-and-tumble places and the municipal records of area towns recorded the ups and downs of social life in these raucous and ribald industrial communities. Court records from Eveleth indicated that the town and its vices seemingly never slept. In a 1904 "Register of Criminal Actions," people were being arrested for everything from prostitution to "abusive language" and drunkenness. More serious problems occurred with "A&Bs" (assault and battery) and destroying property, and there was even one case of murder reported in November 1904.[16]

Prostitution was arguably the next most numerous occupation after mine worker on the ranges. Two enterprising Eveleth women were charged with "keeping a house of ill fame" each month from September 1904 to June 1906. Each month like clockwork they were fined between forty and fifty dollars and charged court costs of three dollars, but they never spent any time in jail. This running bill was charged on the first of each month between the two women and the city. What must have looked like hush money turned out to be just that. In the June 1906 city ledger, the "offense charged" column listed "fees for watchman." That Eveleth was condoning and making a profit from the endeavors of these working women seemed blatantly obvious, but following the column it was spelled out in no uncertain terms: "this is a portion of $65.00 charged by city for Police Protection."[17]

Although the winters in Eveleth were relatively quiet, criminal activity skyrocketed during the summer months, and the city's ledgers provided evidence for this trend. Winter months found only one or two pages of offenses, whereas June, July, and August had four and sometimes five or more pages of offenses. Vagrancy arrests were an especially common summertime offense and often got offenders extended time in jail; in one or two cases of vagrancy, up to sixty days in jail. In another summer offense, a man was arrested on August 3, 1914, and charged with "bastardy." Another man was arrested for being a "non-licensed barber," along with two others who were arrested in the same month for being "non-registered pharmacists." Some summer offenders were committed to the "Poor Farm," a county-owned and -operated shelter for the destitute, and in a few cases the sentence was suspended and the offender was "ordered out of town." In one apparently egregious case, a man who was not a resident of Eveleth was arrested for begging and "given 1 hour to leave town." Other odious summer crimes included being an accessory to a "cow at large" and having "carnal knowledge."[18]

Residents of the jails at any given time represented a multitude of ethnicities. A "Register of All Persons Committed to the Lockup at Eveleth, Minn., 1909–1915" recorded the impressive ethnic diversity of the isolated mining boomtown. Included in the entries was each prisoner's national origin, and those locked up included Austrians, Finlanders, Swede–Finns, Norwegians, French, Irish, Swedes, Bohemians, "Montenegrans," Hungarians, Germans, Hrvotksi [Croatians], Russians, Canadians, Italians, Englishmen, "Indians," Jews, a "Chinaman," Poles, Servians [Serbians], Scots, and Americans. Town banishments mostly happened to Americans or other English speakers; immigrants served time or were "committed to City works," a type of sentencing that included hard labor.

Drunkenness was a standard violation in the Eveleth ledgers and a common problem in range communities. While towns and cities struggled to control the production and distribution of intoxicating spirits, mining companies sought to control the flow of beer into and within

A PLACE HARD AS IRON

During the summer months, criminal activity ran rampant in towns along the Iron Range. This photograph from 1902 shows the debris and wreckage after a bomb planted by robbers exploded the safe at the Duluth, Mesabi and Northern Railroad depot in Eveleth. Courtesy of Archives and Special Collections, Kathryn A. Martin Library, University of Minnesota–Duluth.

mining properties. Company managers allowed private individuals to sell alcohol in company-controlled spaces. Matt Pretnor, an immigrant entrepreneur, was given sanction by the Oliver to sell liquors and non-alcoholic beverages in Coleraine, Oliver's model company town. Pretnor was apparently keeping his business open past 11 p.m. each night, an hour determined to be too late by the Oliver. The company wrote Pretnor a letter stating that the privilege of selling alcohol to a somewhat captive audience would be pulled unless he abided by the restrictions.[19] Mining companies walked a fine line as they attempted to pacify laborers with alcohol in controlled, corporate-owned spaces while at the same time regulating the consumption and sale of liquor so that it was not abused.

This finely toed line became more important during strikes. The upheaval of the 1907 Mesabi strike caused the Oliver to forge an alliance with large breweries to regulate the flow of alcohol onto the ranges. Pentecost Mitchell, vice president of the Oliver, wrote: "Shortly after the strike of 1907 we reached an agreement with the Brewers Association, whereby they consented to stop the sale of liquor at any place on our locations to which we objected, and if you will kindly notify the representatives of the different agencies in Ely that you desire the delivery of liquor to these places stopped, we believe your request will be complied with."[20]

Similar to antilabor sentiments from mining companies, there was an equally effusive anti-immigrant dimension to alcohol regulation. Mining companies often distinguished between "good" immigrants and "bad" immigrants based on their propensity for drinking, labor organization, or cultural festivities. A "Good Finn" went to the local temperance society's picnics on company property and never missed a day of work. A "Bad Finn" was a member of the local socialist organization and spent his free time reading or educating himself at the People's Library in a labor hall—perhaps reading some Marx on a day off. Similarly, a "Good Austrian" went to church on Sunday and took out citizenship papers, while a "Bad Austrian" ran a "blind pig" or an illegal alcohol business out of a company-owned residence.[21] In the eyes of J. H. Hearding, an Oliver mine manager, John Capan was one such "Bad Austrian." In 1908, Hearding launched an investigation into Capan's business dealings with the intention of having him arrested and possibly thrown out of his house and off company property if he was found to be operating a blind pig.[22]

Mining companies were much more successful in regulating alcohol in company locations than the ranges' towns and cities, and their monitoring and controlling of the consumption and sale of alcohol was impressive. Towns had to work through the legal process in alcohol-related cases, but mining companies could serve up swift, autocratic consequences. In one such case, a night watchman at the Spruce Location near Eveleth had a run-in with three men who were drunk and disorderly. The hired mine guard wanted to restrict the sale of alcohol to the men because, according to the watchman, "these men are pretty good men until they get beer into their systems, when they become noisy and disorderly." The guard warned that if they did not change their drunken

Thomas Roddy's saloon in North Hibbing was one of several establishments that served liquor to mine workers and locals at the turn of the twentieth century. Women were often not allowed in saloons of the time. Between 1919 and 1921, the town of Hibbing was moved, wholesale, from its location near the Hull–Rust–Mahoning open-pit mine. More than two hundred structures were moved from what became "North" Hibbing to the town's present location. Courtesy of the Hibbing Historical Society.

behavior, "we will put them off the location, but I thought we would first try the practicability of stopping them [from getting] beer."[23]

In Capan's case, the company concluded that he was probably running a blind pig and that "the house . . . on the extension of Adams Avenue [near Eveleth], has been very disorderly for the last few nights. Capan has but two or three boarders but there are a great many men going to get beer there."[24] In lieu of kicking Capan out of his house, the Oliver concocted a plan to restrict the flow of alcohol into the location where Capan lived. Instead of posting more men to monitor the situation, the company contacted regional breweries to enact the 1907 strike-related alcohol regulation agreement in the hopes of shutting off Capan's supply. An amazing exposition of regional power began to unfold as the Oliver wrote Duluth brewing magnate August Fitger to ask him if he "would notify them of such [blind pig] houses," and then, if necessary, "refuse the man any beer until such time as the man obtained permission to receive same, from the mining company."[25]

The Oliver went about notifying other regional breweries of the blind pig and inquiring if they had sold beer to Capan. These letters also included an edict declaring that no alcohol was to be sold to men in Capan's company location. The Oliver promptly received a letter back from August Fitger, and then another from the Hamms Brewing Company in St. Paul. The correspondence from Hamms read: "In reply, beg to state that after searching our records at this office we find that we have never had any business dealings with the above parties. However, we have notified our representative in that district that in case he was approached by such parties to absolutely refuse to sell them any goods until otherwise notified." Fitger replied, "We will say that we have given strict orders to our Agent in the Eveleth district to deliver no beer whatsoever to [the location] named in your letter, and will say that we shall always be most willing to abide by your wishes in matters like the above." The Oliver received similar responses from the Blatz Brewing Company of Milwaukee, the Gund Brewing Company of La Crosse, Wisconsin, the Minneapolis Brewing Company (Golden Grain Belt Beers), the Duluth Brewing & Malting Company ("the Monarch of all Pure Malt Beers"), the Virginia Brewing Company, and the Schlitz Brewing Company of Milwaukee.[26]

The strict and well-orchestrated monitoring and regulation of alcohol went on unabated in mining company locations. "Beer is still delivered in small quantities to the boarding houses [at Fayal location near Eveleth], but as far as we know we have no 'blind pigs.' Our policemen watch the delivery of it and if we think any place is getting more than necessary for the number of boarders, we notify the party to move off the location, and if employed at the mine he is discharged. In this way we have had but very little trouble with 'blind pigs,'" wrote one Oliver mine superintendent. The catch-22 in such aggressive alcohol management was that if the men could not obtain a drink at company locations, they would head into the ranges' municipal centers where mining companies had little control in monitoring or regulating the consumption of alcohol by their workers. The same Oliver superintendent wrote of the problem,

At the time of the 1907 strike, beer was brought to the iron ranges by train and was then transferred onto horse-drawn wagons. August Fitger's brewing company out of Duluth was a leading provider to the region's urban areas. In this photograph, Louis Sadar delivers a shipment of beer to a merchant in Eveleth. Courtesy of Christine Sadar and Steve Ketcham.

"We are satisfied, however, that if we were to prohibit the delivery of beer to boarding houses the men would go into saloons in the village [of Eveleth], and we believe the effect would be worse than at present."[27]

To rectify this situation, the Oliver sought the partnership of Eveleth's business community in general, and specifically the Eveleth Business Men's Association. Not only did the company have the support of many of the Upper Midwest's major breweries in regulating the consumption and sale of alcohol on its properties, it also gained the help of local businessmen's groups. A January 30, 1908, letter from the superintendent of Eveleth's schools, on behalf of the town's business community, to Thomas F. Cole of the Oliver highlighted the partnership:

As per our conversation of Saturday evening, I am writing you on the subject of your company's regulating the sale of intoxicating liquors on your mining locations. You people are the best judges of how this may be most easily done, but it seemed to the Eveleth Business Men's Association that forbidding the Brewers the locations or evicting from your houses tenants who persist in retailing beer, etc., illegally, would be sufficient. The processes of law seem slow and rather ineffective to us. We find life in mining camps not an unmixed joy. Your company has never disregarded the public's wishes.

Again, may we presume to say that the labor situation is ripe for such action. In the bargain you well know that drunken men are expensive on any job, and more especially a mining one. Finally, the burden of the swarm of degenerate children will be felt by you in the future as it is now by me in the school.[28]

Consequently, the rather corrupt, but somewhat whimsical, irony in all of this intrigue regarding social ills on the ranges, and Eveleth in particular, had unethically come full circle. Eveleth's local government officials, some of who were likely in the businessmen's association, had accepted hush and protection money from prostitutes. Now, however, when the Oliver came calling, Eveleth's businessmen suddenly found the moral high ground and decided to work with the company in curing the intolerable social ills of alcohol abuse. Worse still, and with an almost unbelievable sense of hypocrisy, Eveleth's superintendent of schools had the audacity to complain about a "swarm of degenerate children" under his care morphing into debauched workers while his community was sanctioning prostitution to bolster the city's municipal coffers.[29]

While some mine workers did in fact seek escape or happiness in the bottom of a bottle or in the arms of a "working girl," many others sought to elevate their spiritual or social consciousness in the midst of the raucous and unruly iron ranges. For many men with families, getting their children an education was of utmost importance. Slovenian American Veda Ponikvar recalled: "The schools on the Iron Range began to be built at a very early time. For example the [mine] locations surrounding Chisholm had small wooden schools."[30] Although the small, impermanent school buildings of mining locations could be swallowed and lost to expanding pit mines, large schools in the ranges' municipal centers were constructed to last. The schools became home to a vibrant multiethnic culture, and also mirrored the somewhat rough exterior of life in an isolated industrial region. Polly Bullard commented on her experiences in an early Iron Range classroom: "As to school, I have a funny little room, with the leavings of several rooms in it—quite a handful therefore. They are Italian, Austrian, Finnish, Swedish and Irish—only one American, I believe, and some of them have only been in this country a year or so. Most of them are good children, but I have two or three in need of a good deal of squelching."[31]

Churches and organized religion were another place that mine workers turned to for uplifting interactions. Mining companies were generally supportive of religious life because ministers and priests advocated sober and industrious lifestyles. For many with families, churches were the only place where salvation and sobriety could be expressed. The spires of Italian, Croatian, and Slovenian Roman Catholic churches dotted the landscape, while Finnish Lutheran houses of worship occupied the same streets. Along with spiritual enterprises, laboring men and their families also began founding organizations that examined economic and social concerns. The Croatian Fraternal Union of America, headquartered in Pittsburgh, Pennsylvania, had several branches on the iron ranges, and Slovenian National Homes in cities such as Ely and Chisholm provided immigrants with a chance to engage in debate, participate in theatrical productions, or host weddings and other rituals. For many single immigrant Finnish men, *poikatalos*, or cooperative boarding houses, were their first contact with collective action. In these houses, mine workers lived communally, sharing resources, reading ideological tracts, and discussing labor and social conditions. Although these organizations and places were a type of mutually funded, class-conscious undertaking, they were not overt forms of unionist or political organization.[32]

Many in the ranges' temperance societies, and especially in the Finnish immigrant temperance societies, were unwilling to accept spiritual answers to what they saw as material problems. Fred Torma was one such person. A Finnish immigrant from an agricultural background, Torma immigrated to the United States in the early twentieth century. He had been exposed to socialist thought while in Finland but was unfamiliar with industrial work. Once in the United States, he began working in the Mesabi Range mines and quickly developed an oppositional attitude toward the exploitation he saw around him. Wanting to find an outlet from the doldrums of industrial life while escaping the ubiquitous saloon scene, Fred joined with fellow immigrants and began to organize. Their goal was to organize a socialist group, but the route to achieving such an organization, and the procuring of a coveted social hall, went through a Christian temperance organization:

> There were temperance halls in almost every town. At first we tried to take over these temperance halls for socialist uses. The first place was at Stevenson Mine—temperance hall. I joined that temperance league. At that time the Finns were very much enslaved by liquor. When the boss went for his morning drink the working men followed. I began organizing work to get members into that temperance league [to then vote the temperance society into a socialist local].[33]

The major obstacle in Torma's plan was not converting members, because many were receptive to socialist principles of cooperative economic action, working-class expressions of culture, and sobriety. Instead, the difficulty lay in the hall's being located on company land in the Stevenson Location north of Keewatin. Torma recalled: "We tried to take over that hall then so that we could also take up working people matters, but the mining company intervened. They sent representatives to say that they had provided the money and materials for the hall and it would not be used for any labor movement purposes."[34]

Much like temperance societies and religious groups, socialists sought to identify, explain, and change social ills. The primary difference was that socialist groups provided a material explanation for the problems that plagued life on the ranges. This explanation, often originating from a Marxist, class-based perspective, spoke to the roots of socioeconomic inequality. Early class-conscious immigrant societies looked to cure social ills, while simultaneously addressing the dangerous and deadly working conditions in the region's pit and underground mines. Thus, while municipalities, mining locations, and the men who ran them allowed prostitution and the sale of alcohol to pacify labor, they frowned on and actively sought to stamp out the influence of class-conscious workers' groups and organized labor. Nevertheless, it was the dangerous and deadly working conditions that necessitated such working-class advocates.

2 THE SEASONAL STRUGGLE

Labor and Politics in Northern Minnesota

There is a strike going on here [in Eveleth] . . . there are 100 stooges with guns paid by the mining companies harassing the workers just like some animals. People are jailed every day . . . they say this America is the land of the free but that's a lie.
—*Finnish immigrant Victor Myllymäki during the 1907 Mesabi strike*

AS MEN AND WOMEN IN POLITICAL AND SOCIAL ORGANIZATIONS BEGAN to contemplate the ills of the iron ranges' social landscapes, dangerous working conditions and the inequitable distribution of wealth became parallel concerns. Labor unions emerged in the late nineteenth and early twentieth centuries on the ranges and began to publicly address questions that immigrant laborers were talking about in private. Immigrant political and social organizations soon were combining social problems, such as intemperance, with grievances about working conditions in area mines. This led to the formation of a growing sense of class consciousness among the immigrant mine workers. Almost inevitably, revolts against working conditions and the inequitable distribution of wealth followed.

Many involved in the immigrant organizations read about, advocated, and clamored for a revolutionary change to such social and working conditions. Because many of these immigrants worked in area mines, these industrial workplaces became a type of contested space where immigrants sought to change their material conditions through collective action. These industrial locations where immigrants agitated and organized against capitalist bosses became contested workscapes—an important subsection of the industrial landscape, which mining management believed it controlled and owned. By taking action in such contested work spaces, immigrant employees were attempting to assert control over the conditions of their labor. This perspective deeply troubled area mine managers and repressive actions were taken to ensure that the "bug" of socialism and unionism was controlled and monitored, if not eradicated, from these contested workscapes in particular and from immigrant populations in general.

The growing tension that existed between immigrant workers and mine management in the early twentieth century led to several intense, but truncated, labor actions. Immigrants were not the only people who noticed such problems. Middle-class, mostly American-born reformers on the ranges were mindful of the same inequalities but espoused a different, more moderate course of action. Progressives, and the synonymous political party they founded, advocated a political campaign to gradually identify and change the inequitable distribution of wealth and social ills of the ranges. Like immigrant labor and socialist organizations, progressives saw the inherent contradictions of capitalist production—accumulation of wealth by the few to the detriment and exploitation of the many—as the root of workers' discontentment. Unlike radical immigrant unions and political organizations, progressives did not advocate revolutionary aims in addressing these socioeconomic problems. This discrepancy between progressives, most of whom were fully enfranchised with the vote, and immigrant workers who did not have access to a political voice, is the focus of this chapter.

Contested Workscapes on the Ranges

Because of its boom-and-bust, seasonally structured occupations, mine work and the iron ranges' labor force should be understood in connection with the region's other industries. During the late nineteenth and early twentieth centuries, most of the labor force on the ranges was made up of itinerant workers. Mining companies did employ family men over extended periods of time, but largely the workforce was composed of young men who were laid off in the winter and subject to the whims of fluctuating iron ore prices. When the price of ore fell, mine workers, sometimes by the hundreds, were fired or laid off; when the price was up, or ore stockpiles were depleted, there were jobs aplenty. When work was thin, posthumous mine workers headed by foot into the massive forests of northern Minnesota and Canada, to family farms on the industrial periphery, or to the flowing wheat fields of the Dakotas. Some, in search of work, wandered to other mining districts in Michigan or Montana. The sporadic employment of northern Minnesota's iron mines led to an army of job seekers seasonally wandering the northern climes of the Midwest.

As we have seen in Cronon's metropolis–hinterland model, the physical interpretation of landscape can be used to study the intersections between industry, people, and their surrounding environments. In a similar way, Rodolfo F. Acuña's *Corridors of Migration* studies geographic spaces that determined the movement of Mexican miners and agricultural workers as they crossed the United States–Mexico border in search of work. His historical insights related to the United States' southern border are also useful in understanding the struggle of mobile and oftentimes radical (im)migrant workforces, such as those found in northern Minnesota.[1]

Instead of a corridor, many of the iron ranges' workers formed mobile communities of itinerant laborers who traveled in a triangular, seasonal pattern from the iron ranges to the Dakota wheat fields to the logging camps of extreme northern Minnesota and western Ontario, Canada. Sam Swanson was one of these workers who found himself caught in such a seasonal, triangular work pattern. His recollections of this itinerant life provide a useful case study in understanding the tenuous relationship between employment and survival in the Upper Midwest. Swanson was born in Chicago and moved to work on his uncle's homestead in Clearwater County, Minnesota, after his mother died. At age fifteen his uncle became disabled and Sam was forced to strike out on his own. He headed for the wheat fields of northwestern Minnesota and northeastern North Dakota. Paying a dollar a day plus board, the employment was steady, if not for a few days when a rainy spell would halt the harvest. According to Swanson, the food served for meals was good and there was plenty of it, except during rainy periods when farmers refused to feed idled workers. Remembering these times and his healthy appetite, Swanson recalled, "[the farmer] would take me into town and

I would have to stay there and pay for my hotel and restaurant until the fields dried up sufficiently so I could go back to work."[2]

Work in the wheat fields was consistent in the late summer and early fall, but also migratory. Swanson remarked that "after we had finished the harvest in the Red River Valley, I drifted westward where the grain ripened later and, of course, the wages were 50 cents a day higher." His travels west took him to Minot, North Dakota, where he met a group of workers who had organized themselves into a "hobo jungle" that was partial to the revolutionary industrial unionism of the IWW. Swanson recalled that "a lot of the men that worked the wheat fields who were known as bums, tramps, hobos, and farmer boys [were] looking for a few dollars. I went down to one of these jungles to look it over . . . there were about twenty or thirty fellows sitting around. They didn't seem to mind my coming and looking at their group. In fact they offered me a cup of their bouja and mulligan or whatever you call it. After looking it over I decided I wasn't that hungry."[3]

When a few local farmers noticed missing chickens that were being found in the bottom of hobo stews, Sam and his newfound friends were escorted out of town and loaded onto boxcars headed for points west by armed sheriffs and their deputies. After his deportation, Sam helped a farmer in another part of the state finish his year's threshing; later, he returned to Minot, where he attended his first meeting of the IWW's Agricultural Workers Organization (AWO). The IWW had made significant "hay" in organizing agricultural workers and founded the AWO in 1915. The organization mostly represented wheat-field hands, who worked the United States' and Canada's breadbaskets from Texas in the south to Manitoba in the north, and from northwestern Minnesota in the east to Washington State's Palouse in the west. In the Upper Midwest, Minneapolis came to represent a regional headquarters, had a strong local organization, and in October 1916 hosted the AWO's national convention. Given the AWO's strong advocacy of wheat hands, Swanson felt "I had to join the union." "It cost $1.00 in initiation fees and 50¢ for a stamp or my first month's dues." Sam's initial IWW meeting consisted of listening to the complaints of overworked and underpaid harvest workers. After the grievances had been registered, the union meeting broke into song, and the Wobblies (known as the singing union) filled Minot's nighttime skies with the music of solidarity. Recalling the meeting, Swanson remembered, "it was the first time I had ever heard 'Solidarity Forever' . . . what our singing lacked in quality, I think we made up in quantity. We really were a loud group, considering the number that attended the meeting."[4]

Swanson's itinerant routine is an example of the Wobbly's unique, roaming culture. The proletarian hobo's lifestyle was a celebrated aspect of the union's mobility and portable organizing methods. As an industrial worker on the move, Swanson's life was the stuff of IWW legend, a legend that had been recorded and praised in a song titled "The Mysteries of a Hobo's Life":

> I grabbed a hold of an old freight train
> An' around the country traveled,
> The mysteries of a hobo's life
> To me was soon unraveled.
>
> I traveled east and I traveled west
> And the "shacks" could never find me,
> Next morning I was miles away
> From the job I left behind me.
>
> I ran across a bunch of "stiffs"
> Who were known as Industrial Workers,
> They taught me how to be a man—
> And how to fight the shirkers.
>
> I kicked right in and joined the bunch
> And now in the ranks you'll find me,
> Hurrah for the cause—to hell with the boss!
> And the job I left behind me.[5]

Leaving his job in Minot, Swanson went back home for a short respite and then left for northern Minnesota's large tracts of pine forests. In Bemidji, he came into contact with what the Wobblies called a "labor shark," an employment agent who sold jobs but then worked with the company so that when a worker was fired, often purposefully or for no reason, he or she then had to buy back their former job or pay to get another job from the very same job peddler. After paying the labor shark two dollars for a job, Swanson signed on as a bull cook in a logging camp. Bull cooks fed the fires of the camp's stoves, and while the job offered little prestige and even less in wages, it was good enough for Swanson, who was sixteen at the time. He gradually moved up the pay scale to become a "skidder," helping to ferry cut timber out of the woods before the spring breakup. Work in the woods was difficult and daunting. During one especially wet spring, Swanson and the logging crew were "wet clear up to the arm pits, and walking home at night our clothes would freeze. I decided that this was not the life for me and I quit." Although Swanson disliked the working conditions associated with logging, he would find his way into the woods often and the cycle between fields and forests continued until one spring when he went to work in the mines near Hibbing.[6]

Swanson became a pitman in one of the Oliver's open-pit mines. His insights about work in the pits of the Mesabi Range give a technical understanding of a mine worker's job: "Now, a pitman is the man, or the group of men, who work around a steam shovel. The steam shovel operator was the boss. He had an engineer up in the boom, called a craner. A fireman kept up the steam. There were from four to six pitmen, depending on the bank [of ground] that you had," and "there was a flunky who carried water and did other jobs . . . while the 'walker' was the superintendent of the pit." Working with the pit crew was a new experience for Swanson and being one of the only people who could speak English was difficult. "I was put to work with three other fellows, who didn't know very much English. They were pretty good at swearing, but outside of that they hadn't learned many English words" (ibid.).

Working in the pits was very labor intensive and Swanson estimated that "of the men who worked in the mine at that time, about eighty percent were classified as [unskilled] laborers." Pit mining became deskilled as machinery and mechanized production replaced backbreaking work. This, of course, meant that low-paying jobs in the pits were easy to get but hard to keep. Pit bosses were paid more, but still not the wages of skilled machinists or surface crews (ibid.). Swanson's recollections of work in the pit emphasized the almost mechanical rhythms of a Minnesota iron ore mine: the clank, moan, and whirs of huge steam shovels as they swal-

Mechanization by railroad and steam shovel came early to the Mesabi Range.
This early photograph by Frances Benjamin Johnston from the 1890s conveys
the sheer human and mechanical labor needed to extract iron ore from open-pit
mines. Courtesy of the Library of Congress Prints and Photographs Division.

lowed mouthfuls of earth, the thousand-pound thud of debris dumped
into railcars, and the ear-piercing creaks and clangs of wheels on steel
rails as the cars hauled materials up and around narrow-gauge railroads
and out of the pit. It was an industrial tune that Sam Swanson grew to
know well each summer, until every fall when he was laid off. Work in the
pits slowed considerably at the end of the ore-shipping season. Autumns
were spent in the far-stretching harvest fields followed by a trip into the
freezing winter woods of northern Minnesota, where men would wait for
the opening of the next ore-shipping season in the spring (ibid.).

Some workers chose to stay on the ranges, eking out a living through
the winter on the summer's wages. Living unemployed during this time
was difficult, but it was better than working on a skeleton crew in the
open pits during the bone-chilling Minnesota winter. One mining cap-
tain wrote of the harrowing weather in the late nineteenth century:

Mine supports and narrow-gauge rail tracks highlight this haunting look at an underground mine between Tower and Ely, Minnesota, circa 1915. Many Vermilion Range mines were underground, or shaft, mines versus the Mesabi's mostly open-pit mines. Photograph by Hugh McKenzie. Courtesy of Archives and Special Collections, Kathryn A. Martin Library, University of Minnesota–Duluth.

"How can men do a day's work with the thermometer at 45–50 below zero? We have not had but two days above zero since winter started. One day this week 76 men were off—if it were summertime these men would have made full time."[7] The weather of Minnesota's North Country was a safety hazard in its own right for open-pit mine workers: blazing hot and mosquito-infested in the summer, and damnable cold, frostbitten conditions in the winter.

Underground mines provided steadier year-round employment but were more dangerous than work in the open pits. Beholden to the whims of financial market fluctuations, early underground mining was characterized by labor-intensive human production, while speedups and cost-cutting measures, such as the introduction of new yet unproven produc-

Underground petty bosses were distinguished by their white coats, which were worn as a sign of authority and identification in the dark, underground workspaces. These bosses often sold choice working conditions to miners, a practice described as a type of graft or corruption in the administration of a mine's labor force. Photograph by Frances Benjamin Johnston, circa 1903. Courtesy of the Library of Congress Prints and Photographs Division.

tion technologies, endangered the lives of the underground workforce. All the elements for dangerous job conditions existed in the underground mines. Traveling hundreds or thousands of feet underground (depending on the age of the mine) into a shaft, mine workers extended drifts (horizontal tunnels) to work areas or set about drilling in cave-like hollowed-out areas to set up a "blast pattern." Skilled miners drilled blasting holes, packed them with a blasting agent, and then exploded the hard rock. Following the blasting, unskilled laborers would load the material into a car and ferry the containers to the shaft to be pulled to the surface. Disaster was only a blast away in an underground mine.

The iron ranges' largest loss of life occurred in 1924 at the underground Milford mine on the Cuyuna Range. On February 5, forty-one mine workers died when water from Foley Lake spilled into the mine after a cave-in. A warm rush of air preceded the gushing waters and as the mine's forty-eight-person day shift attempted to scramble to the only exit shaft, the water overtook mine workers one by one. The mine's skip car, the conveyance to transport workers (and ore) up the shaft, was at the surface and the men were forced to climb to safety. Only seven made it out alive. Several bodies were recovered over the course of the following year as the mine was slowly drained.[8]

The daily, deadly serious working conditions in the mines were grueling. As illustrated by the Milford Mine disaster, underground mines were certainly dangerous, but workers in the open-pit mines were just as susceptible to death and injury. Many immigrants coming from southern and southeastern Europe where agricultural work was the standard means of making a living were shocked by working conditions in both pit and underground mines. In one instance at the Holman pit mine, two Italian miners were killed in 1908. A company letter explained that both miners were "gopher hole" contractors:[9] "The evidence now at hand would indicate that they were preparing to fire a small 'pop' in the breast of their 'gopher hole' and probably accidentally exploded the cap, which set off several sticks of dynamite." The accident was a particularly gruesome one: "The bodies were frightfully mutilated and dismembered. There were three other 'gopher hole' men within 150 feet of them. Their attention was directed to the matter by the explosion and seeing the bodies hurled in the air." In almost every such case of death, mining companies found fault with the men working in their employ. Predictably, mine manager John C. Greenway was less concerned with the mine workers' deaths than with the bottom line: "[the coroner] ruled that these men met their deaths by an accidental discharge of dynamite, the cause of which is unknown, and that no one was to blame other than themselves."[10]

In a similar case from 1913, a mining company sought to cast off blame when it fought a lawsuit that demonstrated that the dangers of mining were not confined to the work areas of open pits. According to a personal-injury complaint originally lodged in a St. Louis County court, a twenty-year-old immigrant woman who was visiting a Hanna Mine boardinghouse was struck by falling debris from the Brunt Mine while walking on a public highway. Knocked unconscious and hospitalized, she sued the two companies for more than $30,000, but a judge dismissed the case against Hanna while ruling in her favor for $7,000 against the Brunt Mine's owners. Apparently believing that even bystanders walking on public highways were part of collateral damage in

Injuries in the mines were frequent and, in many cases, debilitating. This unidentified mine worker has been hobbled and is living in one of the Mesabi's mining camps, circa 1905. His barefoot children carry a pail, which may contain the family's drinking water. Many mining camps, like this one, were little more than a collection of tar-paper shacks situated next to the open pits. Courtesy of the Library of Congress Prints and Photographs Division.

the making of profits, the Brunt Mine managers fought the woman's legal case all the way to the Minnesota Supreme Court. For the mining company, the problem was not in paying the $7,000; rather, it was that it did not want to set a precedent in being found at fault for an injury in or around the mine. According to a report on the incident and

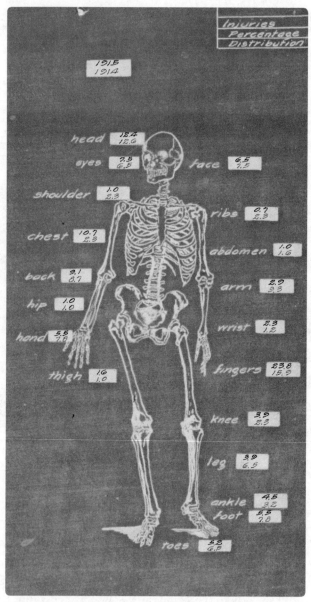

This diagram from the records of the Oliver Iron Mining Company from 1915 illustrates mine workers' injuries in 1914 and 1915. Head injuries accounted for around 12.5 percent of all injuries during these years, while fingers were by far the most injured body part in 1915, tallying 23.8 percent of all injuries. Courtesy of Archives and Special Collections, Kathryn A. Martin Library, University of Minnesota–Duluth.

subsequent lawsuit, lawyers for the mining companies argued that "if the plaintiff was injured as a result of the defendants' blasting operations, the same was the result of her own negligence and disregard of warnings and knowledge on her part that she was in a place where she was likely to be struck by material from the blasting operations in such mine, and that she voluntarily assumed the risk of such danger." To make matters worse, the mining company responsible for the woman's injuries was eventually found not to be at fault because no one (according to the court) could irrefutably prove that the debris came from the Brunt Mine—though the Brunt was the only mine blasting in the area.[11] It seemed that not even the public streets on the ranges were safe.

Manipulating the workforce—and the general public—to avoid liability, ensure profits, suppress wages, and pit ethnicities against one another was a common tactic in controlling the mines' mostly immigrant employees. Keeping surplus pools of laborers at locations with few jobs to offer frustrated attempts to organize workers and was a common practice to avoid strikes. One letter written in the spring of 1907, just before a large strike began on the Mesabi Range, indicated, "I note your intention to commence importing common labor to the Range at once with an idea of maintaining a large floating labor supply with an idea of relieving the tension of the usual situation which arises in the Spring."[12] Communications between management regarding the workforce reflected the harsh attitudes of mine managers toward their immigrant employees: they were not individual people but rather a group commodity to be bought and sold, used, and discarded. There was seemingly little difference in the way managers physically ranked their purchases of wage slaves from how chattel slave owners assessed their acquisitions in the American antebellum South. Correspondence from John C. Greenway to Oliver labor agents spelled out the situation quite clearly: "At the present time we are not in shape to take any more [men] at the Holman Mine but can take two gangs of twenty-five men each at the Canisteo Mine. Would prefer Northern Italians, Bulgarians, or Austrians in the order named."[13]

While immigrant workers were preferred for physically demanding mine work—often work that native-born American workers refused to do—the expectation was that they would become assimilated to American social values and a Protestant work ethic. As Greenway commented on promotions, "I would also be in favor of making it clear to our men that when we make promotions, either from common labor to foremanship, or increases in the pay of foremen, that, other things being equal, that the man with full citizenship has a better chance for promotion and will be favored over the one without citizenship."[14] Immigrant mine workers were seemingly good enough to produce, toil, and die in the mines, but without assimilation they were not good enough to receive a promotion for their efforts. The socioeconomic status of an immigrant, no matter his work ethic or meritorious service, was fixed and controlled by the mining companies. Even when workers were set to get a conciliatory gesture, it came with strings tightly attached to maintain the companies' bottom lines.

For example, in March 1912, a number of mines on the Vermilion Range switched from ten- or twelve- to eight-hour shifts as a test to determine if the new schedule would improve productivity in Oliver mines. Managers spoke of the change in glowing terms and rejoiced that the tonnages of ore were the same or improving. The view of the miners was somewhat different. Joseph Mantel, a chairman for an underground workers' committee in Ely, wrote to the Oliver that same month reporting that "a meeting was held here in this City, last Sunday March 17, in presence of about one hundred underground miners." At the meeting, Mantel and the other mine workers read a story aloud from a company-influenced Ely newspaper that decreed, "Vermilion Range likes new system. Eight hours for underground miners gives much satisfaction."[15]

Mantel and his one hundred or so fellow workers disagreed. On the contrary, they argued that, as practiced, the eight-hour shift was robbing miners of well-deserved break time. At 12:10 p.m., when mine workers were supposed to be hoisted to the surface and on their way to eat lunch in the company dry house or break room, the ore skip was still hoisting ore to the surface. The first cage of workers was not hoisted to the surface until 12:15 and the hoisting of workers continued until 12:30. This was also the time when the supervisors began to call "All aboard for the first cage to go into the mine." Men had to be in their respective places of work at 1 p.m. sharp. Mantel asked, "Now how much time have the men for their dinner if any?" He also noted that shift bosses walked up and down the dry house during lunch showing "the men how to eat quick and to put the lunch down into their stomach fast, if [the mine worker] doesn't obey he is taken by the arm and pushed out of the dry house and told to go home if he doesn't want to work."[16]

Mantel and the workers he spoke for then respectfully petitioned the Oliver to "use the miners more liberally in the future than at present time and furthermore, to allow the said miners a reasonable time for their lunch time between working hours."[17] For attempting to communicate with the Oliver in this penitent manner, Mantel seems to have been fired. Oliver general superintendent W. H. Johnston explained that "the change [to an eight-hour day] has given very general satisfaction at all our mines. We have had only one complaint and that was at our Queen Mine by a chronic kicker who seemed to think they had too little time at noon. His services have been dispensed with." Johnston went on to opine that "just as soon as we commence listening to suggestions—either on the part of the men or of outsiders—there is no telling where the trouble will end."[18]

Additionally, the remuneration for shorter shifts was brought up in regard to the institution of an eight-hour day. Mining companies expected the men to do ten hours of work during the eight-hour shift and be paid the same contract prices for delivering more tonnage. Johnston remarked:

> There is a feeling among the men, however, that on account of the fewer hours of work it will necessitate an increase in the rates per car or foot, to make wages equal to those now prevailing. In this matter, I wish to state we have made it very plain to the men that there is to be no increase in contract prices, and all miners are expected to do as much or more in the eight hours than they formerly did in the ten. The men, I believe, are doing better work per hour than they formerly did, and when they find no increase will be made on their contract prices, they will see that they equal their former earnings.[19]

With men like Johnston at the helm of the Iron Range's mines, it became clear to the workers that if they were going to have a voice in the conditions of their labor, it would not come without a fight.

Early Immigrant Labor Organization on the Ranges

Even more difficult than work life on the ranges was the struggle of mine workers to gain a voice, or small increments of control, in the conditions of their labor. Certain skilled occupations were organized by craft or trades unions, but most unskilled immigrant workers—tasked with the mines' most dangerous jobs—were not allowed union representation. In many cases, such representation was violently withheld from these workers. From his experiences in labor organization, Sam Swanson concluded, "In the past, the mining companies had their men in various political offices and had exerted a strong influence on the community, not only as the principle [sic] employer of labor, but politically and socially and by having many of the business men on their side."[20] If a mine worker ran afoul of the company, there were significant consequences. Being blacklisted did not simply mean losing one's house and income, it meant engaging in a struggle for survival. Company blacklists loomed large on the ranges because once a mining manager had deemed someone a union sympathizer, it was also difficult to get work from other employers. Swanson remarked that "to be fired by the company meant being cast out."[21]

Despite the concerns and pitfalls of labor organization, agonizing working conditions and the exploitation of immigrant laborers actually spurred efforts to organize those deemed to be unorganizable by the then conservative, often anti-immigrant American Federation of Labor (AFL). The barriers to organization were many. Company subterfuge, violence, and social reprisals all speak to the incredible struggle and undeniable character of those who fought for industrial democracy and social justice on the ranges. Most often mine managers such as John C. Greenway, Pentecost Mitchell, and Thomas F. Cole are celebrated for their contributions to Iron Range history. But what about people like Sam Swanson, Jospeh Mantel, and Fred Torma? Because these people fought to give workers a voice, and because those workers were the people who made the actual wealth, their stories are just as important, if not more so, as the mining men who denied so many people their basic human rights.

One of the first major fights for such basic rights occurred, fittingly, at the first commercially profitable mine. Workers at the Minnesota

Mine on the Vermilion Range commenced an impromptu strike on June 23, 1892, when mine management laid off 315 men for fourteen days. The context of these layoffs speaks volumes to the social inequalities common in early labor on the ranges. Days before being put out of work, hundreds of the mine's Austrian workforce took the day off to observe Corpus Christi day, an important religious holiday for Catholics. The mining company retaliated with layoffs and further refused to give the mine workers their wages. The *Vermilion Iron Journal*, a company-affiliated newspaper, spun the story: "On Saturday, the crowd of strikers called in a body at the [mine] office and demanded their wages. Although it was the company's intention to pay the roll that day, for the welfare of the community and the safety of its own property payment was postponed, it being anything but advisable to furnish the half-drunken mob the wherewithal to purchase more intoxicants." Here again, the overt anti-immigrant sentiment of range bosses and their newspapers reared its ugly head. Understandably infuriated by the wholesale punishment, approximately four hundred immigrant workers took to the streets, shutting the mine down. Three companies of the Minnesota National Guard were called in, the strike leaders were arrested, and gradually "peace was restored."[22]

Such loosely organized confrontations between labor and management occurred with some frequency, and often these actions were confined to workers of a similar ethnic background. Finnish immigrants quickly gained status as the most proficient striking population. The Oliver's fear of and animosity toward organized labor, and those Finns affiliated with it, were well established. A 1903 letter from General Manager John Penguilly urged President Thomas F. Cole to be wary of Finns with an organizational impulse:

There has been, during the last part of the week, a man by the name of "Nasula," a Finlander, who hails from Hibbing, and he has been working among the Finlanders of Soudan and Ely. He is trying to start a labor union among the employees of the mine here. The matter was brought to my attention early, therefore I took steps to drive him from the places mentioned, and he has already retreated from the Vermilion Range and gone to the Mesabi Range, in which he claims he could start a union. This [information] may be of benefit to the Mining Men under you located on the Mesabi Range, so as to keep a look out for him and suppress him as soon as possible wherever he should turn up.[23]

In Minnesota's Iron Country, Finns became a primary agitator in labor confrontations during the early twentieth century. On June 6, 1904, for example, four hundred mostly Finnish mine workers walked out at the Drake and Stratton Stripping Operations of the Oliver's Fayal Mines in Eveleth. The company had just announced a wage reduction from $1.75 to $1.60 per day. On the third day of the strike, a clash between the strikers and armed mining company police elevated the stakes considerably, as two strikers ended up in the Eveleth hospital. One man died with a bullet in his skull and the other suffered a jagged shell wound to his chest. This clash set the tone for the turbulent years ahead, as Finnish mine workers continued to strike amid shutdowns and armed company guards.[24]

Previous labor actions on the ranges had lacked formal union representation. On April 13, 1905, however, a committee of unorganized mine workers' representatives appeared before OIMC Mine Superintendent Pentecost Mitchell. When Mitchell refused the committee's demands, the workers laid down their tools. Two days later, the OIMC ordered a general shutdown of its operations. Into this labor action was thrown the Western Federation of Miners (WFM). An industrial union born in 1893 out of mining struggles in the American West, the WFM brought in organizers from other states to help unify the Mesabi's largely immigrant workforce. "The strikers' organization at Hibbing is very complete," wrote the OIMC's Mitchell on April 15, 1905. "I find that there is a number of outside men from Colorado, Montana and Wyoming; they are looking after this strike; they have been here for four or five weeks, but have done the work so secretly and quietly that it leaked out only after the strike had been called . . . there are twenty of these men, representing all nationalities."[25] In spite of its efforts, the WFM had little impact on the Oliver's treatment of the mine workers. When the strike broke down, many of the miners returned to work at the $1.60 a day wage. Although the WFM continued to organize workers after the 1905 labor stoppage, the Oliver continued to meet its attempts with disdain and repression.[26]

Labor Organizing and the 1907 Mesabi Strike

Between 1905 and 1907, the WFM increasingly sent recruiters into the iron ranges. By 1907, it was already a well-established militant industrial union with a reputation for combativeness that had been exacerbated by its union with the IWW two years earlier. As A. M. Stirton, editor of Michigan's pro-IWW newspaper the *Wage Slave*, remarked about the merger, "Let us get busy then and organize into great Industrial Unions competent TO STRIKE AND STAY, that's the word, not to strike and leave as the manner of the Craft Unions is. Get busy and build up the I.W.W. Let every miner in the country join the Western Federation of Miners, and let the Western Federation of Miners swing into line and take its place where it ought to be in the I.W.W."[27]

Founded in Chicago in 1905, the IWW was a grand aggregation of radical organized labor, and the WFM was the largest body pulled into the Wobblies' orbit. The express purpose of this new conglomeration was to seize control of the means of production for the benefit of the workers who lived and died in industrial settings. As one Wobbly treatise argued, "the power of the workers in production is the power of the life and death over society." The Wobblies offered American workers a unique, non-Marxist critique of industrial labor, which maintained that human labor power was the source of all wealth and that capitalists sought to fragment and conquer labor through compartmentalizing production. Although other aspects of life, such as media, politics, and religion, reinforced the exploitation of the working masses, the IWW situated their revolutionary impulse directly at the point of production. It was on the shop floor, under towering stands of white pine, in the wheat fields, and in the open-pit mines that inequitable economic and power relations were experienced most directly, and it was in those settings that the true source of socioeconomic power was located.[28]

The IWW was unlike other unions during the nascent years of organized labor in the United States. The main impact of the IWW to the North American labor movement was in placing a revolutionary aim and purpose alongside the industrial unionism that was gradually developing among the American working class. Industrial unionism was a response to the dominant craft or trade form of union organization.

Craft or trade union organization, according to the founders of the IWW, was becoming outmoded and ineffective owing to the rise of mass-production industries that were replacing craft production. The application of machine technology and the subsequent industrialization, standardization, and de-skilling of the labor process—already well under way in the early twentieth century and later expanded by assembly-line production and scientific management techniques—was beginning to make some skilled trades obsolete. The IWW sought to counteract this march toward industrialization with controversial tactics that included organization of unskilled workers, industrial sabotage, and the ultimate weapon: the general strike, which was designed to shut down entire economies.[29]

To the Wobblies, craft unions divided workers in the same workplace or industry into multiple bargaining units. Craft or trade union autonomy, which provided the restrictive rules for each compartmentalized industrial unit, meant that only a certain portion of workers, usually skilled laborers or craftspersons, in a given industry were available to organize. During labor actions, this restriction often resulted in the defeat of unskilled workers who had little economic, political, or shop-floor status. The Wobblies argued, therefore, that craft and trade union segmentation undermined working-class unity. Its proposed alternative model of industrial organization would place all workers in a single workplace or industry into the same union, regardless of the tools they used in the process of production. All industrial departments would similarly be combined into One Big Union or the OBU. Perhaps most important, unlike many craft unions, such as the AFL during the early twentieth century, membership in the IWW was open to any worker regardless of gender, race, creed, or ethnicity.[30]

Wobbly historian and political scientist Saku Pinta argues that "this approach was designed to maximize the class solidarity necessary for countering the increasingly concentrated power of employers in industrial disputes" and cites an IWW edict that "the longer the picket line, the shorter the strike." Pinta's work has indicated that improvements in wages, hours, and working conditions were essential, but the ultimate aim of the IWW was the overthrow of the capitalist system. The industrial unions of the IWW were structured in such a way as to organize the working class into various branches and departments that would approximate new ways of organizing a future society, known as "building the new society within the shell of the old." The Wobblies did not base their vision of a socialist society (sometimes referred to as "industrial democracy" or the "cooperative commonwealth") on an idealized conception of the past, but rather looked forward to an epoch when human creativity, ingenuity, and technology could be harnessed to benefit humanity as a whole, rather than a privileged elite. Under such a system, the state apparatus would be replaced by industrial administration, while class divisions and the wage system would be abolished in favor of common ownership, with production for use rather than profit as the guiding principle. For the Wobblies in the early twentieth century, industrial unions were to be the embryonic form of an approaching socialist society.[31]

By 1907, with a well-formed ideology in tow, the WFM was successful in signing up approximately 2,500 miners on the Mesabi Range and was set to make another attempt at a significant labor stoppage. Immigrant Finns were at the forefront of the WFM's rank and file, but the administration of the 1907 Mesabi strike came under the supervision of Italian immigrant organizer Teofilo Petriella.[32] On July 19, 1907, Petriella and the WFM demanded two concessions from the OIMC. The first demand was that the company end the dubious "contract system of mining," which provided numerous opportunities for graft on the part of petty mining captains. The contract system paid miners for iron ore extracted in a day. If a miner were stuck in hard rock with little ore, the payment for the day would decrease. Conversely, if a miner found himself in soft, workable rock, the payment for that day would increase. Mining captains sold the soft rock jobs to miners for a price. The contract system was a point of contention between labor and the mining companies for years to follow. The WFM's second demand was that the mine workers receive a flat wage for an eight-hour workday. For a common mine laborer, the wage was to be $2.50 per day, $3.00 for foremen, and $5.00 for engineers.[33]

As might be expected, the OIMC failed to meet the demands of the WFM. Petriella retaliated by calling out the mine workers of the Mesabi Range on July 20, 1907. WFM officials in Denver had intended to call the strike a week later, on or about July 26, but when organizers caught wind of a mining company plan to jettison hundreds of workers before the labor action began, the WFM sprang into action. Almost from the beginning, the WFM, Petriella, and the striking workers who followed them were branded as good-for-nothing anarchists mainly because of the socialist Finns who swelled the Federation's ranks. In a July 23, 1907, newspaper article, the pro-company *Mesaba Ore* editorialized that "it was a mark of note that fully ninety-percent of those in line at the Hibbing Miners' Parade were Finlanders—fiery followers of the Red Flag in that procession." The rampant anti-immigrant attitudes of the ranges' American-born population were on display in the *Ore's* chronicling of the strike: "Of those marching, not one American appeared in line. It was a representative gathering of a class that wants this country run on the socialist plan, and who are willing to resort to all meaning of lawless acts to instill the reform they seek." Because of the strike, not a shovel moved on the Mesabi Range. Activity at the Oliver's mines came to a standstill in Hibbing, Eveleth, and Virginia—shut down by labor agitators and immigrants who had, in most cases, been in the United States for less than a decade.[34]

The Oliver was terribly concerned that the strike activity of the Mesabi Range would filter to the Vermilion. In a letter to the Oliver's General Superintendent Charles Trezona, Assistant Superintendent P. F. Chemoream reported, "Last Monday night a couple of Finns, from the Missabe Range, presumably Socialists, attempted to get the Finn Hall here to talk to the miners. The hall was refused them, as it has been in one previous instance." The Oliver was willing to use whatever means necessary to stop the strike from spreading, including violence, as Chemoream continued: "I am equally positive that in case of interference from the Western Federation of Miners we can raise 175 men, who want to work and protect their homes, to escort these Socialists to the Town line South and help them on their way. However, I am hopeful that such a measure will not be necessary and that we can work without any trouble."[35]

After hearing from Chemoream, Trezona was keen to put necessary measures in place to guard against the strike's northeasterly flow from the Mesabi to the Vermilion Range. On the same day that he received

Chemoream's letter, Trezona wrote to the assistant superintendent at the Soudan Mine in Tower on the Vermilion:

> I would be glad to have you report to me daily, by letter, the situation at the Soudan Mine. Also, I think it would be a good scheme if you could interest the mayor of Tower in this matter, and see whether or not something cannot be done in the way of appointing deputies to cope with any crowd of men that might come over from the Mesaba Range and attempt to stop work at Soudan Mine. I think it would be a good scheme to take this matter up with the mayor, in a quiet way, and see if you cannot get him interested, as well as the businessmen.[36]

From management's perspective, Trezona's trepidation regarding the strike could be seen as understandable in light of events, but his inkling to scheme in secret regarding scurrilous company tactics bordered on unethical. That he was downright immoral regarding the Oliver's efforts was furthered by a handwritten addendum in his letter to Chamberlain, which read, "Paul, you should have the matter taken up with the mayor so that it will appear that the citizens are doing it and not the mining co[mpany]."[37] These back-channel communications, elusive dealings, and scheming sessions would come to characterize mining company subterfuge during strikes. Wanting to seem as if they were above the fray, company managers relied on others to do their bidding and dirty work, while attempting to keep their own actions and intentions hidden from legal recourse and public awareness.

Another example of mining companies' subterfuge during times of labor unrest was employment of out-of-state residents as deputies, detectives, spies, and company police during the strike. Not only was the practice unscrupulous, it was illegal in Minnesota during the 1907 strike. According to revised 1905 state statutes, an armed mining company agent had to be a "legal voter" in Minnesota. This prohibited the importation of gun thugs from outside the state. Violation of this prohibition was considered a gross misdemeanor. A more stringent section of the statutes provided that the hiring and arming of private armies was illegal, again punishable as a gross misdemeanor.[38]

An investigator for Minnesota's Federation of Labor found evidence that mining companies and local law-enforcement members on the

Mesabi Range had, in fact, imported and armed men to harass and hassle strikers. The federation published its findings in an October 1907 edition of *Labor Review*, a magazine geared toward organized labor in Minnesota. *Labor Review* documented the investigator's findings as to whether Minnesota's governor, John A. Johnson, and Commissioner of Labor, Industries, and Commerce W. H. Williams had fully enforced the relevant sections of the 1905 law, known then as the Stockwell Law. Among other findings, the investigator found that the "Employers' Detective Service of Chicago had shipped 145 men from Chicago and Milwaukee en route to Duluth and the Iron Ranges." As evidence for the assertion, the investigator produced a number of affidavits that substantiated the claim that mining companies and local sheriffs from St. Louis and Itasca counties had imported and armed men from out of state for the purposes of quelling labor actions and that Johnson and Williams had done little to hold mining companies or local law enforcement accountable for their actions. One affidavit from a hired Chicago strikebreaker named Benno Kirdier outlined the harsh actions of the imported strikebreakers:

> I was furnished with a gun and a [sheriff's] deputy star and went to work that night. On that same night a raid was made on the boarding house of Peter Zagar where some of the strikers boarded. Capt Kelly [head of the strikebreakers] gave us instructions to load our guns and get ready, and when the signal came to shoot, to obey the order and shoot . . . the next I saw the deputies took the people that were there out and put them in a line and the boarding house keeper was handled pretty roughly . . . they marched the strikers down to [the deputy sheriff's] camp and searched them. There were over 100 strikebreakers there at the deputies' camp, and more than half of them I heard state were from Chicago.[39]

Hired thugs from Chicago, New York, and Milwaukee attempted to break the strike using whatever means necessary. In an August 5, 1907, letter back to his family in Finland, recent immigrant Victor Myllymäki recalled the violence: "There is a great strike going on here [in Eveleth]. There are many of us out of work. I don't know how long the strike will last. It's been only two and a half weeks since it started and this isn't a very pleasant time at all. There are 100 stooges with guns paid by the mining companies. . . . A worker can't peacefully walk down the street anymore. People are jailed every day."[40]

Allegedly, the most heinous act of violence committed by strikers occurred on August 8. Finnish immigrant strikers went to a boarding-house maintained by two women near the Burt Mine in Hibbing and demanded that the house accept no "scab" miners. When deputies ar-rived on the scene, the strikers dispersed. Law enforcement officers seized nineteen of the men and brought them before Judge Thomas F. Brady in Hibbing. Ten received jail sentences for inciting and participat-ing in a riot. While area newspapers bemoaned the scourge of immi-grant workers organizing to better their lives, the Oliver imported more than 1,100 immigrant Austrians to fill gaps in the workforce. Finnish socialists tried their best to rally the rank-and-file miners by opening their social halls on the Mesabi. Such measures were of little use when the OIMC reopened the Mesabi mines with the strikebreaking South Slavic replacement workers.[41]

The Mesabi strike of 1907 lasted for roughly three weeks, and the *Virginia Daily Enterprise* declared the action all but broken on August 9. The WFM, in its own analysis of the strike, was unsure if the organizers' efforts ever had a sustainable foundation:

> The inauguration of this strike by the Minnesota District Union . . . was very unwise, owing to the conditions which surrounded them at the time, as at the time the strike was called, there was less than two thousand members on the Mesabe Range out of about twenty thou-sand men employed by the Iron Mining Companies. They had none of the mechanical forces in the organization, but on the other hand steam shovel men, craners, and engineers, were organized in the American Federation of Labor and fighting the Western Federation of Miners . . . many of those who responded to the strike call and were not members of the organization claimed they did so on the assurance of strike bene-fits (and when they didn't get strike benefits) there was general tur-moil throughout the Range . . . Executive Board Member MacKenzie took charge of the strike [from Petriella] in the latter part of August, straightened out all of our obligations, and while the strike was never officially called off, the fight was dropped and the men secured employ-ment wherever possible.[42]

The WFM's less than enthusiastic endorsement of the strike angered some of its most ardent supporters. While many of the immigrant mine workers were preparing to return to work within the next week, there was one major exception: holdout Finnish immigrant strikers and their families. Of the striking Finnish immigrant mine workers, the *Enterprise* editorialized on August 9, 1907: "Thus far no definite sign of weakening has been manifested on the part of the Finnish miners and workmen constituting in great degree the striking element." Advocates for immigrant workers were few and far between on the ranges, but a growing political reform movement that called for the curtailing of big businesses' influence and the reining in of oligarchy across the nation was making its presence felt. It was not the revolutionary movement supported by many of the Finnish and Italian immigrants during the 1907 strike, but the progressive movement would change the face of politics on the ranges nonetheless.

Range Politics in the Progressive Era

As strikes and labor disputes continued to permeate the Iron Range, the fight for better wages, working conditions, and an improved social safety net was bolstered by a growing political movement. In contrast to the revolutionary industrial unionism advocated by many of the Range's disenfranchised immigrant voters, the progressive movement was a reform-seeking political ethos that was home to many educated, middle-class Americans. Progressivism proved to profoundly shape political and social landscapes on the Iron Range. During the early twentieth century, most of the Range's immigrant mine workers and their families had little say in the conditions of their labor. Their work, and in some instances their cultural, domestic, and social lives, were handed down to them from managers at the mining companies. Lacking the right to vote, these immigrants had even less of a say in the election of public officials. During this time, men partial to mining company interests dominated range politics. A glimpse of change appeared with the rise of the progressive movement, led by English-speaking, educated, middle-class reformers who sought to study, report, and ultimately change socio-economic ills. Progressives were steered by strong winds of change, but not revolutionary gusts, and they differed greatly from the IWW in this

Hibbing's mayor Victor Power was a formally educated lawyer from an Irish Catholic background. He was a member of the Republican Party until being elected as a progressive in 1913. Courtesy of the Hibbing Historical Society.

regard. While the Wobblies sought to "create a new society in the shell of the old," the progressive movement advocated reform and metered socioeconomic change. Although they advocated similar ideas, progressives and the IWW were, at times, in bitter opposition to one another. Thus, revolutionary industrial unionism was not just kicking against mining companies on the Iron Range; it was also at an impasse with the surging progressive politicians who were winning municipal elections.

Perhaps the best known of these Iron Range progressives was Victor L. Power, whose dynamic character, forceful speaking style, and vaunted legal degree set him apart from the region's other political leaders. Early in his life, Power had worked in an area mine, but then attended college and eventually set up a law practice. He entered politics in 1913 when he was elected mayor of his hometown of Hibbing. In what was called a "Sweeping Victory" for progressives, the *Hibbing News Tribune* lauded Power's win along with that of a host of other progressive politicians: "Victor L. Power, attorney-at-law, yesterday defeated Dr. H. R. Weirick, for seven years mayor of Hibbing, by a vote of two to one, receiving 722 to Mayor Weirick's 362," and "the landslide which resulted in the defeat of the administration ticket was one of the most pronounced in the history of the city . . . it followed a short but heated campaign in which both sides put up a brisk fight and was a big surprise to those who have heretofore been a strong influence in controlling city elections."[43]

After his election, Power took direct aim at curtailing the large measure of control mining companies had in municipal politics. In 1915, he squared off directly with mine managers over taxes. In an effort to keep some of the wealth created on the ranges in the ranges, Power took his case to J. A. O. Preus, state auditor of Minnesota, in a wonderfully crafted letter dated August 31, 1915:

> Some considerable time ago I wrote you informing you of the condition that existed in Hibbing with respect to the payment of taxes. I informed you that several of the mining companies had conspired together for the purpose of acquiring control of the village government of the Village of Hibbing, and, in furtherance of that conspiracy, they had agreed together to withhold the payment of their taxes justly and legally due, at the same time demanding from the Village of Hibbing that it surrender to them control of the Village government. The village being a branch of the state government and the village council believing that they were acting in accordance with the duties incumbent upon them by reason of their office, refused to surrender the rights of the people to the mining companies. Thus there was precipitated a fight over the amount of taxes that was justly due from these mine owners and especially from the United States Steel corporation to the State of Minnesota, to the school district of this vicinity, to the county of St. Louis and to the Village of Hibbing.[44]

During his tenure as mayor, mining company managers accused Power of extravagant spending at the expense of taxpayers. In turn, Power blamed the mining companies for pilfering the resources of the state. It was an elegant and populist argument that began with the concept of public ownership of resources: "The people of the Village of Hibbing believe that these ore bodies are not and should not be the property of individuals and in exclusion of the people, who are the rightful owners thereof, and they do not feel that it is extravagance to expend taxes for the purpose of bettering their condition and the condition of the state." Power ended his argument by suggesting that it was a waste to surrender Minnesota's resources to "non-resident capitalists for expenditure outside of the state" and that "the pine timber of our state and the iron bodies were not created or enhanced in value by the act of these non-resident operators, but they were the gift of Providence for the benefit of society."[45]

Power's strong language and populist position appealed to many who understood the inherent inequalities of daily life on the Iron Range. In his campaign to wrest authority from mining companies, he skillfully appealed to the civic sensibilities of Rangers against pro-business provocateurs in Duluth, who were rumored to be associates of mining company management. Power's written assault on the mining companies and thus their Duluth business associates and interests caused the *Duluth Herald* and the *Hibbing News Tribune* to wage a war of words in 1915 over Hibbing's alleged affluence.

As a result of the acrimony between Power and mining company managers, a bill rumored to have come directly from the desks of Oliver management was put before the Minnesota legislature to "limit the expenditures of villages and cities on the ranges." Hibbing's newspapers took to task those looking to defame the city and its call for a larger piece of mining company profits. Chortling about "facts" published in the *Duluth Herald*, one Hibbing paper chastised C. O. Baldwin and W. D. Bailey of Duluth, along with Edward C. Hale of Minneapolis, for inaccurate claims about Hibbing's supposed posh infrastructure. Power also took out an advertisement in the same edition admonishing that Baldwin, Bailey, and Hale's "facts were developed by representatives of eastern capitalists who fear that the people of Minnesota will get hold of some of Minnesota's wealth before they succeed in dragging it out of the state."[46]

It seemed that Power and the IWW might have been natural allies in the struggle for industrial democracy and against the exploitation of mining companies. Ideology, however, split the two populist camps, and the revolutionary goals of the IWW never matched the political reform perspectives adhered to by Power and the progressives. Power flatly refused the revolutionary impulse and his allegiances to organized labor rested squarely with the craft and trades unions of the AFL. Although his oratory and letter-writing campaigns forcefully called for public ownership of natural resources, he could never quite make the jump to a revolutionary restructuring of society. For their part, the Wobblies were dismissive of electoral politics and staunchly antiestablishment. If the Wobblies were fanning the flames of discontent on a tinder-dry landscape in hopes of firing socioeconomic revolution, Power was looking for ways to make it rain. Thus, three distinct and prominent players occupied the cultural, economic, political, and social landscapes of northern Minnesota: mine owners, reformers, and revolutionaries. The tense interactions between all three would create a volatile scene as each attempted to assert their identity and ideology on the Iron Range's dynamic populations.

3 WOBBLY FIREBRANDS

Organizing the Finnish Working Class

Are you poor, forlorn, and hungry?
Are there lots of things you lack?
Is your life made up of misery?
Then dump the bosses off your back.
—*"Dump the Bosses Off Your Back," song lyrics by John Brill, 1916*

ALONGSIDE THE IWW's REVOLUTIONARY INDUSTRIAL UNIONISM, which advocated for a union of all workers, a dynamic, robust, and vibrant cultural apparatus began to develop in the early 1910s. This significant assemblage of cultural forms included art, athletics, debating societies, libraries, social halls, songs, street speaking, union meetings, and the publishing of informational, literary, and ideological texts. The IWW created and nurtured this vibrant popular culture by mixing didactic ideological messages with a stylized medium to foster a unique sense of radical and apolitical working-class solidarity. Especially influential in the shaping of this dynamic culture were the IWW's graphic communications, songs of protest, and cultural spaces of discontent. These media offerings and venues created an immersive sensory experience that audibly, spatially, and visually represented common, everyday themes of class struggle, solidarity, and working-class emancipation. Most often, these sensate experiences appealed to passionate union members who were committed to the IWW's organizational goals, but underlying these emotionally charged media offerings and social gatherings was a strong sense of organizational credibility and thoughtful design and development, which guided the IWW's cultural contributions to the American labor movement.

The IWW's unique proletarian culture has been the subject of debate in labor and cultural history circles. In his important book *We Shall Be All: A History of the Industrial Workers of the World,* labor historian Melvyn Dubofksy argued that the IWW organized around what he termed a "culture of poverty," which brought alienated and disenfranchised industrial workers together to ease the loneliness of life on the road to working-class emancipation.[1] Dubofsky's book was a key early academic examination of the Wobblies, but his culture of poverty thesis was questioned by some who believed that his argument shortchanged the historical agency of the IWW as an effective organization in early-twentieth-century labor relations. It was argued that the poverty thesis relegated Wobblies to being acted upon by capitalist and statist hegemons, instead of portraying the union and its members as fully engaged and mindful participants in their own destinies. Often portrayed as hoboes or itinerant laborers, the roaming, revolutionary culture of the Wobblies has been both celebrated and jeered. This portrayal also had geographic dimensions because Dubofsky's culture of poverty thesis rested in the IWW's fight to organize rural mining and logging landscapes in the American West. The itinerant worker characterization best fit the West's industrial milieu, as thousands of men—often second- or third-generation Americans—wandered from field to forest to mine to mill looking for work. Conversely, the IWW was also active in organizing immigrant workers in the eastern United States. In fact, some of the union's most important and successful labor actions occurred in Massachusetts and New Jersey and included the organization of immigrant women working in industrial factories located in teeming metropolitan areas.

In contrast to Dubofsky's characterization of the IWW's culture of poverty, Verity Burgmann and Salvatore Salerno both posit the idea that its unique, revolutionary culture was more complex and nuanced with regard to ethnicity, gender, geography, and mobility. Burgmann's examination of the Wobblies shifts focus on the organization to Australia, where the IWW sought to organize workers away from the continent of its founding. With regard to Dubofsky's culture of poverty thesis,

Burgmann writes that "the hobo stereotype has persisted because it has served varied purposes: to belittle the Wobblies and to dismiss their criticism [of industrial life and work]; or to proclaim [the positive benefits of the itinerant worker] in the dispossessed status of the membership, in the essential accuracy of the hobo caricature, lay the true strength and vitality of the movement and the source of its distinctive morality and incorruptibility."[2] Similarly, Salerno dispels the rural/urban, native/immigrant binaries by pointing out that "it is apparent that the I.W.W. drew its radical sensibility from a mixture of cosmopolitan and rural experience. Therefore, attempts to locate the I.W.W.'s labor radicalism in a native incarnation of class struggle or as an exotic manifestation of a European revolutionary tendency merely simplify and dichotomize the complexity of the cultural sources influencing the I.W.W.'s development."[3] Expanding on Burgmann and Salerno's interpretations, and in an effort to provide the Wobblies with a much-deserved voice of their own, I argue that the IWW's culture was a carefully crafted representation of a rebellious, yet skillfully ordered, revolutionary industrial union.

Arguably, those most enthusiastic to embrace the IWW's unique, revolutionary union culture were Finnish immigrants. Even before the founding of the IWW in 1905, the Finns had developed a well-organized cultural life in the United States. It did not take long for Finnish immigrants, who mostly worked in the industrial mines and forests of the United States' northern tier and Canada's central and western provinces, to turn that vibrant cultural life into a functional critique of exploitative American labor practices. Perhaps more than any other immigrant group, they gravitated toward the IWW's unique proletarian culture, and in some ways embraced the caricature of the IWW as a hobo culture. A graphic representation of this portrayal appeared in Lapatossu (Shoepack)—a little hobo character "born" in 1910 and featured in a satirical periodical of the same name. Finnish immigrant Wobblies even approved of the moniker when a rival conservative newspaper characterized their 1910s headquarters in Hancock, Michigan, as "Jatkastaapi," or Hobo Headquarters. What many did not know, however, was that the "hoboness" of the IWW, and its Finnish immigrant followers, was a satirical reappropriation of the term that was meant to confound, confront, and confuse capitalist bosses. Finnish immigrants

Often depicted as the "Happy Hobo," Lapatossu, or Shoepack, was famous for his wit and ability to get one over on the bosses. He was a type of mythological working-class hero created for Finnish immigrants struggling with life in industrial America. Illustration from *Työmies*, 1914. Author's collection.

boldly admitted as much when they began publishing *Lapatossu*. Kalle Suvanto, the Finnish immigrant cartoonist who created the Lapatossu character, commented on his wandering proletarian:

> My pencil began to create the figure of Lapatossu on my drawing table this way: mouth in a wide grin, surrounded by stubble, with an American corn-cob pipe hanging down from one corner. A small nose, the right eye far-reaching, round and bright. The left eye closed. On his head a worn bowler hat, pulled down to the ears. In the hat-band a little flower, as a symbol of idealism. In the picture Lapatossu comes from afar, walking along the railroad tracks like hundreds of immigrant boys have had to do in this wide land as they've searched for work . . . Tossu is a cheerful worker who lives on the borders of society. The name has been given by other workers. He is always ready to trade word for word with his fellow workers as well as his employers.[4]

In many ways, Lapatossu encapsulated the cultural values of the IWW and its fervent supporters in the Finnish immigrant community; on one hand, the organization was a bit bawdy, satirical, and scruffy, while on the other, this sense of chicanery was a confident and carefully crafted image—a guarded statement of identity that worked to confound efforts to characterize or define the organization and its members from the outside. In much the same way, the IWW was a keen protector of its own sense of self, and this understanding of who and what the union was about was the exclusive right of the organization's membership. So, although the Wobblies as a cultural organization (and some of its members) could verge on being downright (and intentionally) disorderly, they were also a well-organized, purposefully structured industrial union. Although this latter characterization is often overlooked, there is ample evidence for the IWW's almost scientific organization of industrial workers.

Structuring a Radical Organization

In various complaints and criticisms registered against the IWW by outsiders, the union was depicted as a group of chaos-inducing nihilists, prone to haphazard walkouts and wildcat strikes. Especially dismissive of the IWW were American communists. In his article on Canadian bush-workers, J. Peter Campbell wrote that American communists derisively compared the IWW to a "Cult of Spontaneity."[5] These characterizations, some advanced by competing leftist movements, were derogatory defamations to make the union, its organizational techniques, and culture appear jumbled and reckless. Although these portrayals of the IWW were accurate in alluding to an active cultural organization that was artistic and boisterous, the characterizations downplay and devalue the logical organization and structuring of a revolutionary industrial union, which helped to ground the IWW as an effective representative of America's industrial workers. The Wobblies' inclusive ethos guided most of their cultural expressions. In texts about the IWW's history and organizational goals, the union's publishing department worked to combat contradictory and dismissive characterizations.

Graphic arts were a very important part of the IWW's working-class culture. Arguably the most revolutionary work of Wobbly "art" is Father Thomas J. Hagerty's "Wheel of Industrial Unionism." Father Hagerty was at one time an actual Catholic priest, but an unusual one at that. He finished seminary in 1895, served as a priest in Chicago for a short time, and then relocated to the American Southwest. At first he advocated working-class issues according to ecclesiastical custom, but his views grew more revolutionary and he fell out of favor with the church. As a member of the Socialist Party of America, he edited the American Labor Union's newspaper, the *Voice of Labor*. As he became more involved in socialist causes, the Socialist Party of America became too restrictive for his growing revolutionary perspective, and by 1905 he had drifted into the IWW's fold.[6]

Much of what the IWW published were carefully constructed images and texts of working-class discontent designed to pull on the heartstrings of future and present union members. While emotional appeals to stir the rank and file helped to grow membership, the apparent need for some type of logically conceived structural platform was evident as early as 1905. Into this organizational quandary strode Father Hagerty and his experiences with the highly structured Catholic church. Hagerty proposed and rendered a coherent organizational structure for the IWW, which took the form of a wheel with equally apportioned industrial units. The intention was to unite workers of all crafts, trades, races, political affiliations, and both genders into one big industrial union. His wheel was composed of numerous jobs and general membership branches as spokes

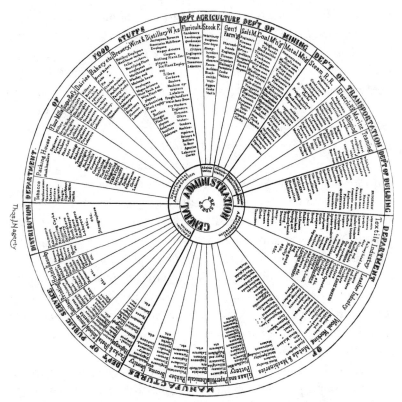

The original 1905 rendering of Father Thomas J. Hagerty's "Wheel of Industrial Unionism" featured eight departments of industry around a central administration and president. The wheel first appeared in the Western Federation of Miners publication, *The Miner's Magazine*, and proposed a radical new way of organizing labor.

that led inward toward departmental administrations, which in turn led to a central administration that radiated around a president at the center of the organization.

Father Hagerty's wheel was a one-dimensional disc of logically ordered industrial classifications. It was, in essence, a taxonomy of industrial work. Hagerty's artistic rendering appeared as an industrial unionist's Periodic Table of Elements. Unlike the Periodic Table, however, which separated elements by composition, Hagerty's classifications brought workers together in one synergistic union that was stronger because of its separate parts. Each department of industrial jobs from the Department of Food Stuffs, which included workers in dairies and breweries, to the Department of Public Service, which included postal workers and hotel chambermaids, had a place in the One Big Union. This highly organized wheel was antithetical to outsiders' conceptions of the IWW's haphazard "Cult of Spontaneity." While the union's radical literature nurtured revolutionary ideals, Hagerty's wheel seemed to represent a steadfast organizational structure.

As a cultural artifact, Hagerty's wheel was different in form and function from the IWW's other revolutionary imagery, which was created to elicit an emotional response. In total, the wheel encompassed resistance to laissez-faire forms of capitalism, the apprenticeship system of craft and trade unions, and socialist and communist forms of hierarchical bureaucracy. In this way, it symbolized the values that were present in the IWW's revolutionary union culture by proposing a radical, new way to structure union organization. Over the years, the renderings of Hagerty's wheel became more stylized, but its original purpose as a logically derived symbol of resistance to customary union organization remained intact well into the 1950s.

A stark contrast between Hagerty's 1905 wheel and later versions was the absence of a "president" and "central administration." Hagerty's original version met with stiff resistance from anarchist-minded members at the IWW's founding convention. The general concept of Hagerty's vision for industrial unionism was accepted, but the particulars of the administration were debated. The IWW had a type of centralized structure, but it refrained from electing presidents or having official, principal figureheads, instead choosing to situate administration in the hands of an elected group of leaders, with the union's general secretary being first among equals. This organizational structure, inclusive at its core, was especially receptive to immigrants, of whom Finns were the most numerous and boisterous, particularly on Minnesota's iron Ranges.

Red, Wobbly Finns

Finnish immigrants contributed greatly to attempts to transform the inequalities of industrial life and bring about a new society on the iron ranges. Often described as agrarian, clannish, socialistic, and slated for exclusion under early-twentieth-century immigration policies, Finns were a small but well-known immigrant population in the Lake Superior basin.[7] As sociologist Peter Kivisto notes:

Finns occupied the status of a definite "out-group" even though they are white Protestant. They were depicted as "Jackpine Savages," Mongolians (in 1907, an attempt was made to deny them citizenship by invoking existing anti-Oriental legislation), and violence prone revolutionaries. As a consequence of this prejudice, the climate was favorable for a variety of repressive actions, including imprisonment and blacklisting.[8]

The number of Finnish immigrant socialists grew as they encountered American industrial life and in a short time they gained a reputation for leftist politics. As Finns began to clash with American industrial and conservative political practices, their penchant for protest and organizational skills catapulted them to important roles within early-twentieth-century social and union organizations. Finnish immigrant socialists were the first and largest ethnic group to set up their own internal language federation within the Socialist Party of America. The Suomalainen Sosialistijärjestö (Finnish Socialist Federation—FSF) was founded in 1906 and organized on the Mesabi Range in Hibbing. Two dozen delegates from regional Finnish socialist organizations came together to form this socialist federation. Regionally, the FSF grew meteorically in the following years as successive waves of Finnish immigrants settled on the iron ranges. Membership numbers of local chapters grew from 2,622 people in 1906 to 13,667 in 1912. By 1912, the FSF constituted approximately 15 percent of the Socialist Party of America's membership.[9]

In the midst of the FSF's rapid growth, a schism developed between revolutionary and parliamentary factions within its membership. This division had its roots in the 1907 Mesabi strike. During the strike, Finnish mine workers looked to the Western Federation of Mineworkers (WFM) union for support, but the WFM (now a part of the IWW) lacked funding to prolong the strike and received no backing from the much larger craft union amalgamation, the American Federation of Labor (AFL). The AFL's disassociation from the WFM was owing to the Wobblies' radical organizational tactics. The AFL was also at ideological odds with the WFM and IWW on the practice of dual unionism—members belonging to two unions at the same time—as well as the practice of extending union membership to unskilled immigrant labor. Consequently, the 1907 strike ran out of momentum in the rank and file of immigrant mine workers did not receive anticipated funding from the WFM and met overwhelming opposition from the Oliver. These setbacks surreptitiously broke the strike as hundreds of mine workers were blacklisted from employment on the Mesabi and Vermilion ranges.[10]

The relatively young Finnish Socialist Federation was rapidly learning the "hard lessons of the School of Morgan and Rockefeller."[11] As a result, disillusioned socialists began to doubt the course of the FSF. The Oliver had not met any of the WFM's demands in the 1907 strike, the death rate of mine workers on the Mesabi Range between 1905 and 1906 was high at 7.5 people for every one thousand workers, mine guards had shot five Finnish mine workers between 1888 and 1905, and the WFM's leadership failed in efforts at long-term organization of the rank and file. There was great dissatisfaction within the ranks of the FSF after the 1907 strike and members of the FSF who were partial to the IWW's revolutionary industrial unionism began to agitate for a more militant organization. Adding to the problems with the WFM leadership, Finnish strikers began to feel that the WFM's leaders exploited immigrant strikers. As mine workers suffered to put bread on the table, WFM organizers such as Teofilo Petriella were reportedly living lavishly. Ethnic rivalry and suspicion had played a major role in organizing difficulties, and blacklisted, sometimes bitter Finnish immigrant mine workers resorted to farming marginal lands in northern Minnesota's turbulent hinterlands just to make ends meet.[12] The 1907 strike fostered strong feelings of discontent within the FSF, setting the stage for an important ideological split between so-called parliamentary and revolutionary socialists. The parliamentary faction saw electoral politics as an effective tool for change, while the revolutionary group saw voting as a bourgeois tool to pacify the working class. This schism festered until 1909 when open conflict enveloped the proceedings of the FSF's national convention. By 1914, after Michigan's Copper County Strike, the two sides had parted ways, cleaving the FSF's membership almost in half.[13]

The 3Rs of Proletarian Literacy

As Finns were arriving in the United States during the early twentieth century, a number of socialist or labor colleges were springing up across the country, such as the Modern School of New York City, founded in 1911; the People's College of Fort Scott, Kansas, founded in 1915; and the Brookwood Labor College of Katonah, New York, founded in 1921. The Work People's College (WPC) was a precursor to many of these class-conscious colleges. Founded in 1907 in Smithville, Minnesota (now within Duluth's boundaries), the WPC's proletarian curriculum was heavily influenced by the IWW's ideology. The college was a center of proletarian education that based its curriculum around a "propaganda of the deed" or direct-action ideology, which advocated revolutionary action over the ballot box. The school was a bastion of socialist and industrial unionist thought, with many of the professors teaching direct-action tactics such as industrial sabotage.[14]

The WPC worked to educate students in the 3Rs of proletarian literacy: reading, (w)riting, and *revolution*. The school's objective was to create an identity for the college, its students, and its faculty that stressed the development of class-conscious workers who were familiar with the goals of industrial unionism. In addition to introductions to ideology, the school worked to develop practical applications of socialist society such as bookkeeping, literacy, artistic endeavors, and publishing as a way of transmitting that ideology to the masses. This approach differed from other general literacy programs; education was not just concerned with the mechanics of reading and writing, but rather with using literacy as a way to break the bonds of repressive institutional hierarchies such as religion, statism, and, most significantly—capitalism. In this way, the literacy gained at the WPC was a cultural, class, and philosophical competency in working-class movements and ideology. As imagined, this revolutionary approach met with great opposition in many reactionary, liberal, and progressive circles. It was a radical curriculum, much like Francisco Ferrer's earlier anarchist-inspired Escuela Moderna for primary school students in Spain, which fomented later iterations in the United States' own Modern School movement.[15]

The WPC focused on adult and continuing education, and also offered summer school to working-class children. Although proletarian

EDUCATION

ORGANIZATION—EMANCIPATION

The Work Peoples College at Smithville, Minn., near the city of Duluth, is the only institution in the United States that gives instruction in industrial unionism and also in all such theoretical and technical subjects that are necessary in the industrial labor movement.

This school is controlled entirely by members of the I. W. W. which is a full guarantee for the fact that this institution is serving the purposes of the organization of the I. W. W. and its membership by teaching various subjects pertaining to social sciences, economics, and technical matters which all are useful in the revolutionary labor movement.

The Thirteenth annual convention of the I. W. W. fully endorsed in principle this college and promised its moral support and publicity through the various publications of the organization.

All this shows that the Work Peoples College is the only place of learning for revolutionary workers, that it serves the revolutionary labor movement, and is, so to speak, one of the necessary organs for building up industrial democracy.

In order to emancipate ourselves from industrial slavery we must know our aim. Taking this into consideration the Board of Directors for the Work Peoples College sends an appeal to workers who wish to obtain education that they would make use of this in satisfying their desire for learning.

Following courses are offered:

COURSES OF INSTRUCTION

1. Scientific department.
2. Technical elementary sciences and practise.
3. English department.
4. Organization bookkeeping department.

SCIENTIFIC DEPARTMENT

Lectures in this department will be given on the following subjects: The construction and procedure of industrial unionism, commencing with the preamble of the I. W. W. and concluding in industrial society. Economics, Sociology, Geography and Biology.

KNOWLEDGE IS THE MOTHER OF PROGRESS

PRACTISE DEPARTMENT

Among other work in this department, two hours per week will be devoted to correct pronunciation, reciting poetry, reading and platform department.

Two hours per week will be given to public speaking and presentation, debate, parliamentary drill, and organization work.

In addition to these hours the student body will arrange for two meetings per week in which subjects of the hour and other discussion will be carried on so as to give the students practise in speaking and conducting meetings according to parliamentary rules.

DEPARTMENT OF ENGLISH

The teaching of English language is divided into four classes. The first class learn the fundamentals of grammar, pronunciation and the diacritical marks.

The second class goes through the grammar thoroughly and in detail. Considerable attention is given to composition in connection with the points raised in the grammar. Attention is also given to sounds and the pronunciation.

The third class concentrates on composition with reviews now and then in grammar. Considerable time is given to reading.

The fourth class gives most of the time to the study of rhetoric; several long themes are written.

DEPARTMENT OF BOOKKEEPING

I. The duties of a delegate.

II. The duties of a secretary.

III. Fundamentals of double entry bookkeeping according to the Rowe system. The student can take up the work where he had formerly left off, or depending on his former preparation.

Additional information regarding the school year, fees, etc., may be obtained by addressing THE WORK PEOPLE'S COLLEGE, Box 39, Morgan Park Station, Duluth, Minnesota.

A 1918 English-language advertisement for the Finnish immigrant–founded Työväen Opisto, or Work People's College. Located in Smithville, Minnesota, outside Duluth, the college operated in the shadow of U.S. Steel's Duluth Works and the planned company town, Morgan Park. Courtesy of the Institute of Migration, Turku, Finland.

literacy was the desired outcome, early on it became apparent that the need for basic literacy programs was required because of the lack of formal education among the WPC's students. According to historian Richard J. Altenbaugh, "the rudiments of mathematics and the basic rules of Finnish grammar had to be taught to worker-students who, although literate, came from poor rural backgrounds in Finland, which required a minimal amount of formal schooling."[16] The need for basic forms of education was apparent early in the school's history, as Finnish-American historian Douglas Ollila Jr. detailed:

> Of the 123 students enrolled in 1911–1912, forty had had no previous education whatsoever, while fifty-seven had had at most two years of training in the elementary schools of Finland. The educational level of the Finnish immigrant was thus quite low, in contrast to the stereotype that Finns had attained a high educational level in Finland. It is interesting to note that the need to master basic educational skills was so imperative that the college founded a correspondence school whose chief aim was lessons in English.[17]

Courses in basic literacy accompanied accounting, mathematics, and science courses in Finnish and sometimes English, which supplemented highly didactic course work centered on the cultivation of reading, (w)riting, and revolution.

For a time, the WPC's tempestuous early existence mirrored the split in the Finnish immigrants' divided labor and proletarian political movements. During its early years, the school teetered between parliamentary socialism and industrial unionism (some might opine anarcho-syndicalism), but, as Ollila writes, "at the 1909 meeting of the Finnish Socialist Federation, industrial unionism and especially the IWW were condemned as being anarchistic, but radicalism persisted in the Midwest, especially at the school" (103). The WPC offered courses in subjects such as political theory, but also provided students with more practical classes aimed at training labor agitators and organizers for work in the field. Professors were generally older and battle-hardened Finnish immigrants associated with the labor movement, such as Leo Laukki, Yrjö Sirola, and Fred Jaakkola. But the institution itself was also home to young proletarian students looking to shape the world,

Students and faculty pose for a photograph inside a science classroom at Work People's College, circa 1915. Prominent orator, editor, and writer Leo Laukki is standing fifth from the left. Courtesy of the Institute of Migration, Turku, Finland.

starting with the Lake Superior region, into a more equitable place. For many at the WPC, it was likely a great place to be young, passionate, and radical while absorbing the revolutionary topics that dominated the college's curriculum:

> While basic education was a primary aim, nevertheless a good many students absorbed socialism in a greater or lesser degree. For many, it was perhaps a very superficial mastery of the theoretical ideas of Marx, Engels, and Kautsky. No doubt the most important learning which took place could be described as "experiential" in the sense of emotional commitment, comradeship, and a faith that "the world would soon be ours." (106)

The college took a further swing to the left when the faculty and students began to advocate the ideology of anarchist philosophers and implement propaganda of the deed curriculum. The turn toward anarcho-syndicalism did not go unnoticed by the parliamentary elements of the Finnish immigrant socialist community. Ollila relates that "alarm was expressed when Haywood and Bohn's text, *Industrial Socialism*, was made a standard textbook for classes, and when students had concluded at a 'tactics' session that the McNamara dynamiting episode [of the *Los Angeles Times* office] had been of benefit to the socialist movement because it showed the poverty of craft unionism" (107)

The WPC's radical curriculum found a willing audience as enrollment numbers consistently hovered above one hundred students during the 1910s, reaching a high of 157 students during the 1913–14 school year. This high-water mark in the early 1910s was an upward swing during an otherwise tenuous period. The fractioning of the FSF after the 1913–14 copper strike in Michigan's Upper Peninsula and the repressive social measures of the World War I and Palmer Red Scare eras made the college's existence fleeting at best. Although the WPC survived the repressive era after World War I, it did so with a pronounced institutional limp. Official affiliation with the IWW brought increased recognition from the Wobblies following the First World War, but this never really translated into increased student numbers, nor did it attract non-Finnish students to the college (110–13).

Literacy at the Work People's College

The importance of multiple media formats in advancing the cause of proletarian education and literacy cannot be overstated. Efforts concerned with the promotion of literacy in the movement, the WPC, and the immigrant population were enacted primarily through print media, and in more popular culture by song. Print media was so important for working-class literacy that the WPC even advertised its correspondence school in a Finnish-language IWW-affiliated newspaper. Primary sources relating to the literacy programs of the WPC and the IWW illustrate the multimodal, multiple-format efforts used to create a literate Finnish immigrant working class. The school and its supporting media outlet, the Workers Socialist Publishing Company (WSPC), produced a broad array of publications that brought the printed word, cartoons, and photographs of industrial union–themed topics to the student body and faculty of the WPC, as well as to the larger Finnish immigrant community.

The WPC housed its own publishing company on the college campus in Smithville as a sort of practical training ground for future cartoonists,

Front cover of a Finnish-language songbook titled *Proletaari Lauluja* (Proletarian songs). The songbook, published circa 1920 by the Workers Socialist Publishing Company in Duluth, featured artwork by a local Finnish immigrant. Author's collection.

An interior view of *Industrialisti*'s offices and store in downtown Duluth, circa 1920. The Finnish-language newspaper was a leading voice for Finnish immigrants associated with the IWW and continued publication in Duluth until the 1970s. Courtesy of the Institute of Migration, Turku, Finland.

editors, journalists, and press and typesetting operators. This faculty- and student-run press printed numerous titles, but the astutely titled periodical *Ahjo* (The Forge) was the most important means of increasing literacy efforts at the WPC. *Ahjo* discussed current issues in industrial unionism and official IWW business, and was a forum for student-generated essays, prose, and poetry. There simply was no better way to encourage ascending levels of literacy in reading and writing than to provide a place for students to submit and read the fruits of their proletarian education.

The WSPC, also located in Duluth, published companion print media that promoted the college, but also the industrial union movement and the IWW in general. The WSPC was a full-fledged publishing company and its newspaper underwent several name changes that reflected strengthening ties with the IWW between 1914 and 1917. In 1915, when the newspaper split from the FSF's official media offering, *Työmies* (The workingman), the WSPC chose a new title, *Sosialisti* (The socialist). Little more than a year later, the publishing company changed the name of the newspaper to *Teollisuustyöläinen* (The industrial worker), indicating a commitment to industrial unionism more generally. By 1917, the paper underwent its last name change, a name that stood until the mid-1970s when the paper folded owing to declining readership. This new title, *Industrialisti* (The industrialist), suggested full support and affiliation with the IWW, which had positive implications for the industrial union movement within the WPC and the Finnish immigrant population more broadly.[18] By 1929, the WSPC began printing its own periodical, *Tie Vapauteen* (The road to freedom), a monthly look at IWW issues, literature, and industrial unionism. The magazine had migrated from New York, where it was founded, to Chicago in 1921. From Chicago, it came to rest—or, more appropriately, agitate—in Duluth in 1929. *Tie Vapauteen's* lavish cover art was a monthly celebration and exhibition of proletarian-inspired creativity, while the magazine's interior art, articles, and agit-prop (agitation and propaganda) materials, such as cartoons, plays, and poems, demonstrated a thoughtful but didactic and radical message.[19]

Although the IWW did not recognize the Finnish immigrant population as a separate ethnic organization within its ranks, it did print numerous agitation and organization materials in the Finnish language. One such title from the WSPC provided an intimate look at just what the industrial union movement's education and literacy campaigns demanded from would-be devotees. *Nuoriso, Oppi ja Työ* (Youth, learning and labor) was a truly unique publication because it was bilingual—the first section was printed in Finnish and the latter half in English. The book contained an exclusive glimpse of what was important to the cultural, historical, and philosophical literacy of Finnish immigrant and Finnish-American industrial unionists. For example, the book included an English-language account of human history from the evolution of life and "man," a short history of black slavery, an introduction to wage slavery, a discussion of feudalism and capitalism, the fight for public schools, and a condensed history of the American labor movement. This short, whirlwind history of humanity leads to a detailed discussion of the IWW, the merits of

This cartoon was published in the nationally syndicated Finnish immigrant magazine *Tie Vapauteen* (Road to freedom), circa 1925. The illustration stresses common themes found in the magazine, such as workers' emancipation, the futility of craft and trades unions, and the corruption of capitalists and capitalism. Author's collection.

industrial unionism, the differences between syndicalism and industrial unionism, and the misrepresentations of direct-action tactics.[20]

This wrestling between ideological terminologies was a theme that dominated the IWW's English-language publications as well. The distinction between anarcho-syndicalism and industrial unionism was an important one that could be easily misunderstood by rank and filers. Although the distinction between competing unionisms was opaque philosophical material, *Nuoriso, Oppi ja Työ* took the time to address the differences and educate readers in the terminology of IWW issues:

> Modern industrial unionism is not syndicalism, as it is no "syndicate" or federation of old craft unions. Its construction and scope of action are entirely different from those of the craft unions and different from all political and non-political parties . . . No old form of labor union can be made to fit the entirely new conditions in production; and no mere change of ideals, no matter how radical, can possibly make them conform to the new conditions. The entire structure and scope of action of the labor organizations must change . . . It [the IWW] is by no means perfect, but it has a mighty good outline and a firm basis upon which to stand and develop.[21]

The texts printed by the WSPC were certainly an assertion of ideology, but they were also a statement of identity. These books, magazines, newspapers, and pamphlets expressed what it meant to be a member of the IWW and how membership in the union differed from other organizations. Toward this end, many IWW media outlets reprinted the union's preamble, a definitive statement of identity, which was adopted at the union's founding conference in Chicago in 1905. Literally, the preamble spelled out the aspects of an IWW-sanctioned working-class identity, prescriptions for revolutionary union activity, and how the Wobblies' sense of class consciousness put them in direct conflict with capitalist bosses:

> The working-class and the employing class have nothing in common. There can be no peace so long as hunger and want are found among the millions of working people and the few who make up the employing class have all the good things in life.
>
> Between these two classes a struggle must go on until the workers of the world organize as a class, take possession of the earth and the machinery of production, and abolish the wage system.[22]

The preamble was a straightforward assertion of intentions, but the union took proletarian literacy a step further when it produced a dialogue to explain the ideological and philosophical foundations of industrial unionism. In a booklet titled *What Is the I.W.W. Preamble?*, two characters identified as "Bob Hammond, a laborer, hardworked, but anxious to know" and "Henry Tichenor, a technical engineer, his boyhood friend, eager to tell" talk about all things IWW, including the importance of the preamble. The dialogue is somewhat formulaic and outdated by contemporary standards, but the rather plain, folksy tone and friendly manner used by the characters' attempt to mediate the rough image and violent portrayal of the IWW in reactionary media of the era. In one section titled "Wages vs. Profits" the dialogue reads:

> *Tichenor* (amazed): What are all these conflicts, if not manifestations of the antagonistic interests of capitalists and laborers? What do they prove, if not the truth of the statement that, "the working-class and the employing class have nothing in common"?
>
> *Hammond* (puzzled): Well, I guess you are right. There is no getting 'round those facts. They show a wide, impassable gulf. But, how comes it that, despite all that, employers inaugurate welfare departments and workers' republics, and give the workers the privilege to buy shares? Surely, they are looking after the workers and giving them something in common.
>
> *Tichenor* (uproariously): Say, those are all methods to keep the workers docile, underpaid and unorganized. Welfare departments are cheaper than union wages and union control. They are also paternalistic . . .[23]

The IWW's status as a direct-action, fighting union put its members squarely at odds with American capitalists. Perhaps the most evocative and provocative of the IWW's union ideology celebrated in text, tract, and tune was the use of sabotage in the class war.

Sabotage as IWW Ideology

The advocacy of industrial sabotage as a weapon in the class struggle was a hotly debated issue in IWW circles for two reasons. Primarily, the IWW's members argued over what constituted actual industrial sabotage. Was sabotage the breaking of machines (industrial violence), the application of "bum" or lackluster work to production, or the enacting of a labor strike to curtail output? Pamphlets and treatises written by

IWW organizers were published to engage members in this ongoing discussion. Secondarily, some in the IWW debated whether the use of sabotage was ethical in the class war. Most Wobblies accepted sabotage as a tool in the IWW's revolutionary actions, but some deliberated over ethical versus unethical usages of the tactic. The promotion of sabotage also plagued the union's public image as the U.S. government and capitalists decried the tactic as an un-American, destructive measure aimed at crippling the national economy.

For mine workers, the most stalwart and well-heeled resistance to the IWW's tactics, including sabotage, came from the Oliver Iron Mining Company. Although other mining companies occupied the Range, including Hanna, Pickands-Mather, International Harvester, and a host of smaller corporations, Oliver had the most might to wield a powerful hand in influencing the Range's economics, culture, and politics. The sheer size and political power of the company meant that any attempt to organize workers would be a battle like that of David versus Goliath. Tactics used by the IWW to combat the Oliver's blacklist, intimidation, and violence were certainly not unique to 1916. The Wobblies had clashed with American industrialists on many occasions and with Iron Range capitalists in 1907 during the Mesabi strike. The use of sabotage as a defined IWW strategy had, however, gained momentum since the 1907 labor conflict and one of the most feared aspects of industrial sabotage came to be the calling of a general strike. Conceptualized as a regular strike on steroids, the general strike's aim was to shut down all aspects of an industry's productive components. For Iron Range bosses, then, a general strike meant not only the stoppage of work in mines, but also the freezing of ore shipments via rail, the prevention of loading ore on boats at docks, and the curtailing of ore shipping down the Great Lakes. The general strike was designed to cripple entire industries, if not entire local, regional, and/or national economies.

As immigrants on the Range began to think about union representation, the IWW and its advocacy of industrial sabotage were central to the decisions workers made regarding organized labor. The iron-mining companies owned the mines, machinery, and mills. Even the roofs over mine workers' heads were most often owned by the mining companies. Moreover, mining companies heavily influenced the iron ranges' educational, political, and social landscape, in addition to owning most of the actual physical landscape. Quite often, workers owned nothing but their labor and combating the lock, stock, and barrel ownership of resources on the iron ranges was a key part of the 1916 strike. Sabotage was one tactic that could effectively checkmate such lopsided power relations. Ultimately, sabotage became an ideological construct associated with the union and, fairly or not, a term that came to define what it meant to be a Wobbly. What sabotage was, how it should be used, and whether it was an acceptable form of class struggle were commonly debated questions by the IWW leadership. These questions even made their way into Wobbly popular culture. Industrial sabotage, be it a conscious withdrawal of efficiency on the job, outright destruction of company property, or a general strike, came to be an enduring symbol of the IWW's primary ideology—direct action at the point of production. Public debate regarding such action and ideology most often occurred among the membership in social spaces designed to fan the flames of working-class discontent.

Finn Halls: Cultural Spaces of Discontent

As the roughly three hundred thousand Finnish immigrants entered the United States between the late nineteenth and early twentieth centuries, they looked for familiar or recognizable social activities to supplement their work lives and to ease the transition to life in America. According to Finnish-American historian Michael G. Karni, many Finns sought to maintain and disseminate their values in their new country: "most Finns were determined not to be passive recipients of American culture. Whether associated with the church, the temperance movement, the cooperative movement or the radical labor movement, they believed they could shape the American environment and shape it into what it was not."[24] Finnish immigrants established cultural organizations that nurtured and supported their transition to life in the United States. Because of this, organizational societies grew in popularity as Finnish immigrants developed vibrant associational lives. Social halls emerged as the venue of choice for Finnish communities, including those on Minnesota's Iron Range. "Finn halls," as they came to be known, served as incubators for a unique, concerted response to their new life. From these halls, Finnish immigrants responded to their material conditions in a proactive manner.

Fred Torma, an early socialist and union member, remembered the importance of halls in the creation of working-class culture. Temperance halls devoted to abstinence from alcohol were often permitted on mining company property. However, once socialists like Torma moved into town, working-class groups slated these halls for takeover. As Torma recounted: "the first place was at Stevenson Mine . . . I began organizing work to get [socialist] members into that temperance league [so we could take over the hall]. I was always somewhat successful at that . . . we tried to take over that hall then so that we could also take up working people matters, but the mining company intervened." Labor halls were, of course, not welcome on company property and "[the company] sent representatives to say that they had provided the money and materials for the hall and it would not be used for any labor movement purposes."[25]

Socialist and labor organizers then turned to other locations and at times existing buildings, which were in urban areas off company property. After being turned away from the hall located near the Stevenson Mine, Torma and other like-minded Finnish immigrants targeted a building in Nashwauk, a municipality in Itasca County, Minnesota. Torma remembered that "it was November maybe October when we bought that hall. Then the question arose—how would we pay for it?" Cultural activities such as plays, concerts, and dances were as much an economic necessity to support the hall as they were ideological disseminators of working-class culture. Torma led the way in turning the Nashwauk hall into such an enterprise: "since I had learned the carpenter's trade from my father I said I'd lead. I made drawings as best as I was able. The older ones thought we should merely put planks on top of beer kegs and keep performances on top of that." Pride in their working-class culture may have led many to expect more from their social spaces and Torma spearheaded an effort to build a proper stage (35–40). In addition to plays, the Nashwauk Finn Hall served as a location for other functions, including committee meetings, debates, and rehearsals. Games and dancing occupied the children as well. It was a

An exterior view of the socialist Finn hall at Nashwauk, Minnesota, circa 1910. Finn halls were the centerpiece of Finnish immigrant life where people often gathered to celebrate special events in the community. Courtesy of the Immigration History Research Center, University of Minnesota.

busy cultural life, all housed in a building dedicated to the promotion of working-class culture (1–4).

At times these cultural activities were not overtly didactic and so were designed to simply get people together and mitigate the drudgery of industrial life. There were, however, plays, debates, lectures, and other activities designed to instruct in the ways of agitation and organization. Especially important was the establishment of a library and, as Torma recalled of the Nashwauk hall, "at that time everyone had a desire to learn. For example because wages were, at the most, $2.00 for a 12 hour day no one could afford to purchase books." As a result, the Nashwauk local chapter of the FSF planned for a library composed mostly of socialist literature to elevate the members' intellectual lives (ibid.). Most important, socialist Finn halls became a cultural core to their members. Aarre Lahti, who grew up in Ironwood, Michigan, recalled the Palace

Finn Hall as the place of his "most vivid memories of the town [with] the most formative impact on me." Lahti was especially taken with and proud of the work that went into the development of class-conscious culture: "these immigrant laborers, without any assistance from the town's financial institutions, used their own energy and determination to erect this huge hall in a series of work bees. The hall, after completion, boasted the best dance floor in the county and a stage with all the necessary scenery, costumes, and mechanical equipment for a first class little theater."[26] Athletics was another important aspect of hall life. For immigrant socialists, the revolution was a mind *and* body experience. Lahti remembered that the Palace Hall "was the only facility in town with gymnastic and track paraphernalia. The athletic sessions were held on Tuesday and Thursday evenings and again on Sunday morning when the hall's auditorium was set up with parallel bars, a high bar, 'horses,' mats and other gymnastic equipment. The weekday sessions began about five o'clock to accommodate those who were on the night shift."[27]

Finn halls across the Lake Superior region were shaping up to be social spaces of fiery opposition to American capitalists and capitalism. Immigrants could attend classes on Marxist economics, debate the shortcomings of capitalism, join unions, stage theatrical productions that lampooned the bosses, and even participate in athletics. In short, halls offered immigrants, as Karni noted, "[involvement] in a movement which promised to bring the good life to all through social and political revolution."[28]

Social Spaces of Discontent at Virginia and Hibbing

The Finnish immigrant socialist halls of Virginia, Hibbing, and smaller municipalities such as Nashwauk provided a staging area for agitation and organization across the Iron Range. In the early twentieth century, Finns were the main beneficiaries of this vibrant cultural life, but after 1907, they began to agitate and organize outside the doors of their own social spaces. The FSF and its members learned an important lesson from the 1907 Mesabi strike and carried it over into the years before the 1916 strike. Working with the WFM during the Mesabi strike and the 1913–14 Michigan Copper Strike had brought the socialist-unionist Finns to see their halls not as closed, walled-off ethnic social spaces, but as vital components of a unified struggle in times of industrial unrest. From the 1907 strike experience, according to Auvo Kostiainen, Finns "came into close contact with American labor organizations, and they stuck together with other nationalities on the Mesabi Range." The lessons of cooperative labor organization became firmly entrenched in the collective consciousness of Finnish immigrant organizations like the FSF. Furthermore, the FSF's close association with the Wobblies led many Finnish immigrant socialists to become, over time, Finnish-American Wobblies who were receptive to seeing class struggle as an international fight and not an intra-ethnic struggle for bread, jobs, or respect.[29]

Because of this, Finn labor halls were open not only to Finns but to others engaged in the ongoing class struggle. On one level, the IWW operated as a national rallying institution, while Minnesota's socialist-unionist Finns provided a regional and local structure that could offer a grassroots organizational foundation with social spaces to serve local populations involved in labor actions. While the IWW contributed funds, muscle, and the prestige of a nationwide union, the FSF and its social spaces of discontent afforded several strategic loci for agitation and organization. Across the ranges, Finnish immigrants' political and social spaces became important rallying points for the IWW's efforts at creating cultural solidarity within a previously divided working-class culture.

The central venue of Finnish Wobbly activities, and later strike activities in 1916, was the well-adorned Socialist Opera House in Virginia, Minnesota. A brick structure with ornate architectural elements, the Socialist Opera House was designed to impart the credibility, permanence, and stability of the FSF on a landscape dominated by mining companies. Previously the home of Finnish immigrant cultural endeavors, the opera house became a focal point of multiethnic organizational efforts during the strike. The building's elegant architecture ran counter to the bloody reality of the strike as it played out on the grizzled setting of the Iron Range's industrial landscapes. According to historian James A. Roe, the builders of the opera house "brought together a curiously contradictory assemblage of images and ideals. Even the name 'Socialist Opera'—so boldly displayed on the façade—joins elements

Constructed in 1913 by Finnish immigrants after several years of fundraising, Virginia's Socialist Opera House was a finely adorned showplace for the Finnish immigrants' socialist movement. Courtesy of the Institute of Migration, Turku, Finland.

from two usually differing worlds; the working-class ethic of socialism and the high culture of opera." The opera house was so ornate and skillfully designed that the conservative press in Virginia even called it "one of the most substantial structures on the Range, modern in every detail." In a 1913 *Työmies* newspaper article, A. F. Heiskanen wrote of the opera house, "our new hall . . . is the epitome of the struggle up to this time of the Virginia working-class." To some, the hall and the refinement of socialism, which the opera house symbolically represented, were a source of pride and organizational affirmation.[30]

Whether dogmatic socialists agreed or not, the Socialist Opera House and its cultural activities were less about strident working-class culture and more about recreation. This was a new strategy in the recruitment and retention of members as the fancy opera house stood as a motivational symbol and source of great revenue for the socialist-unionist movement. Additionally, and more covertly, the opera house and its cultural activities beckoned as a purposeful enticement for non-socialists to walk through the hall doors and hear the proletarian mes-

The Socialist Opera House's elaborate interior included a chandelier, box seats, finely constructed stage and scenery, and even a small pool for staging water scenes during plays. Courtesy of the Immigration History Research Center, University of Minnesota.

sage. As James Roe deduced, the mission of the Virginia Workers' Organization as builders of the opera house was to get people in the seats and then convert them: "it was possible to draw audiences unaware of the movement to hear agitators' speeches, poems and songs and such material with which it was possible to elevate their knowledge." The opera house opened on April 13, 1913, with more than eight hundred people enjoying a play by Goethe. Mixed in with subsequent farcical comedies and high-tech bourgeois stage productions were educational and dramatic plays designed to elevate class consciousness and create proletarian solidarity.[31]

True to its form and function, the opera house became the central meeting place for Finnish immigrant members of IWW, though its artful ornamentation at times clashed with the revolutionary goals of the union. Unlike more modest halls and theaters, such as the Nashwauk Finn Hall, the design of the Socialist Opera House competed architecturally with American vaudeville theaters. In this way, the building dazzled visitors with excessive decoration that visually invited audiences to escape the drudgery of their ordinary world.[32] The opera house would become home to many raucous working-class entertainments amid the fancy chandeliers and ornate woodwork. Daisy Nelson-Walkama was among those who grew up in the comfort of the opera house's cultural offerings. She recalled the grandeur of the historic space in the 1920s and 1930s. Rows of folding chairs lined the wooden floor in the main level's beautiful multipurpose room. Wall boxes and balcony seating hung over the auditorium. The basement housed a kitchen and dining room for services of *kavia* and *pulla* (coffee and Finnish bread).[33]

The Virginia Socialist Opera House was nominally the official strike headquarters in 1916, but the Hibbing Workers' Hall was equally important to organizational efforts on the Iron Range. Hibbing was especially vital to the Finnish immigrant socialist-unionist movement. In 1906, formerly unaffiliated Finnish immigrant socialist locals in the United States came together in Hibbing and voted to create and join the federation of socialist organizations that became known as the FSF. The organization became the first and largest foreign-language party within the Socialist Party of America.[34]

For the IWW, the Hibbing hall was mostly important because of its location in the largest metropolitan area on the Range. In 1916, the hall became the locus of action for striking workers on the western edges of the Mesabi, which included the tightly controlled Itasca County iron mines. Located on land once owned by the Oliver in what became known as North Hibbing, the hall was a stately, wood-sided balloon-framed structure, utilitarian in all of its trimmings. The Workers' Hall was not nearly as ornate as Virginia's Socialist Opera House and was more akin to a traditionally conceived working-class space. Nevertheless, the hall's activities and physical size mirrored those of the Virginia Opera House. Plays were an important way to express political ideology and bring in revenue, but over time, the Hibbing Workers' Hall gained great importance as a meeting place for workers during labor conflict.

The hall's importance to Finnish immigrant socialists dates back to 1909. For the building's grand opening, the Hibbing FSF local decided to overlap its festivities with a daylong New Year's Eve celebration. For the opening affairs, the local scheduled a speech by Leo Laukki, professor at the Work People's College, a reading by Finnish immigrant poet Aku Päiviö, and another speech by Hibbing local member Wilho Leikkas. That night a performance of Gustaf von Nurmer's *Elinan Surma* (The death of Elina) was scheduled, featuring a cast of eighteen actors to cover all the parts. One of the play's characters was Vappu or Freedom, likely a tip of the cap to the industrial democracy called for the by IWW.[35]

In halls like the Virginia Opera House or the Hibbing Workers' Hall, at the Work People's College, and in houses of the immigrant rank and file, a unique amalgam of immigrant and American working-class culture was taking shape. A variety of media was shaping the message. Along with immersive, first-person media such as plays, debates, and the ever-popular sing-along, the IWW used periodicals and texts to reach people who were not able to hear the message firsthand. Of this mobile messaging, images, such as photographs of events or radical cartoons, took on an especially important role in the class-conscious education of immigrants. The use of visual media was powerful, and especially relied upon by organizations that sought to bring immigrant groups together under one cause. The IWW skillfully used images to reach working-class individuals who were illiterate or who could not read or speak the English language. The IWW's visual depictions of class struggle were perhaps most important for its attempts at organizing immigrant workers who understood little or no English. Additionally, images were a sort of quick and dirty ideological summation for those who could not spend long hours reading philosophical tracts or IWW preamble dialogues.

The Singing Union

The IWW was proudly known as the "Singing Union" to foe and friend alike. The building of working-class cultural identity through music was an important part of organizing immigrant workers. Through song, locally robust Finnish organizations, replete with a dynamic, fiery hall culture, engaged with the vibrant and melodic culture of the IWW. The IWW's assertions of identity and ideology was appealing to many young, disaffected, and disenfranchised children of Finnish immigrant laborers, as well as to their American fellow workers. Arguably, the most cherished of all IWW publications was the oft-memorialized and popularly known "Little Red Songbook," officially titled *I.W.W. Songs: To Fan the Flames of Discontent*. This songbook was an ever-present feature of the union's cultural activities and was an essential component to the process of crafting working-class literacy. Even if a worker could not read, the songs of the IWW offered an opportunity to understand the basics of industrial unionism. Additionally, many IWW songs were easy to memorize and had familiar melodies. Even old religious tunes were appropriated with lyrics crafted specifically to fit the industrial wageworker's situation. One popular song, excerpted here, was "Dump the Bosses Off Your Back," written by John Brill and sung to the tune of "Take It to the Lord in Prayer":

> Are your clothes all patched and tattered?
> Are you living in a shack?
> Would you have your troubles scattered?
> Then dump the bosses off your back.
>
> Are you almost split asunder?
> Loaded like a long-eared jack?
> Boob—why don't you buck like thunder?
> And dump the bosses off your back?
>
> All the agonies you suffer,
> You could end with one good whack—
> Stiffen up, you orn'ry duffer—
> And dump the bosses off your back.[36]

More than any other expression of culture, singing in the local Finn halls was *the* shared experience for both FSF and IWW members. As a form of cultural expression, music became an intangible part of the working-class experience.

In most, if not all, labor halls across Minnesota's Iron Range, songs of industrial revolt and protest filled rooms up to the rafters with conceptions of what it meant to be a class-conscious worker. Some of these songs traveled with immigrants from Finland, but over time the songs became derivations of IWW songs sung in Finnish with borrowed words from the American working class. Some members knew the songs by heart, but others learned the songs from books published by the

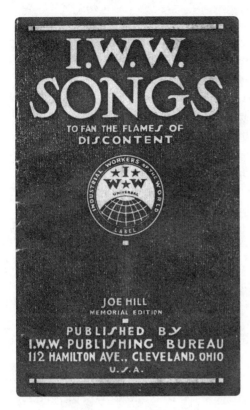

This edition of the IWW's "Little Red Songbook" was published after Swedish immigrant Joe Hill's 1915 execution in Utah. The memorial edition celebrated the life of the famous songwriter, laborer, and union organizer. This copy was once owned by an unknown Finnish immigrant who pasted in copies of songs, some in the Finnish language, that he or she preferred to the songs in the original publication. Author's collection.

Workers Socialist Publishing Company. Within this immigrant press, songbooks took on a critical purpose as transmitters of cultural values. Both Finnish- and English-language songbooks were treated with a kind of sanctity that resembled religious hymnals. The Wobbly songbook is an example of the personal connections that were established between songbook owners and the material culture of the industrial union. The book's owner so strongly felt the connection between his or her Finnish roots and the American Wobblies that the English-language songbook was augmented with Finnish lyrics. This type of cross-cultural expression was an important amalgamation that deserves additional emphasis because singing and songs were one of the most proficient ways of transmitting American working-class culture, identity, and ideology to an immigrant people. Once in the United States, the traditions of the Old

World came into direct contact with other cultures and musical traditions. Other working-class groups inevitably influenced Finns, and their music was surely shaped by such interactions as intersectional members of an immigrant *and* an American working-class group.

The multitude of intersections between Finns in the United States and conceptions of what it meant to be a part of the American working class demonstrated the interplay between culture, organized labor, and class-conscious literacy. As instrumental communicators of culture, songs had the power to teach those who did not have the means to acquire a formal education. The songs danced to in Finn halls, caterwauled in boardinghouses, woods, and lumber camps, and sung in part harmonies around a kerosene lamp in the family kitchen fostered a type of class-conscious literacy. It was a form of education that could not be bought at the finest collegiate institution, divined by the most pious religious organization, or taught at the most bureaucratic primary school. Finnish immigrant songs, as well as the musical history of other immigrant groups, related what it was to be working-class, giving expression to the joy, pain, triumph, and struggle of newly American, yet somehow "foreign," toilers.

Like other immigrant groups, the Finnish immigrant population had little say in their future (or past) education. For members of the working class, therefore, literacy programs and educational opportunities free from other class backgrounds had to be created in accessible, sometimes clandestine ways. Working-class songs provided a useful platform to pass along such a system of literacy via cultural expression that was free from class control. Stylistically, the IWW's musical culture contained a unique subversive character regarding the struggles of the working class. This sense of irreverence was conveyed in political cartoons and, even more so, through song. IWW songs employed this sense of humor, sarcasm, and satire to create a cheeky and irreverent musical culture that endeared listeners and imbued them with a sense of power through mockery. Songs were a relatable method of transmitting elements of the IWW's sarcastic, vibrant, and whimsical cultural apparatus, and Finnish immigrants heartily embraced this cultural expression.

In turn, Finn halls became the cultural space most affected and appreciated in this working-class social exchange, while songbooks were important transmitters of such cultural dialogue. The extensive printing of IWW songbooks in multiple languages supported the dissemination and retention of working-class overtures. It was in this lyrical expression of culture that the IWW's ideology and revolutionary message were conveyed most memorably. Prior to the 1916 labor upheaval, Finnish immigrants were the Range's most receptive audience. This changed with the coming of the strike and the IWW's push to actively engage a multiethnic audience in northern Minnesota. While the message was being expanded to new populations, the location of the transmission of these important cultural ideals remained situated in the revered Finn hall. Thus, the importance of these halls to the cultural imperatives of the IWW and the 1916 strike was extremely significant. The halls stood ready to become local centers of organization that could unite immigrant workers from numerous nations in a structured revolt against Minnesota iron ore companies. There was, however, the formidable task of doing the actual work of bringing these immigrant voices together into One Big Union. Getting South Slavic workers, onetime scabs during the 1907 Mesabi Strike, to stand in solidarity with Finnish and Italian immigrants would prove to be a significant challenge to organizing the immigrant workforce across the Iron Range.

4 FROM STRIKEBREAKERS TO SOLIDARITY

The Slavic Worker Revolt

[South Slavic immigrants] began to realize in their own mind
that they were human beings, with certain inalienable rights . . .
and they began to realize that there were certain things that they
would have to fight for.
—*Slovenian American Veda Ponikvar*

FOR INDUSTRIAL UNIONS SUCH AS THE IWW, WHICH SOUGHT TO
unionize workers across jobs and industries, much of the difficulty in
organizing workers on the Iron Range was compounded by ethnic frag-
mentation. During the late nineteenth and early twentieth centuries, the
ranges were a rough-and-tumble landscape in an isolated region that was
profiting from an increasingly exploited multiethnic population. At the
same time, the ranges' economic, cultural, social, and spatial landscapes
were subjugated by powerful men running million-dollar corporations
who sought to shape the identity of workers, their families, and their
institutions into a profitable expression of American capitalist ideals.

There were few independent expressions of identity on the iron ranges
that did not revolve around company-controlled or -sanctioned lives. As
we have seen, Finnish immigrants directly, and at times violently, collided with American capitalist expectations of assimilation by forging
their own unique cultural, economic, political, and social institutions
and cultural artifacts. In many instances, this push for industrial freedom landed many on company blacklists. For the Range's other immigrant workers, the struggle to craft an autonomous identity that existed
outside the sphere of mining company influence was difficult. The need

for powerful expressions of independence had to become an ideological imperative if working-class populations were to assert a self-determining identity forged in their own image and interests.

The tension between being a new American and simultaneously belonging to a native culture has come to characterize the study of immigration. In chronicling the lives of workers on the iron ranges, the term "intersectionality" can be applied. Kay Deaux defines the term as "the condition in which a person simultaneously belongs to two or more social categories of social statuses and the unique consequences that result from that combination."[1] For immigrants on the ranges, this kind of intersectional existence was a common part of everyday life. They lived lives in which their native culture as members of an immigrant group—be it Italian, Slovenian, Croatian, or Finnish—collided with and was simultaneously shaped by their status as members of an unaffiliated international, often itinerant, working class. At the same time, these immigrants existed on the margins of the American working class, which at times did not want to acknowledge any ties to these mostly unskilled, underpaid, and derisively mocked "un-American" immigrant laborers. For immigrant mine workers, identity was a precarious, shifting construct for strangers in a strange land who were actively being assimilated, exploited, pulled across cultures, and (ideally for American bosses) shaped into ideal workers by capitalist overseers.

As the IWW worked to organize immigrant workers, it carefully crafted and communicated symbolic representations of what it meant to be an industrial worker in both an American and an international working class. The melding of immigrant identities with that of new American identities was the IWW's goal as it hoped to cultivate solidarity among its ethnically diverse immigrant rank and filers. The Wobblies hoped to forge this identity and then transmit ideological beliefs that stressed collective action against a mutual adversary: industrial capitalists. Such ideological representations of identity sought to cultivate the "commonly shared and collectively elaborated beliefs about social reality consensually held by members of [the IWW's] culture or subculture."[2] Because cohesion of practice and thought was important among IWW members, it was the job of ideology to link disparate communities— members of ethnic brotherhoods, radical political organizations, and various religious benefit societies—in the goal of taking on powerful mining corporations.

Immigrant identity on the ranges was defined by adoption of, or more important, resistance to, the normative behavior expected by mining companies. Mining corporations were not anti-immigrant; most mining managers understood that their profits relied on immigrant toilers. Immigrants were often treated poorly by petty bosses in mines, but upper management understood that immigrants were a key part to a company's profit-and-loss statement. In fact, many companies offered "Americanization" and English classes to immigrants with the goal of assimilating them to the doctrine of American capitalism. This assimilation provided one route to establishing a new identity. Another identity, however, came with resistance to the capitalist system. For this perspective, immigrants had to look outward to organizations that were antithetical to, or at least critical of, American capitalist institutions. The IWW was one such hostile organization. Unlike the companies' attempts to assimilate immigrant workers, which were a "one-way street," these immigrant workers were not passive, submissive recipients of Wobbly ideology. They actively aggregated, created, and reshaped the IWW's culture and philosophy. Unlike their dogmatic collision with American capitalism, immigrants' relationship with the Wobblies' ideological constructs was a reciprocal relationship that benefited both the union and the immigrant rank and file. Immigrant success in joining an American working-class organization such as the IWW, however, did not ameliorate the perils of industrial life in northern Minnesota. All that mining companies had to do to reject immigrant Wobbly identity was to ignore, imprison, or imperil the IWW's administration, organizers, and rank and file. This antiunion strategy would work for a time before 1916, but as the IWW's leaders developed more effective organizational strategies, dissenting immigrant workers became more difficult to control. The struggle to gain union recognition in contested workscapes, however, was just one aspect of the forging of immigrant working-class identity. Even after the Range's immigrants were affiliated with an American labor organization, they were still in a precarious situation: they were still workers in a dangerous industrial landscape without the power to assert a democratic voice in determining their sociopolitical surroundings—in short, they still could not vote in local, state, or national elections.

Membership in the IWW was certainly one way to gain some semblance of a voice in the workplace; the predicted sociopolitical revolution would follow after the democratization of industrial spaces—according to the IWW. Development of an ideological political consciousness was another means for immigrants to assert their independence, but to an extent, the Wobblies disregarded the political process. The IWW denounced politics as a tool for the bosses and the bourgeoisie that concentrated power in the hands of a political elite, and away from the working masses. This was one critique of electoral politics in a defined political landscape that was dominated by American-born white men. The people interested in politics on the Iron Range, however, were not limited to the ruling elite. Perhaps more than anything, in forging new identities, many immigrant workers wanted a political voice in the conditions of their labor and their social lives. Most wanted access to the American Dream and understood that it came through a political involvement that was previously denied by political elites.[3] Thus, in many ways the development of a political identity, because it highlighted the disenfranchisement of immigrant workers, illuminated the inequalities of life on the Range. This intersection between working-class identity and political ideology provides a nascent examination of identity politics for the Range's immigrant populations of the early twentieth century.

Identity politics, as a field of study, seeks to understand the inherent contradictions and inequalities of marginalized populations. In short, identity politics sheds a light on oppressive sociopolitical institutions, landscapes, and political structures. For immigrants on the Iron Range working to forge a sense of identity, the most overtly denied expression of socioeconomic engagement was the right to vote. Most of the working masses were disenfranchised immigrants and this lack of political autonomy in such a polarized landscape had exploitative and repressive consequences. In his "Five Theses on Identity Politics," Richard D. Parker argues that "political freedom is shaped by three simple norms: political equality, popular sovereignty and, therefore, majority rule."[4] In contrast to Parker's standards, these sought-after democratic norms were conversely situated in northern Minnesota. For the Range's immigrant populations, which could have constituted a majority of the vote, there was no political equality as most immigrants were not citizens and could not vote. Let us also not forget that women could not vote at this time either. Essentially, the iron ranges were composed of closely monitored work spaces and social spaces where a few men and their managerial representatives ruled a large, voiceless body politic that could not vote. This changed somewhat with the coming of the Progressive Era, but even the Progressive movement was largely headed by middle-class, American-born men, and this was especially true on the iron ranges.

Ideological expressions of autonomy and working-class identity such as workers' cooperatives, ethnic benevolent societies, and, increasingly, organizations opposed to capitalism were the only means for immigrants to achieve Parker's political equality in their lifetime. Corporately controlled, disenfranchised, and exploited immigrants found that unions such as the IWW, which argued that politics was a tool of company bosses to keep workers subservient, were sometimes the only points of access toward the expression of an autonomous working-class *and* immigrant identity. For this reason, the IWW's distrust of electoral politics gained many converts on the ranges in the years preceding the 1916 strike. The alliances between immigrants, particularly Slavic immigrants, were not always easily brokered. Many Slavic newcomers were brought to the ranges for the express purpose of breaking a strike, and this put them in direct conflict with the IWW and other immigrant groups—Finns and Italians, especially—who had chosen to partner with organized labor in the struggle to find a voice in the oppressive political landscape. This chapter is concerned with the struggle of immigrant groups, especially "Austrian" or South Slavic immigrants, as they attempted to forge a self-determined industrial identity; chronicles their efforts to assert their collective voice in the face of industrial exploitation; and considers their contributions to organized labor leading up to the 1916 strike.

Immigrant Labor by an Industrial Lake
As the Lake Superior basin, which included the Minnesota Iron Range, the Michigan Iron Range, and Michigan's Copper Country, grew in industrial importance from the mid-1840s to the dawn of the new century, the battle for industrial democracy intensified. At first, small wildcat

labor actions and walkouts announced the displeasure of workers with the "bosses," but as the output of copper and iron increased, so too did the organization of wageworkers. Unions such as the Knights of Labor and the Western Federation of Miners (WFM) began to organize an effective response to working conditions and industrial control of wages. From the rather demure incantations of talks between labor and management in early disputes, more proactive and provocative methods toward the instillation of industrial democracy, such as those espoused by the IWW, came to color industrial relations in the Lake Superior basin. As the intensity and tactics of organized labor matured, the methods used by capitalists to increase efficiency through machinery, management, and social controls were also amplified. When mines reached full production, the need to find cheap labor intensified, causing mining companies to hire tens of thousands of immigrants. The stage was ultimately set for multiple clashes between immigrant labor and management regarding industrial democracy, and, more specifically, the power of immigrants to gain some type of voice in the industrial workplace and social landscape.

The presence of WFM recruiters in the Lake Superior basin increased considerably in the years leading up to the 1916 strike. The confrontations their efforts triggered were not limited to northern Minnesota. On July 4, 1906, a labor organizer was in Rockland, Michigan, a small, boomtown hamlet close to an area copper mine. The organizer requested to speak at a local Finnish immigrant temperance society and proceeded to pontificate, telling the gathered workers to strike for better wages and industrial democracy—fitting for an Independence Day speech. The organizer's words did not take long to incite action—on July 30 the workers walked off the job at the Michigan Mine. A dispute followed between the impromptu strikers and Ontonagon County's "peace" officers. Two Finnish workers were shot dead and nine more were wounded. Reportedly, one of the slain strikers was even left in Rockland's downtown for a day as a warning that martial law was in effect. Finnish-American historian Arthur Puotinen wrote of the event, "Ludvig Ojala's head was shot off at point-blank range." The other striker, Oscar Ohtonen, was shot in his stomach, receiving fatal wounds to his lower intestine.[5]

By 1907, the WFM had succeeded in signing up approximately 2,500 mine workers in Minnesota and was set to attempt a major labor action. This massive, conscious withdrawal of efficiency occurred on July 20, 1907, when Italian immigrant organizer Teofilo Petriella called out workers across the entire Mesabi Range. The WFM's national offices in Denver were reticent to begin such a large-scale labor action, but the work stoppage was driven by a localized, grassroots energy supplied by Finnish and Italian mine workers. Mining activity at Oliver mines came to a standstill in Hibbing, Eveleth, and Virginia. The strike was the largest and most prolific in the Lake Superior region to that date. The 1907 Mesabi strike was so effective that to break it and salvage production in the idled mines, the OIMC imported more than a thousand South Slavic scabs between August 1 and August 29 to replace striking mine workers. The tactic of pitting working-class immigrants from different ethnicities against each other was a steadfast approach used in the Lake Superior basin. The shuffling of low-wage employees to force striking workers back on the job or replace a workforce with new, unseasoned workers was a common response to worker grievances.[6] Known to the mining companies as "replacement or imported workers," but as "scabs" to those out of work, the Austrian strikebreakers were distributed to mines and locations across the Range. In all, the Oliver imported 1,124 men to the Mesabi, according to an August 29 tally. A notation at the bottom of the report added that "we expect about 77 to 80 men on 'South Shore' [Railroad] this morning from the east, whom we expect to send to mines in Hibbing District (8–30–07)."[7] With the addition of the Austrian scabs, mining company managers were able to break the strike in about two weeks' time and union organization ground to a halt.

For six years following the 1907 Mesabi strike, a tense, intermittently fragmented labor peace existed across the Lake Superior basin, while cautious labor agitation and organization continued in earnest, led mainly by socialist-unionist immigrant Finns. Company-hired spies attempted to monitor the situation across Minnesota, Wisconsin, and Michigan mining regions. Although a spark persisted throughout the working-class population, these were certainly dark times for union organization, especially on Minnesota ranges. According to a report given by WFM organizer William E. Tracy in 1909, the WFM was in dire straits owing to

Southern European mine workers photographed on one of the Mesabi Range's many railroad tracks, circa 1911. Immigrants from southern Europe—Italy and the Austro-Hungarian Empire—were often unfamiliar with industrial work as many came from the Old World, where they worked on family or manorial farms. From *Popular Science Monthly*, 1911.

dwindling membership on the Mesabi Range, and was just barely hanging on in the Vermilion Range town of Ely. As part of his duties as an organizer, in 1908 Tracy made the rounds of the Upper Midwest's mining regions; a circuitous route that wound him from Michigan's copper- and iron-ore laden Upper Peninsula to South Dakota's gold-rich Black Hills.

In between was Minnesota's Iron Range, which had, according to Tracy, been quiet regarding union activity "owing to the disastrous results of the strike of 1907."[8]

Tracy traveled a path from the Vermilion south to the Mesabi visiting nearly or already defunct WFM offices in Aurora, Eveleth, Hibbing, McKinley, Sparta, and Virginia, and an almost abandoned WFM local in Ely. His travels put him in touch primarily with Finnish- and Austrian-speaking union sympathizers. Notable among Tracy's reports was his frustration with being unable to speak with potential members because of the language barrier: "with the exception of mechanics, steam shovel men and steam engineers, there are no men employed in the mines of this region who are of American birth, or who are familiar with the English tongue." He stated that "several different languages are spoken, Finnish, Italian and a variety of Austrian dialects, including the Montenegrin. An organizer who speaks only English cannot accomplish anything at all among these men without the aid of competent interpreters and translators" (295). Another hindrance to Tracy's efforts was the intimidation of mining company operatives and spies. In Ely, a local barber and former WFM member was sympathetic to unionism but commented that "he hoped that [Tracy] would not patronize his shop, as that would probably cause him to be boycotted to the extent of forcing him out of business" (ibid.).

Tracy's most promising lead in reestablishing a WFM local was in Hibbing, home to a number of pro-WFM South Slavic mine workers. On September 11, 1908, with the ex-secretary of the Eveleth Miners' Union, "Brother" John Movern, in tow as his Austrian interpreter, Tracy engaged "with a few members of local No. 155, who were of the opinion that there was a chance to rally together enough of the men at that place to reorganize, and still retain at least a foot hold in the Mesaba Range at Hibbing" (ibid.). Tracy made plans to meet with the workers the following Sunday under "great secrecy" to reorganize the Hibbing WFM local. Upon arriving in Hibbing on September 20, the organizer found that the mine workers he was scheduled to meet with were no longer working in the mines. Labor spies had caught up with the group, ascertained the identities of the workers, and reported their activities to employers who then summarily fired the men. Disheartened, Tracy left

Hibbing on September 21 and headed east toward Michigan's Copper Country (296).

Reflecting on his September exploits in Minnesota while in Hancock, Michigan, Tracy recalled, "I was conscious of the fact that I had been followed by two detectives all through my travels in Minnesota, and I had hoped to get away from them when coming to Michigan. In this I did not succeed" (ibid.). Tracy would be back in Minnesota that December, however. Via a request from WFM President Charles Moyer, Tracy met with Finnish immigrant workers in Hibbing's socialist hall on December 16. Using the services of translator John Välimäki, Tracy went to the hall to collect the administrative vestiges of WFM District 11, Hibbing Miners' Union No. 155, and some "belongings" of Nashwauk Union No. 196, and to do a postmortem of sorts on the WFM's dwindling membership.

The collection of these WFM materials and Tracy's missed September meeting with South Slavic workers were metaphors for the union's disconnect with immigrant workers in Minnesota. In general, Minnesota's radical Finns had lost faith in the union, while South Slavic immigrants were dubious of the WFM's overtures. Many Finnish immigrants in Minnesota were ardent supporters of the Wobblies, and thus the WFM, because of the union's affiliation with the IWW. In turn, South Slavic scabs were brought in by the mining companies to break the 1907 strike. Following the strike, the WFM parted company with the IWW, and would soon become affiliated with the conservative-leaning, at times anti-immigrant American Federation of Labor (AFL) in 1910. Because of these changing loyalties, the AFL-affiliated WFM fell out of favor with Minnesota's IWW-supporting Finnish immigrants. While WFM dues and enthusiasm were on the decline among Minnesota Finns, membership in the Finnish Socialist Federation was on the rise. Finn halls were burgeoning centers of activity and the IWW-sympathetic Work People's College in Duluth celebrated its first anniversary in 1908. So, while membership and support for the WFM was on the decline among Minnesota's Finnish immigrant population, ostensibly because of a perceived distrust of the WFM's burgeoning conservatism, support for revolutionary forms of organized labor and working-class politics was likely growing in that same group.[9]

Similarly, in the South Slavic immigrant population there was a well-rounded distrust of the WFM, but for a different reason. For Austrian mine workers, the WFM was *the* union South Slavs scabbed against during the 1907 strike. This negative association caused South Slavic workers to be suspicious of the WFM—possibly fearing retribution from the union or its supporters; or, more simply, perhaps there was not an interest in joining the union that opposed and derided them as scabs during the strike. For whatever reason, Tracy found organizing on the ranges between 1907 and 1913 difficult work. Additionally, the constant presence of company spies on his "tail" caused him to conclude that "in Minnesota I do not believe that it would have been possible for me to have accomplished anything of importance."[10]

Michigan's Copper Country was more active and receptive to labor organization by the WFM after its union with the AFL. The nine-month-long 1913–14 Michigan Copper Strike, administered by the WFM (and somewhat ridiculed by the Wobblies), was the most significant expression of worker discontent in the Lake Superior basin. While Finnish immigrants were major participants in the 1913–14 strike, Italians and South Slavic workers, especially Croatian immigrants, joined with Finns in the strikers' ranks. The WFM sent into the Copper Country a multilingual cadre of organizers who spoke Finnish, Italian, Croatian, Hungarian, Polish, and Slovenian. But mining companies brought in multilingual replacement workers as well. While copper mining companies brought workers in from across Europe and the United States, a large majority came from southeastern European backgrounds, and just as in the 1907 Mesabi strike, there were many imported Austrian strikebreakers. The largest copper company, Calumet and Hecla, alone brought in more than nine hundred immigrant scabs, more than half of whom were South Slavic.[11]

An extremely bitter and contentious strike, the labor action on Michigan's Keweenaw Peninsula brought Lake Superior labor relations to new lows. During the strike, hired mine deputies, strikebreakers, and county deputy sheriffs shot and killed two Croatian strikers in Seeberville, Michigan; shot and wounded a fourteen-year-old Hungarian girl in another location on company property; and may have caused the loss of some seventy-three to seventy-nine immigrant lives, sixty of whom were children, at a WFM-sponsored multiethnic Christmas Eve party for striking workers and their families in Calumet's Italian Hall. The mining company powers also planned the beating, which resulted in an accidental shooting, and deportation of then WFM President Charles Moyer in late December 1913. Seeing the brutality of the mining companies and their hired thugs go unchecked by local law enforcement, the state of Michigan, and federal government bureaucrats, striking workers on Michigan's Copper Range were coerced, strong-armed, and threatened back to work without recognition of the WFM, which was the main goal of the strike.[12]

After the Michigan Copper Strike ended in mid-April 1914, the Lake Superior region's class-conscious Finns were bruised and battered. The events of the Italian Hall tragedy (Finns were the ethnic group with the largest number of deceased at Italian Hall) and the perceived total loss of the strike had taken their toll on the morale of the labor-conscious ethnic group. In addition to the tragedies in Michigan, interest and support for the WFM, which had been on a steady decline since the 1907 Mesabi strike, began to disintegrate. Increasingly, Minnesota's Finns began to look to the IWW for direction. More important, thousands of Finns had been blacklisted from the mining industry in Minnesota. On Minnesota's Iron Range, the massive blacklisting of Finns after the 1907 strike had an immediate impact on organizing activities in the mines. Many Finns had moved on from the area to the copper mines of Montana, begun work in the logging industry, or relocated to the industrial peripheries in Minnesota's hinterland. While a core of committed organizers remained in cities and rural communities, Finnish immigrant labor organizers were standing outside of contested workscapes looking in. Minnesota mining companies had effectively gutted their workforces of organized labor–oriented Finnish immigrant workers. The labor-conscious Finnish immigrant cultural apparatus survived, however, especially Finn halls, which were staffed, patronized, and populated with zealous supporters of organized labor in the iron ranges' urban centers.

In all, the Oliver blacklisted approximately 1,200 Finnish immigrant mine workers across the Mesabi after the 1907 strike. But the blacklisting was not just happenstance. It occurred as an across-the-board Oliver company policy, as communication from Charles Trezona, the OIMC's general superintendent, to Thomas F. Cole, Oliver's president, demonstrated: "on account of the calling out of the miners in this district . . . a great many of the Finns employed here have quit and it appears to me that these men are all members of the Western Federation of Miners. In my judgment, they should not be re-employed and I have given instructions to our Mining Captains to this effect."[13] The blacklisting of so many Finnish immigrants from the Mesabi's mines meant that after the 1907 strike, Finns made up less than 8 percent of workers on the Mesabi. Remarkably, before the strike, Finns were nearly 20 percent of the working population in area mines.[14] The Oliver's Italian ethnic working population—considerably fewer than the Finns—was also reduced after the strike. The importance of the Italian immigrant striking population during the strike was bolstered by the fact that the WFM's lead organizer in 1907 was Italian immigrant Teofilo Petriella.[15]

The Scabs Begin to Revolt

By 1908, Austrian workers were disgruntled, feeling that they had been used in the previous year's strike and then discarded. A letter from a former South Slavic scab sent to OIMC General Superintendent Charles Trezona documented the feeling of the former strikebreakers: "we were good last summer when there was a strike on the Mesabi Range, when you were circulating papers that we should come to the meeting not to strike, truly there we Austrians were honored. Now you have turned your back on us . . . do not think we are such big fools."[16]

Understanding the Austrian immigrant population, as Oliver mining management would find out, was difficult. Partially, the difficulty resided in the fact that while the immigrant population was given the monolithic label "Austrian," they were, in fact, from several different ethnic groups that, in reality, had little to do with Austria or the linguistically linked Germanic Austrians. Arguably, no other immigrant group on the ranges was so misunderstood or affected by despotism and imperialism as its Austrian population. Generally regarded as people having emigrated from the Austro-Hungarian Empire, immigrants from this region of Europe were a unique amalgamation of ethnicities that had been unnaturally coalesced by imperialism in central and southeastern Europe. According to political boundaries of the time, the Austro-Hungarian Empire included individuals from parts of fourteen different present-day nations: Austria, Italy, Hungary, the Czech Republic, Poland, Slovakia, Romania, Ukraine, Moldova, Slovenia, Croatia, Bosnia-Herzegovina, Serbia-Montenegro, and Bulgaria. Added to this multiethnic mix were two main "classes" of Austrians: Germanic and Slavic. In an era when discussions of eugenics pervaded public discourse, the Germanic peoples were desirable, whereas the Slavic peoples were seen as inferior—both within the Austro-Hungarian Empire's ruling class as well as in the United States' employing class.

There was, of course, much more complexity to the cultures, languages, and religions of people from the Austro-Hungarian Empire, but to the managers of mining companies on the iron ranges, the availability of cheap Slavic Austrian labor had the potential to break strikes and increase profitability. More precisely, many from the southern and western parts of the Austro-Hungarian Empire self-identified as "Jugoslavs." Translated, the term meant "South Slav" and included mostly Slavic-speaking peoples from the Balkan region of Europe, which consisted of ethnic Bosnians, Croatians, Macedonians, Montenegrins, Serbians, and Slovenians.[17] Range bosses often lumped these ethnically distinct peoples in the same category and identified the entire population as "Austrian." That their cultures, languages, and ethnic backgrounds were unique and distinct made little difference. More important was the perception that these peoples were subservient and desperate to escape from the bonds of their native homelands. Because of this quasi-refugee status, South Slavic workers were often seen, by organized labor of that time, as a population of strikebreakers willing to do almost anything for a job. Early-twentieth-century depictions of South Slavs did little to dispel the notion that they were anything other than clay in American capitalists' hands. In 1921, for example, Dr. M. S. Stanoyevich of Columbia University wrote of the *entire* South Slavic population:

> Living in the midst of many conflicting forces, the Jugoslavs present the interesting spectacle of a brave, hardy, obedient, and simple people.

They are mostly of dark complexion, possessing considerable powers of endurance. Their brown eyes are indicative of, now of some intense grief, now of some great joy. They are sensitive and emotional, but by way of compensation they have a certain resiliency which saves them from permanent depression or continued exultation.[18]

In short, according to Stanoyevich's account, South Slavs made good, compliant workers. Differing from his portrayal of South Slavs were their own assertions of an independent immigrant identity. Once in the United States, associational life flourished and in these social settings the collective misnomer of "Austrian" gave way to independent ethnic organizations founded by Croatians and Slovenians (with Serbians organizing distinct organizations after World War I). A benevolent and fraternal organization, the Croatian Fraternal Union, was the largest of any such South Slavic group in the United States. Founded in 1894, by 1930 the group claimed almost one hundred thousand members. The first Slovenian organization in the United States, the Carniolan-Slovene Catholic Union, was also founded in 1894. The organization that grew to be the largest among Slovenian immigrants, however, was the Slovenska narodna podporna jednota (SNPJ) or Slovenian National Benefit Society, organized in 1904. By 1930, the society had claimed more than sixty thousand members across the country. While many of the benevolent and fraternal organizations were linked with the Catholic church, such as the Croat Catholic Union (1922) and the Jugo-Slav Catholic Union (1898), others were squarely founded with class-conscious intentions, such as the Slovene Progressive Benefit Society (1909) and the Slovene Workers' Alliance (1910).[19]

Croatians boldly, and repeatedly, asserted their voices through organized labor and leftist political organizations during the early twentieth century. Although it was not a socialist organization, the National Croatian Society, a precursor to the better-known Croatian Fraternal Union, was a cooperative society of working-class immigrants formed in Allegheny City, Pennsylvania. The National Croatian Society formed a loose confederation of organizations across the United States and began publishing a newspaper called *Zajednicar* (Fraternalist) in 1909. At its eleventh convention, held in 1914, the organization's bylaws included

Serbian and Croatian fraternal organizations like this one in Detroit were integral in providing a space for new immigrants to congregate throughout the Great Lakes region. An important part of this gradual assimilation was the recognition of both native and new American identities. Photograph circa 1919. Courtesy of the Immigration History Research Center, University of Minnesota.

strong language against the practice of scabbing: "the members who are taken ill because of drinking, immoral life, venereal disease or because they work during a strike as strike breakers, lose their rights to sickness benefit."[20]

The first socialist organization of Croatians, the Jugoslav Political Club, began in 1903 and was located in the industrial city of Pittsburgh. As with many immigrant organizations struggling to gain a foothold in a new land, there were ebbs and flows of operation. The club folded after two years and then reorganized a year later. By 1909, there were at least fourteen socialist organizations of Croatian immigrants in the United States. Many were located in industrial centers such as Chicago, Milwaukee, and St. Louis. Interest in socialism had grown so much in the United States that by December 1910 a Jugoslav Socialist Congress of America was held in Chicago. At that meeting it was determined that South Slavic political concerns should be merged with the Social-ist Party of America (SPA). Out of this merger, the Jugoslav Socialist

Alliance was formed. This amalgamation of South Slavic socialists was international in perspective and included Croatians, Slovenians, Serbians, Bulgarians, and Montenegrins.[21]

Along with ethnic, political, and social organizations, newspapers served the South Slavic immigrant community as well. Some periodicals, such as the *Glas svobode* (Voice of freedom), were companion publications to organizations such as the SNPJ. Newspapers such as *Hrvatska* (The Croatian) and *Narodni glasnik* (National herald) served as ethnic connections to the Old World. Others, such as the *Amerikanski slovenec* (Slovenian American), spoke to the intersections between immigrant and American identities. In addition to newspapers that cultivated ethnic preservation and religious identity, there were a number of politically engaged newspapers published by South Slavic immigrants: *Proletarec* (The proletarian), *Radnicka borba* (Workers' struggle), *Radnicka straza* (Workers' guard), and *Industrijalni radnik* (Industrial worker) all espoused revolutionary-socialist perspectives.[22]

While many South Slavic newspapers and organizations operated from a working-class perspective, they fell short of being advocates for socialist and union causes. A divide for many in the South Slavic community existed between the materialism of class-conscious socialist organizations and religious life. For many, South Slavic life revolved around the church, and this perspective led many to be wary of participation in organized labor during the early twentieth century. Additionally, South Slavic immigrants were often used as scab labor during strikes, a practice that brought many South Slavs into direct confrontation with American unions and other immigrant populations who had adopted American labor organizations as their own. But, once in America, thousands of South Slavs did end up turning to Marxist organizations for a voice. The SPA and the Yugoslav Socialist Alliance became home to a great many South Slavic immigrants. Although never nearing the participation of their Finnish immigrant comrades—who had the largest ethnic federation in the SPA with almost thirteen thousand members in 1913—South Slavs were the fourth-largest immigrant population in the SPA. South Slavic membership in the SPA steadily increased from 982 members in 1911 to 2,112 in 1916—perhaps in large part owing to a burgeoning class consciousness after negative experiences with American industrialists.[23]

South Slavic immigrants' growing association with class-conscious American organizations had important ramifications for the American labor movement, and especially affected labor organization in the Lake Superior basin. While Finnish immigrants retained a rich class-conscious cultural life after being blacklisted from employment on the iron ranges, much of the work in organizing miners occurred at the local level. These workplace actions and agitations now rested squarely in the hands of South Slavic workers who were brought in to replace the discontented Finnish immigrants. In a truly incredible turn of events indicative of the horrible labor conditions on the range, the very scabs who were brought in to take the place of Finns in the mines were beginning to foment labor unrest less than a decade after the 1907 Mesabi strike. Discontent was building. A 1913 strike on the Cuyuna Range presaged the call to worker revolt in 1916 on the Mesabi. This strike, commenced in April, saw miners demanding an end to the contract mining system, an eight-hour workday, and hospital cost coverage for workers.[24]

This short, truncated Cuyuna strike was somewhat minor compared to the massive labor rebellion that occurred in Michigan's Upper Peninsula beginning in June 1913. While the AFL-backed WFM was administering labor actions in Michigan's Copper Country, the IWW was leading a strike closer to, and directly affecting, Minnesota's iron ranges. This strike, which grew from a memorial for two workers killed on the job into a considerable labor rebellion on the Twin Ports' iron ore docks, was also the first formal meshing of labor interests between Finnish and Slavic immigrants in Minnesota.

The strike was born out of tragedy in early August 1913, when ore punchers Nick Libest and John Koski were crushed to death under a railcar. According to witnesses, the horrific deaths were caused by unsafe labor practices of the Great Northern Railroad, which hauled iron ore from the Mesabi Range to the Twin Ports for shipping down the Great Lakes. The incident occurred on the docks in the working-class community of Allouez, a port town on the outskirts of Superior, Wisconsin. The deaths of Libest and Koski, the serious injury of fellow worker Conrad Hill, who had his "left arm severed at shoulder, left leg

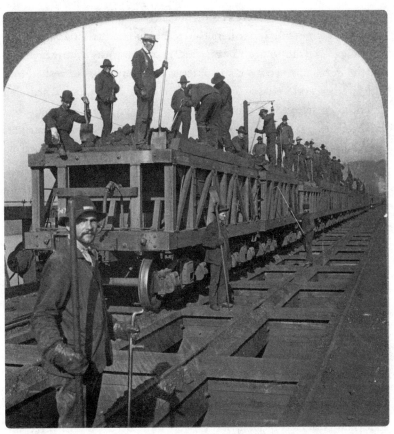

Dockworkers, known as "ore punchers," were tasked with the dangerous job of punching stuck chunks of iron ore through bottom dumping railcars, which emptied down long chutes into massive Great Lakes ore boats. This photograph depicts workers at the docks of Two Harbors, Minnesota, circa 1910. Courtesy of the Robert N. Dennis Collection, Miriam and Ira D. Wallach Division of Art, Prints, and Photographs, New York Public Library.

off at hip," and the injuries of four others caused workers to walk off the docks in protest against the Great Northern.[25]

A formalized labor action quickly spread throughout Superior's docks and into Duluth. The IWW was on the scene to organize and call for improved safety for workers and a fifteen-cent-a-day wage increase. Superior's local newspaper, the *Superior Telegram*, recorded the democracy involved in determining a course of action: "a secret ballot taken at the meeting of strikers this morning resulted in 244 votes to strike against 95 to return to work. The first voting was by informal ballot, the decision to strike being practically unanimous from the Finnish, Swedish and Polish workers. The Belgians, after much discussion among themselves, refused to vote informally, and demanded a secret ballot." The day after the labor stoppage began, newly anointed strikers paraded in two columns down the streets of Allouez. The parade started at the Woodmen Hall and finished at Woodmen Park in an open-air meeting where "more than 400 strikers and sympathizers were in line."[26] According to the *Superior Telegram*, an IWW organizer by the name of Frank Little was in charge of the strike. Within days, the IWW had also brought out men at the Missabe Railroad docks in Duluth. More than four hundred men quit work at the Missabe docks, increasing the tension among workers and railroad management. Organizers and striking workers held meetings in West Duluth's Finnish hall where plans were discussed to forge sympathy strikes, with Frank Little announcing that "word has been sent to the Two Harbors, Ashland, and Marquette docks, announcing the action of the men at the Twin Ports and requesting that the workers on all other docks assist them."

By August 11, however, management of the Great Northern and Missabe docks were claiming victory. The *Superior Telegram* reported that the IWW was brazenly sending in some of its best organizers to continue the fight, but the Wobbly organizers were arriving too late. "The Great Northern Railway company, this morning, through D. M. Philbin, manager of the companies' ore properties, informed George Bubar, chairman of the East End Chamber of Commerce, that the road was ready to take back into its employ all of the ore dock men who are out on strike excepting those of the Finnish nationality." The newspaper reported that Finns were "half the workers' population, while the others were largely Belgians and Poles and a few Scandinavians." Philbin also noted that while the Great Northern would work to make the docks safer, there would be no increase in wages until October 1 when the company would grant a ten-cent-a-day increase in wages, which would be followed by another ten-cent increase on October 15.[27]

So, while the Finnish immigrant strikers were blacklisted from the

IWW organizer Frank Little was the lead organizer of the Superior and Duluth dock strikes in 1913. For his efforts, he was kidnapped during the labor unrest and held at gunpoint outside Superior. Little was lynched four years later in Butte, Montana, for his ongoing participation in the American labor movement. Photograph circa 1915. Courtesy of the Labadie Archive, University of Michigan.

Allouez docks, they had it better than IWW organizer Frank Little, who was kidnapped and deported from the strike zone. The *Superior Telegram* was somewhat dismissive of Little's absence from the strike: "the return of Frank H. Little, the strike leader who was released from his alleged captors in Holyoke on Sunday morning, was the signal for much enthusiasm among the strikers at Allouez this morning. Much capital has been made by the strikers of the alleged kidnapping." Little had been missing for four days, and his whereabouts were unknown from Wednesday afternoon until he returned to administer the strike on Sunday. While the *Telegram* was dismissive of his story, the *International Socialist Review* got the story firsthand from Little and the picture painted was a dire one, indeed. According to the *Review*, Little had been taken from a train car by a mob of men, placed in an automobile, and then spirited some twenty miles south of Superior into Minnesota's Carlton County. He was being held in a house at gunpoint when union sympathizers and organizers discerned his whereabouts and confronted his captors. After a short gunfight and standoff, the Carlton County sheriff was summoned and the kidnappers agreed to his release. He returned to the strike no worse for the wear, but his abduction and deportation sent a strong message to those hoping to increase strike efforts. The strike eventually dwindled and workers returned to the docks with the assurance of increased safety measures and the promise of impending wage increases in the coming months.[28]

Clearly, the pace and intensity of labor organization were increasing in Minnesota after 1913. A major obstacle for the IWW in the years between 1907 and 1916 was turning former labor foes, Austrian immigrants, into friends.[29] As strikebreakers during the 1907 strike, scabs from South Slavic regions in Europe ran into direct confrontation with Finnish and Italian mine workers and their union representatives. During the 1907 strike, some of these same Finnish and Italian immigrant strike activists were intimately involved in the administration and implementation of the strike's activities and goals, and were, in essence, the avowed rivals of South Slavic immigrants.

Ethnic rivalry and distrust of the IWW in the South Slavic immigrant population were substantial problems that concerned Wobbly organizers well before the 1916 strike. Because of this concern, and after learning from previous strike actions that were fragmented by ethnic discord, the IWW called on its ample experience with organizing immigrant workers and brought in a talented cadre of organizers, while also recruiting local, multilingual organizers. The tactic worked. Veda Ponikvar, a child during the strike, relates that many Slovenian immigrants were confused about how the IWW worked in the years leading up to 1916: "There were a few people that were in business, and some who were very active in the SNPJ, who were exposed [to unionism]. They would go to conventions in larger cities and so forth and mingle with people who were working in factories." In these interactions, Slovenian immigrants came into contact with the goals and methods of industrial unionism. As Ponikvar suggests, "they [became] a little bit more knowledgeable about the whole thing. But your total population at that time was wondering about the whole thing." Over time, however, knowledge of unionism and distrust of the IWW dissipated as the Range's

Slovenian population became sympathetic to the strike.[30] This sympathy turned into open advocacy and the former Austrian scabs began joining the ranks of the Iron Range's immigrant class-conscious workers.

Animosity between the Austrian scabs and displaced Finnish and Italian immigrant workers did not disappear overnight, but enmity was relatively short-lived and became negligible only a few years later—in at least one Range town. Ponikvar recalled that in Chisholm, workers "weren't at odds, simply because as a community they were helping each other, and the neighborhood was pretty much intermingled. You had Italians, Finns, [Czechs, Russians,] and Slavs living on the same block." The dissipation of ethnic rivalry after the 1907 strike was likely helped by the growing class consciousness of immigrant Austrians who began to see themselves as part of an American working class. Realizing that they had been used by mining companies during the 1907 strike, Ponikvar surmised, South Slavic workers recognized that their class interests outweighed misgivings about the IWW and ethnic rivalries. The former South Slav scabs were considering becoming Wobblies.[31]

Class-conscious South Slav Strikers

As a result of beginning to find their voice in American industry, former South Slav replacement workers were now subject to the vitriol of Iron Range capitalists. Their association with the IWW drew the ire of mining companies, and the immediate impulse from mine managers and their hirelings was to paint the South Slavs, along with other class-conscious immigrants, as un-American radicals. The burgeoning class consciousness of former scabs found expression in the IWW's open advocacy of direct-action tactics such as industrial sabotage and the strike. Minnesota's iron-mining companies, for their part, developed a company line to paint the calling of labor strikes and sabotage as an un-American act of terrorism. For "respectable" citizens, sabotage—both withdrawal of efficiency and destruction of industrial machinery—loomed like a specter over the Lake Superior industrial region. At the same time, few outside the ranges' industrial setting understood the actual contexts or contingencies regarding the use of strikes or sabotage to voice worker complaints. As one fervently pro-mining company newspaper brutally remarked during the 1916 strike:

Law must be enforced. The rights of all must be respected. Men who go on the property of others and coerce workingmen into quitting jobs they want to keep must be prosecuted. If there is no law by which these agitators can be silenced they can surely be controlled in the same manner that is the Negro in the south. For we cannot sacrifice all law and order at the behest of a few radicals, who would in an instant tear down all that our fore-fathers built in past generations . . .

As near as we can make out this reign of terror is entirely due to that outlawed and unlawful organization, the Industrial Workers of the World well translated in the west, its birthplace, as "I Won't Work." But the fact that the members of this order will not work is not its worst sin. It's an outlaw even among labor unions. Its principle [sic] teaching favors "sabotage," which, translated means it is the worker's duty to do all possible damage to machinery or property both before and after quitting his job. That is anarchy pure and simple . . . we are firmly convinced that every man who becomes a member of the I.W.W. obligates himself in favor of "sabotage" and if he does he is a traitor to the country and should be treated as such.[32]

During the 1916 strike, the intersectional lives of immigrants directly collided with competing definitions of what it meant to be American. From the mining company perspective, South Slavic immigrants were once the expendable saviors of capitalism on the ranges, brought in during a pinch to bail out mining interests and save financial bottom lines. After they had done their duty as scabs, however, they were relegated to second-, third-, or fourth-tier status—disposable cogs in the industrial machinery. After this type of treatment, and with a quickly developed understanding of the system of capitalist exploitation, South Slav immigrant workers hastily became one of the most ardent supporters of organized labor on the ranges. Along with class-conscious Finns and Italians, many South Slavic workers began to understand that if they were to find a voice in America, it would only come by defining their own identities, in their own way, as immigrant members of the American working class.

There was, of course, a company understanding of what it meant to be a "good American": be a forthright worker, avoid labor or socialist organizations, and, more generally, be a malleable cog in the country's

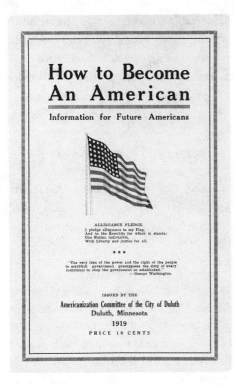

How to Become
An American

Information for Future Americans

ALLEGIANCE PLEDGE.
I pledge allegiance to my Flag,
And to the Republic for which it stands;
One Nation indivisible,
With Liberty and justice for all.

★ ★ ★

"The very idea of the power and the right of the people
to establish government presupposes the duty of every
individual to obey the government on established."
—George Washington.

ISSUED BY THE
Americanization Committee of the City of Duluth
Duluth, Minnesota
1919
PRICE 10 CENTS

Both mining companies and municipal civic groups offered courses and literature designed to assimilate the nation's growing immigrant population. The Americanization Committee of the City of Duluth issued this pamphlet for new immigrants in 1919. Courtesy of Archives and Special Collections, Kathryn A. Martin Library, University of Minnesota–Duluth.

quickly evolving industrial landscape. Companies were so intent on cultivating this type of worker that they offered specialized "Americanization" courses. According to an article titled "Steel Trust Springs a New One: Proposes Establishing Scissorbill Factory to Prevent Strikes" in the IWW-sponsored newspaper *Strikers' News*, "Duluth daily newspapers tell of a proposed plan whereby the Oliver Iron Mining Company is to establish night schools at its mines for the purpose of educating the foreigners employed by them and thus making good citizens." The article, derisive and satirical throughout, opined that in addition to manual training for male employees, the schools would include domestic training for their wives. The training included "a plan of domestic science wherein the wives of miners will be taught to make a very palatable soup from cast-off shoes, old socks, candle drippings and last year's sunbonnets," to supposedly "reduce the cost of living." Ultimately, the role of night schools would be to Americanize, and thus make fit for naturalization, their workers in the interests of the companies and American capital. "The outline given is that the mining companies will encourage naturalization of its employees," the article argued, so that "when there comes depression in the iron business those who have not availed themselves of the company big-heartedness to accept the Stars and Stripes will be the first to be fired."[33]

While it was the job of the company press to draw distinctions between foreign- and native-born Americans, many immigrants wanted nothing more than a mere taste of what it meant to be an American. This was the case with Mike Stark, a Slovenian immigrant, who worked in a Chisholm-area mine and testified to Range municipal officials during the 1916 strike:

> I am a miner for fourteen years—over fourteen years, and I have eight children—I have seven living and one died. I worked now for last three years, I have got $59 check (a month), $61, $62, $63, $67, up to $70 (a month) . . . and I send four kids to the school, and the teacher would like to have the children dressed and clean and everything like that. I like to do that myself. And the children go to church, the priest likes to see that the wife is dressed nice like the American ladies, and the children dressed like the American children. I like that too, but I can't. You fellows think—a single man maybe [can live on my wages], but how can my family live on such wages?[34]

Italian immigrant Fluvio Pettinelli felt much the same: "Gentleman, I like to tell you that I come in here in this country five years and a half ago. I been working in mine ever since." After stints in the Lincoln, and later in the Alpena Mine, Pettinelli was increasingly troubled with the practice of paying to work the more profitable ground in mines. This system found petty mine bosses selling profitable ground to mine workers as a way to supplement income and divide the workforce. Pettinelli, who wanted nothing more than a stable job that provided access to the American Dream, continued: "Two years ago I got married and got American girl. I believe she has right to live as another American, so I believe further I got right to live [as an American] . . . the month when I worked contract [mining] and strike bad place we no have enough to eat . . . nothing. We

Ethnic Populations in Oliver Mines and Their Citizenship Status, April 1916

NATIONALITY	CITIZENS	FIRST PAPERS	FOREIGNERS	TOTAL
Austrian	29 (7.1%)	54 (13.3%)	322 (79.6%)	405
Finnish	50 (19.5%)	54 (13.3%)	122 (47.7%)	256
Italian	21 (12.1%)	25 (14.5%)	127 (73.4%)	173
Northwestern Europe[1]	39 (58%)	13 (17%)	18 (25%)	70

Source: "Nationality Statement, 1916," Oliver Iron Mining Company, Box 2-27, Folder S3021, Richard H. Hudelson Labor History Collection, 1880–2006, Northeast Minnesota Historical Center Collections, University of Minnesota–Duluth, Duluth, Minnesota. In addition to the ethnicities mentioned in the table, the data included information for 35 Russian workers, 13 Polish workers, 1 Turkish worker, and 10 Canadian workers.

[1] This designation counts workers from Sweden, Norway, Denmark, Germany, England, Scotland, and Ireland.

have to go without clothes. If we eat, we don't dress, and if we dress we don't eat. That is fact."[35] For many immigrants who were non-citizens, attaining the fabled American Dream proved a difficult reality.

While many immigrants were working to forge a better life in the United States, it was clear that Austrian and Italian workers were laboring in a "foreigner" status for the Oliver in disproportionate numbers to immigrants from Northwestern Europe (and even Finland). By the spring of 1916, almost 80 percent of the company's South Slavic workforce and 75 percent of its Italian workers had yet to make any overtures toward applying for American citizenship. Many of these immigrants had not even taken the first step of applying for "First Papers." According to Oliver company data, even the highly suspect, pro-labor Finnish immigrants were more likely to become citizens. What, then, could explain why Austrian and Italian immigrant workers were so unlikely to have moved toward becoming U.S. citizens? One answer could simply be the number of years spent in the United States. Italian and especially Austrian mine workers had been present on the iron ranges for less time than other ethnicities. These immigrants, many coming during or after the 1907 strike, were a sort of second wave of exploited immigrant labor, and simply had not been in the country long enough to take concrete steps toward citizenship. Second, and conceivably linked to the first reason, it was likely that some Austrian and Italian immigrants had no intention of remaining in the United States and had plans to return to their countries of origin. Multiple trips across the Atlantic in search of work were commonplace, and many immigrants from a host of countries came to the Americas in search of short-term jobs with no intention of becoming citizens. Finally, but perhaps most important, it was possible that many of these immigrants simply did not feel like Americans. They could not vote, many lived in squalor, and the tiered society of industrial America did not convince them that social betterment—or citizenship—could become their personal reality.

Although many in the South Slavic and Italian immigrant populations longed to become American workers, their experience with American capitalists was a stark reminder of who owned the iron ranges. As the 1916 strike began to rage, Austrian workers ran afoul of the system and began to face the retribution of a capitalist class that felt betrayed by formerly subservient strikebreakers. South Slavic workers and their families began paying the price for their class consciousness and growing identification as American working-class actors with a voice. One such class-conscious immigrant was Mrs. Francis Zbenich who, along with two other women and nine children, was thrown into the city jail in Hibbing for protesting against a union turncoat. The *Strikers' News* caustically recounted her arrest:

> Mrs. Francis Zbenich was arrested Monday night when she attempted to remonstrate with a creature, alleged to be a man, who has been carrying a union card and drawing strike benefits from the union while scabbing on his fellow workers. At the time she was arrested she had her three months old baby in her arms. She was brutally dragged to the patrol wagon and thrown in bodily, the baby getting a severe bump against the seat and herself being badly shaken up. At the jail Tuesday her left arm showed a severe bruise, seemingly made by the Deputy's fingers. Of course, he had to hold her tight. A woman with a nursing child in her arms is so dangerous, you know.[36]

Many like Mrs. Zbenich quickly became enemies of American capital and were treated as such by mining companies. Strikers and their families discovered that retribution for not toeing the company line was swift, as the Zbenich family learned soon after Mrs. Zbenich's arrest. The August 4, 1916, edition of the *Strikers' News* detailed the eviction of the Zbenich family from their home, House No. 39, on company property in Carson Lake (near Hibbing): "You are hereby notified that the lease dated November 1, 1910, between the Tyler Iron Mining company, as party of the first part, and yourselves, as parties of the second part . . . is hereby cancelled and terminated. You are required to remove within thirty (30) days, from said premises, all your possessions and belongings or the same will become the property of the said party of the first as in said lease provided." It was likely no coincidence that the mining company was threatening eviction of the Zbenich family given the matriarch's run-in with the law in Hibbing.

The sense of working-class solidarity across the ethnic divide had reached so far into the South Slavic striking population that some were catapulted into important positions within the strike's administration. John Pancner, an organizer and chairman of the Central Strike Committee, had his name attached to a passionate appeal for working-class solidarity in the *Strikers' News* that spanned ethnic, political, and union divides: "Fellow Workers, Friends, Trade Unionists, and Socialists: The striking miners of the Mesaba Range, appeal in this great crisis to the whole working-class of America . . . our wives and children are being beaten, you can at least keep hunger away from our doors, while we fight the battles." Pancner was a committed advocate for the Wobblies and called for donations to continue the fight. The most amazing part of his appeal, however, was where he asked for donations to be sent: "Fellow Workers, Comrades, Brothers! Don't leave the women and children starve, collect money and send it to JOHN LEPPANEN, Treasurer of Relief Fund, Box 372, Virginia, Minn., or wire Finnish Socialist Hall, Virginia, Minn."[37] A representative of a population that had scabbed some nine years earlier was openly calling for a united front of working-class solidarity. This was a truly remarkable turn of events in the 1916 strike, and a scenario that less than a decade earlier was almost unthinkable as thousands of South Slav scabs filled area mines, taking the place of blacklisted Finnish immigrant mine workers. Now, just before and during the 1916 strike, thousands of Austrian immigrants were filling Finnish immigrant-founded cultural spaces of discontent to hear the message of organized labor. This was, quite simply, a miraculous turn of events.

Organizational and social roles were becoming clearer in the run-up to the 1916 strike. Finnish immigrants acted as the localized structural element during the strike—their halls, political and socioeconomic organizations, and previous experiences with Lake Superior labor organizing gave the labor action a strong foundation. Italian immigrants provided the 1916 strike's organization with some of its most formidable and important organizers, national media, and social connections. Unlike Finns, who were somewhat regional in geographic distribution, settling in northern industrial and frontier areas, Italian immigrants had a national network of labor-conscious organizations and fiery supporters. Carlo Tresca and his numerous social connections—which underwrote his exploits as a national organizer—was a prime example of this committed and well-formed national network. Using national media and big-city connections, Italian immigrants could rally financial and moral support from great distances in a short period of time, which was a boon to the cash-strapped IWW. South Slavic immigrants were the ethnicity with boots on the ground in contested workscapes. The former foes to organized labor had bodies in the workplace, which gave them the ability to agitate, organize, and sabotage against efforts to crush the strike. Sadly, it was also South Slavic immigrants who paid the ultimate price in lives lost and jailed individuals as the strike's tumultuous events unfurled across the ranges.

Not lost in the cultivation of ethnic solidarity and immigrant struggles with joining the American working class are the efforts of the IWW as a union that proclaimed, "An Injury to One Is an Injury to All." The Wobblies worked hard and devoted much time to their primary organizing goal—unite all workers at all costs. This perspective and interpretation of the strike is best illustrated by a short article—or more so, a declaration—in one of the first issues of the *Strikers' News*: "All Nationalities to Lend Support: Finnish, Italian, Russian, and all other locals in Chicago have also vowed to stand by the miners in their brave

A Finnish temperance society brass band provides music for a Slovenian funeral parade through Ely, Minnesota, circa 1910. Few events brought people out like a funeral, and the planning of such an event was an occasion for solidarity among ethnic groups. Courtesy of the Brownell Collection, Iron Range Historical Society, Gilbert, Minnesota.

fight for better living. They have pledged their physical, financial and moral support every one of them." That support led to increasing numbers of striking workers as the ranges became ablaze in working-class strike actions while hurtling headlong into the largest labor action ever seen in Minnesota. The *Strikers' News* was clear about intent and claimed numbers:

> War has been declared against the Steel Trust and the independent mining companies of Minnesota, by the Industrial Workers of the World. The iron miners are mustering. Twenty thousand have left the mines and pits. More than seven thousand have already been sworn in. The Steam Shovels are idle. The drills are silent. The miners are on strike in the following camps: Hibbing, 4,000; Chisholm, 2,800; Virginia, 2,500; Buhl, 1,400; Eveleth, 1,600; Gilbert, 900; Biwabik, 600; Aurora, 900; Kinney, 800, and other camps.[38]

The stage was set for an epic clash between immigrants linked by organized labor and U.S. Steel, one of the largest and most powerful corporations in United States. From an industrial landscape WFM organizer William Tracy described as being "wholly impossible to rally any of our men under such discouraging conditions" in 1908 to a region ablaze in working-class revolt, driven by former scabs—the about-face of organized labor in less than a decade was unprecedented. The strike was organized, but now it had to be waged. This massive labor action would put the newfound solidarity of working-class immigrants and the organizational acumen of the Wobblies to the test.

5 THE RHETORIC OF REVOLUTION

Communicating the Strike

Yesterday afternoon there was a meeting of the citizens and businessmen to take steps against the strike agitators, and they appointed a committee and called for a mass meeting last evening at the curling rink. A committee spoke at the meeting, called for and passed a resolution, practically unanimously, to deport the star strike agitators on this noon's train.

—*James D. Ireland, Hanna Mining Company manager to Hanna Headquarters in Cleveland, June 16, 1916*

THE RUSH TO UNITE STRIKING MINE WORKERS ON THE MINNESOTA iron ranges in early June 1916 taxed the IWW's organizing abilities. The union was taking on one of the most powerful corporations in the United States, U.S. Steel, or, as it was more colloquially known, the "Steel Trust." Well-funded corporations like the Oliver were prepared to spend millions of dollars to break strikes. Additionally, several other well-heeled iron ore operators known as the "Independents" looked to the Oliver's leadership during this time of industrial turmoil and pledged funds and people to rid the ranges of the IWW. Collectively, the Steel Trust had a long reach and its influence reached all the way to the Minnesota governor's office.

In addition to the barriers of organization put forth by mining companies, one of the IWW's most difficult hurdles in bringing about a large, successful labor action was that the union sought to organize immigrant mine workers from many different nations—none of which identified English as a first language. Although seemingly a gargantuan task, the

This group of IWW organizers was the first wave of people "Big Bill" Haywood sent to the Mesabi Range in 1916 as the strike began in June. Carlo Tresca, the Italian immigrant anarchist, is in the bottom row, second from left. Photograph by George R. Dawson. Courtesy of the Iron Range Research Center, Minnesota Discovery Center.

IWW's previous experiences with organizing immigrant workers would guide the union in its efforts to communicate with the ranges' working classes. The great test for the IWW, then, was successfully communicating its revolutionary culture, ideology, and passion across multiple media formats in an effective manner.

In many ways, for the IWW, the 1916 strike can be seen as the culmination of many years of learning how to organize immigrant workers through trial and error. After a number of hard-fought strikes, union leaders began to understand the importance of organizing immigrant workers on their own terms. In short, the IWW's relationship with its members was a two-way street. This meant that strike speakers, publications, and organizers mirrored the numerous nationalities that the IWW sought to band together. In pursuing this goal, the IWW entered the fight of 1916 with a talented, multiethnic mix of local, regional, and national organizers: Italian Carlo Tresca, Slovenian John Pancner,

"Austrian" John Perich, Scottsman Sam Scarlett, Finn Leo Laukki, Swede-Finn Charles Jacobson, Bulgarian George Andreytchine, and half-Native American and half-white organizer Frank Little, among others, were sent by IWW General Secretary "Big Bill" Haywood in an attempt to lead the revolt that was quickly developing on the Mesabi Iron Range. Added to this battalion of organizers, the Wobblies brought with them a savvy array of communication strategies that could agitate across a disjointed physical landscape and fragmented working-class population.

Wobbly Propaganda and the Spark of Worker Revolt

To many the 1916 strike seemed to materialize out of nowhere, but there were indications of labor unrest at least a month before the start of the strike. On May 2, an organizer with the IWW's Agricultural Workers Organization commented that the Range was "ripe for organization and action." The IWW's official newspaper, the *Industrial Worker*, also contained a veiled reference to an impending labor action when it published a letter from a Range mine worker on May 13 that stated that "the spirit of revolt is growing among the workers on the Iron Range," while the same article blatantly called for organizers "who have an understanding of the tactics and methods of the IWW and who would go on the job, and agitate and organize on the job," to be sent to northern Minnesota.[1] The 1916 Minnesota Iron-Ore Strike started on June 2, 1916, at the St. James Mine in Aurora, Minnesota. Mine authorities had tried to suppress the strike, but according to reports of the time, Italian immigrant Joe Greeni bolted from Aurora to Virginia, and the strike followed in his wake and moved west. The strike would eventually reach to the Vermilion and Cuyuna ranges as well, but never with the same intensity as on the Mesabi.[2] Local organizers partial to the IWW supported the strike until the IWW's regional and national leaders arrived on the scene. The union described the push to organize:

> Strikers realized the absolute necessity of a [national] organization. They felt the need of trained speakers and organizers, speaking the different languages of the range. Largely upon the advice of the Finnish miners, the strikers sent word to the nearest organizer of the Industrial Workers of the World in the city of Duluth to come up to the range

and help them. Fellow worker [Arthur] Boose, a teamster of Duluth, a capable I.W.W. organizer, started the work of organizing. Soon he got help from the General Headquarters in Chicago . . . the result of [this] activity was the systematizing of the work in connection with the strike, the issuing of a weekly bulletin, "The Strikers' News," the starting of a country-wide campaign for financial aid and the distribution of aid to the most needy.[3]

With a local, regional, and national organizational force in place, the IWW set up strike headquarters at the Socialist Opera House in Virginia, home of the IWW's Metal Mine Workers' Industrial Union No. 490. While the opera house was the primary center of the strike, Finnish immigrant labor halls across the Mesabi Range served as local centers for "agitprop" (art, agitation, and propaganda) and organization. Especially significant was Hibbing's Workers' Hall, which took on the role as regional headquarters for the western end of the Mesabi Range. Other halls and social spaces operated as nodes of organization across the ranges, transmitting strike news and communiqués along the region's disconnected towns and mining locations.[4]

Landscapes, whether the washboarded dirt roads linking dislocated industrial towns, the route of a parade through a Range city, or the architecture of a building in a working-class neighborhood, played an important part in the 1916 strike. The IWW and the ranges' Finnish immigrant population had learned an important lesson from the 1907 Mesabi strike that would come into play nine years later. Working with the WFM during the 1907 and 1913–14 strikes awakened Finnish immigrants to the important role they could play in *American* working-class struggles. As a result, they began to recognize the significance of their accrued material culture—halls, printing presses, and publications—to labor actions in the United States. According to Finnish historian Auvo Kostiainen, Finnish immigrants "came into close contact with American labor organizations, and they stuck together with other nationalities on the Mesabi Range." The lessons of collective labor organization became firmly entrenched in the Finnish immigrant consciousness as their social spaces were opened to other ethnicities. In this way, Finnish immigrants hastened the unification of labor during the 1916 strike by providing the

Supporters of the IWW draped themselves in "One Big Union" pennants outside
the Socialist Opera House in Virginia, Minnesota, circa 1915. The opera house
served as headquarters for the 1916 strike as workers from all backgrounds and
ethnicities attended events and rallies inside and outside the iconic structure.
Courtesy of the Iron Range Research Center, Minnesota Discovery Center.

IWW with an intact grassroots organizational structure replete with
social spaces that functioned as command centers.[5]

As a social space of worker discontent, the Socialist Opera House in
Virginia made a strong argument for the power of material culture to
act as communicative expression. The building often served as a backdrop for group photographs of IWW gatherings. The staging of these
photographs and the adornments of both the building and the people
demonstrate the power of place in uniting workers around a common
cause. The sturdy brick walls of the opera house mirror the solidarity
displayed by fellow workers who proudly hold "One Big Union" pennants. These triangular cultural symbols that displayed the IWW logo
expressed a sense of belonging, similarity of purpose, and a shared experience. The Socialist Opera House was a heavily stylized expression

of working-class culture, making it a showpiece for organized labor, a social space that evoked sentiments of solidarity, and a brick-and-mortar expression of the strikers' resolve.

It was no mistake that Virginia and the opera house became the IWW's primary headquarters during the labor conflict of 1916. Geographically, Virginia was centrally located in the strike zone and had a large Finnish population. Haywood and other Wobbly organizers had been making overtures to the ranges' immigrants since the union's inception in 1905, and as previous chapters have shown, Finns were especially receptive to these calls. Because of this receptivity, the locus of IWW activities on the Iron Range was situated in the Finnish-immigrant-built Socialist Opera House. In addition to serving as strike administration headquarters, the opera house was the location of mass strikers' meetings, revenue-creating concerts and plays, the venue for blistering strike speeches, and the beginning and end point of strike parades.

The IWW's strongest mine workers' local, Industrial Union No. 490, was also located in Virginia. IWW General Secretary "Big Bill" Haywood noticed the significance of this local chapter and put money toward the printing of a Finnish-language industrial unionism guide, *Teollisuus-Unionismin Opas* (Guide to industrial unionism) to reach out to Virginia's immigrant population. Distributed free of charge, the guide was an attempt to provide the technical details of industrial unionism to nascent organizers as the strike's momentum progressed. The quickly produced booklet was printed on somewhat delicate paper by the union "Quickprint" shop in Virginia and was meant to serve as a portable organizational tool for Finnish-language speakers.

Because the *Guide to Industrial Unionism* was an introduction to the IWW and its ideology, it was perhaps not surprising that the final page introduced readers to Haywood himself. To lend a more colloquial tone to the publication, the booklet included an inked reproduction of his signature and invited readers to write to him personally for more information. Haywood's reproduced signature established a personal connection between him and the audience, establishing "Big Bill" as the de facto leader of the 1916 strike. The importance of fully developing Haywood's ethos as the general secretary of the IWW cannot be overstated.

Teollisuus-Unionismin

Opas

Kustantanut

Industrial Workers of
The World

(Kolmas painos)

Industrial Workers of the World'in
Periaatteiden lyhyt selitys

QUICKPRINT VIRGINIA

This *Guide to Industrial Unionism* was published in the Finnish language to aid in organization of workers during the 1916 strike. The pocket-sized guide, published in Virginia, Minnesota, by the Quickprint Shop, served as a mobile organizing handbook and featured a greeting from the IWW's general secretary, "Big Bill" Haywood. Author's collection.

Haywood's status as the head of the IWW had made him something of a celebrity, a famous, fiery figure in labor and union circles, though infamous on the national scene. Along with establishing his credibility as the point person for contacts with the IWW, the official seal of the IWW adorned the book's cover, giving the entire document an official-looking, working-class integrity.

As a mobile organizational tool, the *Guide to Industrial Unionism* was likely distributed in the streets of Virginia and handed out during parades and street speeches—a common IWW organizational tactic. Strike parades and processions made an immediate impact on audiences. When the 1916 strike began, the streets of Mesabi Range municipalities were filled with strikers, and the critical mass of a strike parade was one of the most impressive displays of union power and solidarity. Strike parades were designed to visually assert the credibility of both the IWW and the actions of striking workers. Fly-by-night organizations with

"Big Bill" Haywood was an imposing figure and noted celebrity of the United States' early labor movements. In 1907 he was tried for the 1905 shooting of Idaho's governor and found not guilty. As a child, he injured his right eye and was often photographed showing his left profile. Courtesy of the George Grantham Bain Collection, Library of Congress Prints and Photographs Division.

limited resources, both financial and human, did not organize orderly parades of well-dressed men, women, and children who were accompanied by boisterous brass bands. In orchestrating such public displays of coordinated working-class culture, the IWW was demonstrating that it had the organizational acumen to get people on their feet and marching to the same beat.

In addition to establishing credibility, parades during the 1916 strike were also emotional appeals to those who watched, or saw photographs in the newspapers, of the mass, mobile meetings. These mobile public gatherings were festive occasions—jovial introductions to the IWW and striking workers. This type of celebratory public introduction was especially important for dismissing company warnings that the IWW was an organization prone to disarray and violence. Neatly organized rows of marching strikers, accompanied by a uniformed brass band, were led by the wives and children of striking workers. The well-dressed participants indicated to audiences that the IWW

A parade of IWW supporters leads a spirited march through downtown Hibbing, June 21, 1916. As with many union parades, women and children led the way in a valiant act of bravery as strike parades could often turn violent. Courtesy of the Iron Range Research Center, Minnesota Discovery Center.

was not a band of ragtag, bomb-throwing anarchists—as the mining companies implied.

Although strike parades were often jovial in nature, it did not mean that they were free from risk. Such public events could become instances of incredible heroism and bravery in the face of strong opposition from law enforcement, mining company police, and hostile members of the public. One *Strikers' News* article concerning the actions of a parading Slovenian man reported that "while the deputies posed with their guns in their hands and a sheepish look on their ugly faces, one of the strikers, a Slavonian, broke the deadlock by marching straight through the line of deputies and shoving them to one side as he went and opening a way for the parade which marched triumphantly out of town toward Eveleth."[6] This newspaper account, likely meant to cater to Eastern Europeans' perceived piety, contained an almost biblical quality that would have appealed to those less familiar with class struggle and more comfortable with accounts of triumphant underdogs.

In pro-union media the strike was envisaged as a David versus Goliath event, but the "parting of gun thugs" during a strike parade also conjured remnants of another well-known biblical tale, that of Moses parting the Red Sea, bringing an oppressed people to a promised land. In this tale of delivery from tyranny, however, a Slovenian led the way, allowing strikers passage to a bountiful feast where IWW orators could deliver a message of emancipation, liberty, and solidarity. The article continued:

> on their arrival [strikers] found a bountiful supply of sandwiches, lemonade, and coffee at the Finnish opera house and after eating lunch and taking a short rest, they attended the meeting, which was one of the biggest in the history of the strike. [Elizabeth Gurley] Flynn and [Joseph] Ettor spoke and the crowd was so large that it was necessary to hold an overflow meeting outside of the hall, where speakers addressed the crowd from the balcony.

Although the effects of strike parades could be felt across several communities, they were a local affair, confined to the social spaces occupied by strikers and an immediate audience. They were an effective method of communicating messages of solidarity, but only to a limited audience in a defined landscape. Because of the sheer size of Minnesota's iron range, strikers were separated by miles of physical space. To combat the separation of the strike's audience over geographic space, the IWW relied on a mass-media machine, and in particular the *Strikers' News*, a pro-union, locally produced newspaper dedicated to reporting the events of the strike.

For striking workers, the *Strikers' News* was a far-ranging mobile mouthpiece, a textual oration of IWW principles, strike activities, and mining company transgressions against the working class. Rhetorically, the newspaper was steeped in passionate appeals that sought to engender interest, empathy, and compassion for striking workers. It was also a locally produced chronicle of strike events. Printing the newspaper locally was a strategic decision meant to combat mining company assertions that outsiders or "foreign agitators" were stirring up the area's contented workers. Homegrown manufacture of the newspaper also highlighted the decentralization of the IWW along with stressing the local control of the ranges' rank and file in administering the strike. The IWW made every effort to convey that the *Strikers' News* was both published and edited by "THE STRIKERS THEMSELVES."

A common feature in strike publications was the strikers' demands. Newspapers printed during times of industrial turmoil, such as the *Strikers' News*, were one such media outlet where strike goals were presented to the public. The original demand of the strikers on the ranges was simple: the abolition of the detested contract mining system. As national leaders of the IWW became more involved, the number of strikers increased and their demands were articulated in a more profound and proficient manner.[7] The updated demands of the strikers in mid-June of 1916 included the following:

> A straight eight-hour day for all men
> A minimum wage of $2.75 for surface labor and $3.00 for
>   underground labor with $.50 a day additional for wet places
> The abolition of the contract system
> A semimonthly pay day
> The men were to be paid when quitting or discharged
> The abolition of the Saturday night shift with full pay
> The return of all strikers
> The abolition of the private mine police[8]

Most important among the strikers' demands was that union recognition was not included. This was a tactic to checkmate corporations' unwillingness to meet and bargain with organized labor. During past strikes in the Lake Superior basin, such as the 1913–14 Michigan Copper Strike, one steadfast demand from strikers was recognition of the union as the elected representative for workers. Knowing that this demand would be a barrier to labor negotiations between the rank and file and mining company managers, the IWW did not ask that strikers require union representation as a condition for the resumption of work.

In addition to the *Strikers' News*, there were several immigrant presses running stories partial to Minnesota's striking iron-ore workers. At least seven non-English, IWW-sanctioned newspapers reported on the strike: the Polish-language *Solidarnosc* (Solidarity), located in Chicago; *Il Proletario* (The proletarian), an Italian-language newspaper located in

Boston; *A Bermunkas* (The wage worker), a Hungarian semimonthly located in New York; the Swedish-Norwegian-Danish *Allarm* located in Minneapolis; the *Darbininku Balsas* (The voice of the worker) located in Baltimore; and *Sosialisti*, a Finnish-language newspaper from Duluth. Arguably, the most important of these non-English periodicals was *Sosialisti*, a publication of Finnish immigrants in northern Minnesota. *Sosialisti* was significant to the strike because of the important roles Finnish immigrants had played to nurture, agitate, and bring about the strike. The newspaper's close proximity to the Mesabi Range gave it great credibility among the region's large Finnish population, many of whom also worked in the extractive and shipping industries in northern Wisconsin and Michigan's Upper Peninsula, where the IWW hoped to forge sympathy strikes in the march toward a general strike in Lake Superior's industrial basin.

The 1916 strike far surpassed all other previous attempts at organization of mine workers on Minnesota's iron ranges. IWW officials claimed that approximately 15,500 mine workers were idled and that more than 7,000 of these workers had joined the Wobblies during the first month of the strike. The mining companies' estimations placed the number of strikers at a significantly lower tally, estimating that between 7,000 and 8,000 men had participated in the walkout.[9] The actual number of men on strike was probably somewhere between these two figures. Enticing more workers out of area mines was the primary function of IWW literature. These mass-produced publications were a running correspondence between the IWW and potential future union members. At first glance, the purpose of the IWW's multimedia offerings may have appeared to be solely antagonistic. However, this would be a simplistic rendering of a dynamic and vibrant usage of communication strategies between the Wobblies and their intended audience during the early days of this industrial conflict. Admittedly, however, there was certainly a sarcastic edge to the IWW's media, but the purposes underlying the careful creation, distribution, and production of the IWW's organizational materials were multifaceted. The goals of the IWW's early strike rhetoric were threefold: (1) to provide, at the very least, a rudimentary understanding of revolutionary industrial unionism. The IWW was aware that the ideological tenets of industrial unionism were complex, but the union made attempts to distill the technical language of ideology into concise texts and visual interpretations of key concepts; (2) to inform and instruct on tactics used in the class struggle. For the IWW, the 1916 strike was a battle in the class war. The IWW was interested in training organizers and agitators for the inevitable commencement of a general strike that would cripple U.S. industry and provide workers with the economic upheaval that would bring about a revolutionary change in society. The IWW had a long-term goal in mind, and transmitting the tactics for bringing about a revolutionary experience were of paramount concern; and (3) to unite the Range's multiethnic workforce. Mining companies attempted to divide the working class by importing scabs and strikebreakers, favoring certain ethnicities over others, and sometimes segregating certain groups in work camps at company-owned locations.

The most difficult bridges for IWW organizers to cross were the cultural, linguistic, and socially divergent pulls of Iron Range populations, some of whom—especially South Slavs—were suspicious of the IWW. An important tool for organizing these multilingual groups was the effective use of radical cartooning. Cartoons provided the IWW with the ability to translate very complex and didactic messages—such as the One Big Union, sabotage, and solidarity—to multiple audiences via a universally transmissible image. As a result, the audience receiving the message did not have to be able to communicate in the same language. Images were a kind of universal visual language because many immigrants had experience with agricultural or industrial work, familiarity with ethnic repression in their home countries, and an understanding of what it meant to be subservient to a ruling class. The IWW was able to translate complex ideological messages via images of exploitation of workers, the perils of dangerous working conditions, the suppression of free-speech violations, and a decidedly underdog status to immigrant mine workers on the ranges in the hopes of creating solidarity across the previously divided immigrant workforce.

One of the most famous images produced during the 1916 strike was the "IWW's Big Stick," which encapsulated most, if not all, of the IWW's organizational rhetoric. The large IWW figure represented the union's collective rank and file, which, when acting in solidarity with one another, grew strong. The huge club in the hand of the "Mesaba I.W.W.

This political cartoon was published in the nationally recognized *International Socialist Review* and is perhaps the most widely known and well-received artwork related to the 1916 strike. The cartoon features common themes of worker solidarity, liberation (the sun in the background is labeled "Emancipation"), and the power of union organization.

Solidarity" figure symbolized what effective union organization could do for strike efforts on the ranges.

Invoking echoes of Teddy Roosevelt's "Walk Softly and Carry a Big Stick" foreign policy, the IWW figure was poised to make his way toward the rising sun labeled "Emancipation." Standing in the path of Mesabi solidarity and emancipation were diminutive Iron Range bosses, led by the primary character, the "Steel Trust." Rhetorically, the impressive and steadfast IWW character made a strong emotional appeal to its audience as he confronts the minute Steel Trust. In this way, the cartoon used juxtaposition to argue that if workers of the ranges would stand together as one, they would be able to turn the tables on the mining companies and gain power over the conditions of their labor.

While cartoons were one form of artistic communication, the IWW also frequently employed literary works to frame the strike as an emotional and passionate cause. The *Strikers' News* printed poetry and other verse as a way to portray events and ideologies of the strike in novel ways. In most cases, working-class poetry was designed to elicit an emotional response. One such poem was simply titled "The Strike":

> Say what ye will, you howls of night,
> The strike upholds the causes of right:
> The strike compels the king to pause,
> The statesmen to rebuild the laws.
>
> Say what ye will, yell without truth;
> The strike tears off the mask of things,
> To mass and class the issue brings.
>
> Say what ye will, the strike is good,
> It clears things long misunderstood;
> It jolts the social mind awake;
> It forces men a stand to take.
>
> Say what ye will, all else above,
> The strike is a war for bread and love;
> For raiment, shelter, freedom, all
> The human race can justice call.[10]

The poem's author, who did not identify herself or himself, was making an emotional appeal through the arrangement of a standard rhyming pattern and the evocation of common socialist themes of class consciousness, ethical actions, and personal sacrifice. The author was also likely attempting to inform and instruct regarding the difficult sacrifice of engaging in a labor strike, but intending to advise the audience that, while difficult, the end results of such struggles were beneficial to all humanity. Shared sacrifice, then, becomes a major theme of the poem and its inclusion in the *Strikers' News* was likely an attempt to boost the morale of striking workers through a type of literature written from a decidedly working-class perspective.

Another method of artistic agitprop used during the strike was revolutionary, even for the IWW. Debuting at a mass meeting in Virginia's

Socialist Opera House, the IWW had filmed a large strike parade and showed the moving picture during a strike meeting. The *Strikers' News* recounted the events of the premiere, touting the use of motion pictures in the class struggle: "Movies of Strikers Parade Shown Despite Chief's Orders," as the article's headline proclaimed. "A packed house saw the motion pictures of the big parade of several days ago lsat [sic] Sunday night . . . the pictures, which were offered to the governor when the 'business men' of Virginia protested against the parade, showed there was no disorder nor violence in connection with the procession." Along with the screening, there was an interethnic showing of solidarity through song and dance. The same *Strikers' News* article commented: "the Austrian Orchestra, composed of Slavonian Socialists, rendered several selections . . . other musical numbers including a violin solo, the Finnish Choir, and two vocal numbers by Finnish girls won the approval of the audience."[11]

Putting moving images of an IWW parade on celluloid strips of film opened new methods of communication between the union and its members. Film, because it was a mechanically reproducible media format, was also a mobile organizational tool—a significant element in the IWW's attempts to bring the class struggle to people at a distance. Supporters in far-off places like Chicago, Milwaukee, Minneapolis, and New York could watch moving pictures of the struggle to organize impoverished, but resilient, immigrants on the Minnesota ranges.

The unique features of film as a mobile organizational tool underscored the fact that the medium could also carry a potent message. Motion pictures as a tool in the class struggle provided a powerful allure that likely created a sense of pride in the IWW's membership. In addition to such novelty, the IWW could leverage the moving pictures to provide factual, seemingly irrefutable visual evidence that the Wobblies were credible representatives of the American working class and not a violent group of chaotic thugs. Through film and what it represented—financial stability, modernity, and technological acumen—the IWW was at the forefront of organizing, and this was a powerful argument in the union's struggle for respectability as a labor organization.

Given the rhetorical appeals and unique methods of communicating with its working-class immigrant audience, it was clear that the IWW had organized a potent media campaign to unite workers and attack the Range mining companies. The commencement and ongoing events of the strike were evidence that the IWW, its cartoonists, writers, songwriters, and filmmakers, had developed and were implementing a dynamic cultural apparatus that challenged the power of corporate giants like U.S. Steel. The opening weeks of the strike in June 1916 were proving to be a decisive time in a period when mining company managers were beginning to understand the rhetorical force of the IWW.

Oppositional Propaganda from Steel Trust Newspapers

In confrontations between the derisively branded un-American, "foreign" Wobbly agitators and American protectors of property and life such as company police, mining company-affiliated newspapers were quick to sensationalize the supposed violence of IWW-affiliated strikers. Newspapers, like one local Hibbing rag, had only to print the last names of the combatants in a quest to delineate Americans from foreigners. In one such ethnically charged clash, the exploits of the Teller brothers took center stage in a desperate fight to ward off hordes of striking Wobblies. In an article titled "MINE GUARDS ARE STABBED; TWO CLUBBED," the author sensationalized the conflict by using emotional appeals to bolster the efforts of the morally upstanding all-American Teller brothers: "Brothers, Fighting Side by Side, Fall Beneath Strikers' Knives." Later in the article it becomes clear that the two brothers had been bested in an all-out street brawl: "Martin Teller, chief of the Oliver Iron Mining Company's special deputies is the most seriously wounded. In the battle he was stabbed four times; twice in the back, once in the thigh, and once between the ribs. His brother Charles, who was fighting at his side, suffered a deep cut on the side of the neck." While Martin and Charles had nice American sounding names, the newspaper made certain to point out that the "three strikers locked up are Steve Dronjack, Eli Manovich and Raphael Pett. All of them are battered up by the billies of the officers."[12]

Lost in the article is the fact that the Teller boys were identified as members of the Oliver's "special deputies" and not St. Louis County deputy sheriffs or local Hibbing police officers. Thus, they had no legally sanctioned powers to arrest or engage striking workers on public property—they were hired by mining companies to police company-owned land and had no authority on Hibbing's municipal streets. Because of this distinction, the Tellers and the strikers were mutual combatants, and the brothers were just as culpable for the violence as those who were arrested. As the article continued, "the trouble started shortly after 6 o'clock on Third Avenue and North Street [in Hibbing] when Marcus Clark attempted to reach the mine entrance through a crowd of about 200 strikers on picket duty. He was edged to and fro and several blows landed on his head. Village police came to his rescue, and Martin Teller and his brother Charles, started to aid them." Perhaps noticing that Martin and Charles Teller were in a precarious legal situation, the article shifted the sensationalism by name-dropping a who's who of Hibbing authorities: "M. J. West, superintendent of the Oliver Iron Mining Company in Hibbing district rushed to the scene the minute news of the clash reached him and remained until all signs of trouble had disappeared." Another Hibbing celebrity appeared on the scene "about 20 minutes after the fight" as "Chief of Police William Dwyer came up with the patrol wagon, walked boldly into the crowd of 200 strikers and picked out and arrested Steve Dronjack, alleged to have been the man who did the stabbing." Although Dronjack was supposedly the culprit, the newspaper was forced to acknowledge that "he was accused of using the knife, although none was found on him when he was searched."[13]

If the sensationalism of the actual event was not enough, the Hibbing paper went a step further and covered Martin Teller's stay in the hospital. This was perhaps the most ludicrous of the skewed journalism as the article recounted that "Teller's anxiety was for his wife, who had left him yesterday to go to Foster City, Michigan. 'Don't let her know,' he instructed." While the angels swirled around Martin Teller, blowing horns of absolution, justice, and mercy in a Hibbing hospital, the newspaper got busy asserting blame for his attack. Yet another article on a different skirmish got more to the point. One wounded warrior who had survived the ravages of another recklessly portrayed "foreign" horde was identified as a hero with seemingly presidential connotations: "John Adams, an American miner at the Sellers Mine was threatened with bodily violence by a group of striking pickets as he approached the mine entrance this morning."[14] Noting that Adams was an "American" worker

The company-influenced press published its own interpretations of the strike. This cartoon from Duluth's *News-Tribune* newspaper indicated that IWW stood for "I Won't Work." Portraying this stylized "I.W.W. Agitator" as a violence-prone revolutionary, the twin boots of "Law and Order" and "Organized Labor" (in this case, the craft and trades unions of the American Federation of Labor) symbolized respectable citizens booting the Wobblies from northern Minnesota.

was just one way of delineating "good" workers from striking "foreign" radicals. The coverage of events like these made it clear that the strikers were under assault by the company-influenced English-language press, and that class, ethnicity, and assimilation were central components of the argument against the IWW.

Company Dispatches from the "Minnesota Front"

While the IWW and mining companies were trading barbs via mass communications, company executives were feverishly writing daily, sometimes hourly, intra-company communiqués updating events of the strike. Daily correspondences between subordinate mine managers on the scene and higher-ups at corporation headquarters darted back and forth in the mail, and over telegraph and telephone lines. James D. Ireland, general manager of the Virginia Ore Mining Company, a subsidiary of independent operator M. A. Hanna & Co., reported back to his bosses in Cleveland almost daily. His reports generally began with an assessment of the day's activities at company properties, after which he included additional information on major events in the region. His assessments of the mines and their risk of being overrun by strikers were a barometer of the labor action, and the daily advances of striking workers in shutting down mines were worrisome to mining companies' financial ledgers.

By mid-June 1916, it was becoming clear that conditions on the Mesabi Range were drifting toward an epic battle between labor and capital—not another idle shutdown of operations. Territory was being staked among the orange-red hills, open pits, underground shafts, and streets of the Iron Range. The Oliver, thanks to its substantial resources, would lead the way, but the Independents were arming as well. Over time, mines on the Mesabi began to look similar to the battlefields of World War I as barbed wire and trenches were used as barricades against raiding strikers looking to cajole workers into laying down their tools and joining the strike. Ireland commented on the warlike landscape: "trench operations of warfare have been instituted in the defense work at the mines. At the Ordean, which is an open pit and where the entrance is by the way of a huge stockpile of ore, a trench or ditch has been dug through the stockpile with a steam shovel, so that it cannot be crossed by the strikers in attempting to enter the open pit."[15]

The Oliver armed its men to the teeth and, according to company-kept press sources, seemed itching to open fire on strikers. One communication read, "Oliver police are guarding the properties in all sections. They are armed with Winchesters and any striker who steps on mining company property does so at the risk of his life, according to warnings issued by the mining companies."[16] From Ireland's correspondences, it seemed there was a looming specter over the ranges that was spreading like the German measles. In one letter, he forebodingly wrote: "I suppose it will only be a question of time before the trouble spreads to [the Brunt Mine and Nashwauk in Itasca County]. They have not pulled off a strike at Eveleth until yesterday, but [the mining companies] are having their troubles there now the same as we are. Of course the strikers are bent on tying up the whole range."[17]

While mine managers had their difficulties dealing with strikers on the ranges, the Duluth–Superior docks were targeted by the IWW as a way to pinch production and distribution on both ends of the supply corridor. Mining companies did all they could to head off sympathy and solidarity strikes by area dockworkers. The Oliver and the Independents were concerned that the ore they had stockpiled in the event of an emergency, such as the strike, would run out during a prolonged labor action, crippling future profits. Ireland wrote of the impending dock strike: "the I.W.W. are beginning to agitate a strike on the docks, and the two Duluth papers do all they can to fan the thing along by interviewing every red shirt they can find and making their headlines give a misleading impression."[18] In another letter, Ireland wrote that information secured from the Thiel Detective Service indicated that a strike was being contemplated by the Seaman's Union, but that the prospects of an actual strike were low because the American Federation of Labor was opposed to a work stoppage. In addition to the docks, rail arteries that connected the Twin Ports with the Iron Range were concerning to mine management because the IWW was sending organizers to railheads like Two Harbors and Duluth/Superior with the intention of provoking labor shutdowns.[19]

As mining managers worked to quell potential agitation, their companies continued to suffer under the decreased output. The sabotage-inspired withdrawal of efficiency was working. By late June, Ireland was reporting back to his bosses that mines across the Mesabi Range were shutting down. He cast most of the blame on the IWW and the strikers for the shutdown. Other managers such as Earl E. Hunner blamed his workers' cowardice, and advised his men that "he would keep their jobs open for them if they came back to work within a short time, but if they continue to be willing to be bull-dozed by the strikers that he would board up the Harold [Mine]."[20]

The situation was the same over much of the Mesabi Range in St. Louis County and the shortage of work was driving men away from Minnesota's iron mines, east to Michigan's Copper Country, west to Butte, Montana, and south to Arizona. Mines in Itasca County on the western Mesabi were faring differently. Ireland attributed the situation to county law-enforcement procedures. He believed that "the Sheriff of Itasca county will . . . prove to be a much more forcible man than sheriff Meining of St. Louis County, and he has a corking good deputy as his assistant at Nashwauk, and the instructions to the police and the sheriff's deputies in Nashwauk are to keep disorderly characters out of Nashwauk."[21]

The strike would become the largest and bloodiest ever in Minnesota up to that time, with both sides claiming atrocities. While mining companies were known to use severe forms of repression against organized labor, the 1916 strike would be the first time that mine workers met the physical force of their employers with a defensive force of their own. The IWW's methods of combating mining company intimidation were detailed in a 1916 article from the *Duluth News-Tribune*:

> Fifteen hundred striking iron miners held a meeting tonight in the Finnish Socialist Hall under the leadership of IWW agitators. They threatened a three for one retribution when informed of a resolution adopted at a citizens meeting ordering the strikers out of the city (Virginia). "For every one of our members who is a victim of the gunmen who will doubtlessly be imported by the mining companies, three mine officials will pay the supreme penalty," declared W. D. Scarlett, IWW leader of Chicago who presided at the meeting. The meeting tonight came as a climax to the walkout of nearly 2,000 miners from the locations of Aurora, Biwabik, Eveleth and Gilbert. Yesterday the strikers started to march upon Virginia and the advance guard arrived late last night.[22]

Mining company managers blamed organized labor for the bloodshed at the onset of the 1916 strike, but an investigation by state-appointed labor investigators Martin Cole and Don Lescohier, submitted to Minnesota Governor Joseph A. A. Burnquist, stated differently:

We are entirely satisfied that the mine guards have exceeded their legal rights and duties, and have invaded the citizenship rights of the strikers. Such violence as has occurred has been more chargeable to the mine guards and police than to the strikers, and the public police departments have entirely exceeded the needs of the situation and have perpetrated serious injustices upon the strikers. Every shooting affray that has occurred on the Range has occurred on public property. The parades of the miners have been peaceful; the public police have had no trouble in maintaining order, and if the private guards had been compelled to remain on company property we do not believe that there would ever have been any bloodshed on the Range.[23]

The Progressive Perspective

The Mesabi Range's progressive government officials were caught in the middle of the escalating turmoil. Victor L. Power, attorney at law and Hibbing's fighting progressive mayor, could only speculate on the coming labor dispute. As the full force of the strike began to unfurl on June 9, 1916, Power's personal diaries indicate that he had little on his mind in the way of labor politics. By Tuesday, June 20, however, the mayor's world had turned upside down as he recorded notes of calls with mining company officials, meetings at the Workers' Hall, and a well-attended IWW parade interrupted by Hibbing police.[24] A friend to organized labor, but no friend to the revolutionary IWW, Power's political life seemingly hung in the balance during the strike. Behind closed doors he was meeting with Wobbly delegations, but he was also holding court with mining company representatives. His general impulse was to support Hibbing's workers, though he simultaneously publicly rebuked the IWW and was all the while critical of mining companies in the early days of the strike. In public, Power's rhetoric was simple and straight to the point regarding the IWW. As one newspaper article heralded, "I am not behind the I.W.W. as an organization," stated the mayor. "It is not organized labor. If the working men however, decide that they want their conditions bettered that is their privilege, providing they go about their business to do it within the laws of the land. We will not allow any threats to be made within the jurisdiction of the Hibbing police authorities and we will offer protection to workingmen that desire to go to work."[25]

Power sought to extend Hibbing's decision-making on municipal administration of the strike to other areas of the Range by writing to each of the Range's village councils to propose a meeting in Hibbing with the goal of bringing about a reconciliation between mining companies and striking workers. While this neutral stance was the Hibbing city council's public response to the growing labor conflict, Power recorded in his diary that "the council members discussed informally at the close of the meeting behind closed doors the question of picketing, the rights of striking miners to do so, and how far they can exercise their power." As a progressive politician, Power was caught in the middle of two powerful ideological forces: the progressives' compulsion to thwart the power of trusts and large corporations, and a strictly reform-minded political impulse that excluded revolutionary organizations such as the IWW. Power was reticent to publicly take sides and his rhetoric in the early weeks of the strike underscored his attempt to appear as an impartial arbiter of industrial conflict, one who applied himself diligently to the preservation of civility on Hibbing's streets. But maintaining this balance was difficult, for in private, his diaries reveal increasing incidents of violence between strikers and mine guards that would come to characterize this period of the strike.[26]

Vigilante Justice: The Violence of Company Men

For mining company managers, the plan to quell the 1916 strike was not complicated: quash worker upheaval by any means necessary, using whatever means were available. In increasing increments of legal pressure, political scheming, and violence, Oliver and the Independents relied on strategies and tactics to run or beat the IWW off the ranges. Company managers had many options, including law-enforcement officers, the courts, a well-heeled private army, and citizens' vigilante groups. The official line from management transmitted in public was that the IWW and strikers were violence-prone, un-American revolutionaries. There was little evidence for this accusation, as Ireland himself wrote on June 23, 1916: "there was no violence or trouble reported [from the IWW], and were it not for the miners being intimidated, practically all of our crew would be out to work."[27] Mining company managers were, in essence, making the claim in private that jeering crowds, scornful of

THE RHETORIC OF REVOLUTION

scabbing workers, were grounds for a concerted, violent reply to organized labor.

Most efficient at intimidation and violence were company police forces. Some corporations, such as the Oliver, had a standing police force made up of heavies and toughs oftentimes recruited from large metropolitan centers. M. A. Hanna & Co., an independent mining company, had to organize a police force specifically for this strike and looked to follow the model put forth by the Oliver. The first step in such a model of suppressive violence was finding a first-rate chief thug who had demonstrated past success in dealing with organized labor. For this purpose, Hanna & Co. called upon the services of Jack Rowett, former sheriff of Gogebic County in Michigan's Upper Peninsula. While mine workers on the ranges were barely scraping by, evidenced by their striking for higher wages, Hanna & Co. was prepared to pay Rowett two hundred dollars a month for his services. Ireland wrote in glowing terms of Rowett's prowess in using physical force:

> Rowett is a peach and the best man I know of with possible exception of Mr. Dave Foley, the Chief of the Oliver Police. As you put it up to me to keep the mines working this summer and to be sure of being able to handle situations right and with force, I have to have a man with guts and experience . . . Rowett is a quiet spoken man but a champion wrestler and fighter and has a great record for nerve and while sheriff of Gogebic made a reputation for himself by not playing politics and by delivering the goods when called on.[28]

Ireland went on to detail how Rowett would act in concert with local authorities to suppress union organization and what lengths and methods were approved of by the mining companies. Like a union-busting superhero, Ireland outlined the process for summoning Rowett: "if trouble is brewing at any point the [mine's] Superintendent will telegraph or phone Rowett and he will be on the job at once and work with the Superintendent and I will have him appointed deputy sheriff and we will of course have to stand back of him if he gets in trouble handling strikers." Ireland boasted that "Rowett is not a gun man but an awful handy man with his fists and putting hand cuffs on, tho I think he has shot a man or two, and I think I have a treasure of a man that I can absolutely bank on if we come to bat with the I.W.W."[29] Having found a man capable of using force and violence to deal with striking workers, M. A. Hanna & Co., like many of the other mining companies, turned to looking for a way to rid the ranges of IWW organizers. Ireland noted that violence was one-way: "Everyone is agreed that the best thing is to beat up the leaders and the Oliver Police do so whenever they get a chance."[30]

The culture of violence that was brewing between strikers and management was becoming deadly serious across northern Minnesota. Conditions were especially dire on the Mesabi Range, where heavily armed mining company police began to take liberties with their powers. The companies in general, and Ireland in particular, grew resentful that St. Louis County Sheriff John Meining would not employ such violent tactics as well. "The Sheriff of St. Louis County is not worth a D——," Ireland caustically wrote, adding that Meining was "playing politics and looking for votes . . . and follows Dave Foley and the Oliver Police about and won't allow [Foley] to muss up the [IWW's] leaders, tho Foley has mussed up a few of them." Ireland was equally upset with the media coverage of the strike. In the past, mining companies had kept staunch allies in the press that publicly justified and rationalized violence against strikers, yet he seemed to think that one newspaper in particular was neglecting its allegiances to mining companies: "the News Tribune of Duluth that you [subscribe to] is a dirty slut and always takes the side of the strikers."[31]

A Failed Plot to Deport the IWW

All told, the violence of hired company goons proved ineffective—the St. Louis County sheriff would not do their bidding, and the newspapers were not printing the right lies. In response, the mining companies attempted to incite a vigilante committee to deport the IWW's leadership from the Mesabi Range. On June 16, Ireland wrote of a rowdy meeting the previous evening at which plans of a mass deportation were discussed. The crowd of between five hundred and six hundred included ex-mayors of Range municipalities, former city attorneys, a onetime judge, and other prominent local businessmen, who urged the formation of a deportation committee. In an almost unanimous resolution and with a subtle nod to the need for physical force, Ireland wrote that the committee would in fact deport the IWW's most adept organizers in the near future and that he was quite certain that "they will carry out the resolution by the spirit of the meeting last night."[32]

On the same night as the citizens' committee meeting, a mass of strikers gathered in Virginia's Socialist Opera House. Labor spies described the meeting as one in which "the hall was crowded to overflowing, but everything was very peaceful, and [the strike leaders] advised the men to be peaceful and to not do any more than they would with their hands in their pocket." But when the strikers learned of the impending resolution at the citizens' committee meeting, strike leaders vowed that "if the operators imported any gun-men, they would organize a vigilance committee and kill three of the operating force to one striker that was killed."[33] No one in the IWW disputed the utterance, even when the local press quoted IWW organizer Sam Scarlett as saying during a speech, "for every one of our members who is a victim of the gunmen who will doubtlessly be imported by the mining companies, three mine officials will pay the supreme penalty."[34]

Scarlett's "Eye-for-an-Eye Speech" was meant to bolster confidence in the face of growing fear over violent vigilante justice. For citizens' associations, often backed by mining company managers, practicing vigilante justice had played significant roles in breaking past strikes in Colorado and Michigan just two years earlier in 1914. The IWW intended to administer a peaceful strike but clearly felt the need to let mining companies and the Range's citizens' committee know that it would not be intimidated. In spite of its attempts at a peaceful protest, mining managers painted the IWW as violence-prone revolutionaries. In reality, however, mining companies continually relied on a systematic campaign of violence to run the IWW and their "agitators" off the ranges. As they had in previous labor struggles, company managers relied heavily on surrogates, such as citizens' committees, to do their dirty work, and as of June 16, they looked toward a swift resolution to the IWW problem.

That was June 16. A day later things had changed. As Ireland mournfully wrote to his handlers back in Cleveland, "the citizens' committee did not eject the agitators yesterday, in accordance with the resolution passed the night before. I really thought they would, but I think they got cold feet." The cold feet came as a result of some skillfully crafted subterfuge by the IWW. Previously, company managers had kept local businessmen on a short leash through a system of coercion, intimidation, and sometimes outright peonage. As a result, businessmen on the Range often cowed to company interests. According to Ireland, however, the IWW had outflanked this coercive system and "informed the businessmen that if they took any action against the strikers they would start a co-operative store [administered by the IWW], and boycott all the other stores." For Ireland and his fellow mining managers, the presence of IWW agitators in Range towns meant trouble for day-to-day mining operations. Recognizing the increase in strikers and sympathizers, he vowed to force the agitators out of the urban centers as a way to regain control over the industrial landscape, claiming that "if the outside agitators were removed from town, and forced to keep away, everything would be going smoothly in a couple of days."[35]

For the once-omnipotent mine managers, the situation on the Mesabi Range was becoming unmanageable. Worse still for the iron-ore bosses, the IWW had come to occupy the moral high ground—even according to Ireland. While the Independents and the Oliver had hired thugs willing to commit violence at a moment's notice, the IWW had resisted such impulses. Meeting after meeting and speech after speech found the Wobblies advising a peaceful continuation to the strike, if left unmolested. Ireland once again admitted as much: "the [IWW] speakers at the meeting asked the men to keep quiet and not use any force," and "they are telling them to not use liquor, and giving them other good advice."[36] This was certainly strange rhetoric for an organization that mining companies had branded as a violence-prone revolutionary union. Yet, the violence advocated by mining companies was institutionalized and present in multiple levels of management. A June 19 letter from Howard M. Hanna Jr. to Ireland confirmed as much: "I am sorry that the businessmen and citizens of Virginia did not have nerve enough to throw the agitators out." Perhaps most disappointing, these educated men of influence, power, and wealth seemed to know that they were acting in an immoral manner as Hanna Jr. advised Ireland to tear up the letter after reading it.[37]

A Shift in Strategy

Without the prospect of using the Range's citizens to break the strike, mining companies had to find other methods of repression. One such cog in this oppressive machinery was the manipulation of the local judiciary. On June 24, 1916, Ireland signaled his approval regarding how some municipal judges were adjudicating during the strike. He confidently wrote to board members in Cleveland, "I must say that our municipal judge is very good at this time. He does not hesitate in giving good, stiff sentences. There were two fellows that threatened our timekeeper the other night, and the city police gathered them in and the municipal judge gave one of them ninety days at the work farm and the other thirty days."[38] One municipal judge in Eveleth, W. E. Moylan, belittled the IWW and its organizers when he commented while sentencing striking worker Ed Mattson for what was likely a trumped-up public intoxication arrest, "Mattson is an I.W.W., but not of the worst type . . . [he] is not a dangerous character, but several offenses made punishment necessary. He is an I Want Whiskey agitator."[39]

Not every municipal judge was opposed to giving IWW organizers a fair shake, even if it took a little direct action to convince justice to remain blind. In one such case, a spirited assembly outside Chisholm's courthouse made a convincing argument that an organizer arrested under suspicious circumstances should be set free. After initially giving ninety days, the judge changed the sentence to a simple fine after the chief of police advised that three hundred to four hundred strikers outside the courthouse disagreed with the sentencing.[40]

As the strike began to impact the political and social landscape on the Range, mining company managers had to deal with the simple fact that much had changed since the labor upheaval that occurred nine years earlier. In 1907, political winds gusted in the direction of company management; however, the progressive pushback of the 1910s had changed the atmospherics of Range politics. By 1916, a number of the area's municipalities were administered by progressive politicians and officials who were elected to office because of their oppositional attitude toward the mining companies. Especially notable were Hibbing's Power and Virginia Mayor Michael Boylan, both of whom were ideologically antithetical to the power exerted by Range mining companies.[41] While progressive mayors caused mining company managers mental fits, they were at the same time opposed to the IWW's revolutionary perspective. Despite mining company accusations that politicians such as Boylan and Power were acting in collaboration with the IWW, Range progressives merely provided the venue in which to allow striking workers, through the IWW, to voice their displeasure with the mining companies.

This balanced administration of the conflict infuriated mine bosses back east and throughout the Great Lakes region. While Power and Boylan were willing to let the IWW agitate, organize, and strike within the letter of the law, the mining companies were fixated on breaking the strike through a mass deportation of IWW leadership. Company managers crafted multifaceted arguments for such action based on innuendos and rumors about the IWW's violent lawlessness and anti-Americanism. In this manner, mine bosses quickly seized upon the anti-immigrant fervor of the World War I era. Many in the industry attempted to portray the IWW's actions and ideology as seditious by implicating the Wobblies as German or Austrian Empire provocateurs. That the union was absolutely opposed to monarchy made no difference; the company line placed the IWW, its organizers, and rank-and-file members as part of the Kaiser's standing army. Ireland even speculated that German money might be finding its way into the IWW's strike coffers.[42]

Portraying the strike as a threat to national security in this time of worldwide upheaval provided further impetus to end the conflict using any means necessary. Mining companies began to gear up for an offensive against the IWW by consolidating various company police forces. The plot to orchestrate the activities of imported gun thugs coincided with efforts in New York among mining executives who were urging the Steel Trust to take a more active role in the suppression of the IWW. In Minnesota, Ireland signed off on hiring twenty-three deputies at five dollars a day for the Virginia Ore Mining Company's private police force.[43] The legalities of importing men, paid by M. A. Hanna & Co., who would be acting in the interest of the mining companies, yet who were oftentimes deputized by local authorities to police public spaces, caused fleeting concern for the men back at Hanna headquarters. Legal liability and public scrutiny were a passing concern.[44] Despite the recruitment, feeding, and arming of a small private army, mining company managers were losing ground in combating the influence of the IWW. Adjudicating the Wobblies off the ranges was not working, the citizens' committee plan to deport the IWW had failed, and the St. Louis County sheriff was not as firmly tucked in the mining companies' back pocket as expected. Fearing an even greater loss to productivity and profit, mining executives appealed to a higher political force in the form of Minnesota's Republican governor.

6 FLASH POINT

Dissent and Violence in 1916

The Governor got his orders for
To try and break the strike.
He sent his henchmen on the Range,
Just what the Steel Trust liked . . .
  —*Song lyrics written by IWW members from St. Louis County
  jail, Duluth, July 1916*

DECISIVE ACTION ON THE PART OF MANAGERS AND MINE OWNERS WAS
needed if they were going to halt, turn back, and dislocate the Wobblies
from the ranges. As we have seen, in attempting to implement such decisive action, mining company managers relied on repressive and steadfast antiunion strategies in an attempt to break the strike. Company
gun thugs, local law-enforcement officers, middle-class business owners,
and judicial maneuvering were all part of the plan to drive the IWW
from northern Minnesota. These tactics, however, were unsuccessful in
crushing the Wobblies, and in a last-ditch effort, mining managers enlisted the help of Minnesota's highest authority.

As the preceding chapter demonstrated, violence was often alluded
to in mining company correspondence, and managers took great pains to
carefully control the public's perception of the developing labor action.
In 1916, most people outside northern Minnesota learned of the strike's
violence from newspaper reports gleaned from articles of the Range or
Duluth's corporate-influenced media. Conversely, politicians and other
officials read about strike events in official governmental reports, which
was especially problematic because of the role Minnesota's Republican

governor played in busting the strike. These sources were mostly written in English and had a definite class-based perspective that was dismissive of actual working conditions faced by immigrant laborers, omitted key facts regarding violence against strikers, and represented mining companies' hostile opinions against organized labor. The bias of these newspapers, over time, has skewed the way people remember the 1916 strike in particular, and, more generally, how organized labor and its contributions to society have been valued. This chapter, however, interprets the violent events of the 1916 strike from the perspective of organized labor, using sources empathetic to the strikers' plight. The following chronicle of the strike's events in late June through July imparts and reasserts a voice to workers who were silenced in their outrage over the violence that was occurring around them, and the partisan stance of Minnesota's highest elected official during this labor conflict. Numerous groups partial to organized labor, and especially the IWW, accused Governor Joseph A. A. Burnquist of acting in concert with mining company managers to break the strike. These claims were dismissed by most at the time, but newly discovered documents from company sources strongly suggest that the IWW's assertions were, in fact, accurate. Ironically, then, the chapter reveals that labor history research should not be confined to labor sources in the attempt to give workers a voice. At times the harshest indictment of unethical historical actors comes from their very own words. This was certainly the case with the tragic, violent, and deadly trampling of strikers' lives and human rights during the 1916 Minnesota Iron Ore Strike.

John Alar: "Murdered by Oliver Gunmen"

The mining companies' use of violence and intimidation during the 1916 strike was well documented, as idle threats turned into street scuffles that gradually increased in violence and frequency. Until late June, however, company tactics, though ruthless, were not deadly. This changed with the June 22 death of John Alar, father of three and an immigrant striker from Croatia. The IWW was quick to print a chronicle of Alar's death in the *Strikers' News*, accusing the Oliver Iron Mining Company of outright homicide:

John Aller [sic] was murdered by the Oliver Mining Company gunmen at his home near the property, Thursday, June 22, 1916, at 6 o'clock in the morning. The strikers who were on the picket line on that morning say that the gunmen deliberately walked into Aller's house and shot him three times in the back. John Aller was a married man and leaves his wife and three children, the oldest being five years old and the youngest is an infant boy. They are orphaned because their father demanded a right for all of them to live. The strikers are supporting this fatherless family.[1]

The company's perspective was, of course, much different from the IWW's. Hanna Company manager James D. Ireland wrote of Alar's death on June 23: "in yesterday's fracas there was one man killed and several badly wounded. It was a fight with clubs, bricks, rocks and guns. The man that was shot was on his knees aiming his gun at another man, and it seems the other man got there first. The man who was shot had a rifle and a revolver, so he was bent on mischief alright." Ireland also seemed displeased by women participating in the strike. In his discussion of Alar's death, he mentioned that "there were a number of women in the fracas also; one of them stepped out of her door and shot three times at the deputies. There were probably twelve or fifteen shots fired. One of our deputies got hit in the breast with a brick, and he was spitting blood all yesterday afternoon."[2]

Regardless of Alar's actual or imagined participation in the altercation, the Oliver's company police shot him off company property, where they had no authority to arrest or detain, let alone shoot, anyone. Concerned about the repercussions for shooting a man off company property, members of the Oliver police quickly sought out St. Louis County Sheriff John R. Meining to offer their side of the story. According to Ireland, however, Meining had disappeared and was putting all blame for the incident on mining company deputies. Disgusted, Ireland opined, "Meining is a yellow pup . . . I feel that this trouble will not end until the Governor can be persuaded to put a regular man in as sheriff who will drive the I.W.W. agitators off the range."[3]

The *Strikers' News* chronicled the funeral rites and procession on Sunday, June 26, which followed Alar's casket from Virginia's Socialist

The death of miner John Alar at the hands of Oliver gunmen was one of the most notorious events of the strike and turned Alar into a labor martyr for the IWW. Mourners and labor organizers voiced their dissent at the fallen miner's well-attended funeral in June 1916. Photograph by George R. Dawson. Courtesy of the Iron Range Research Center, Minnesota Discovery Center.

Opera House to the city's Calvary Cemetery: "Fully seven thousand strikers accompanied the murdered brother to the cemetery [and the] Finnish Socialist band of Virginia played the funeral music and marched at the head of the parade. At the grave of John Aller, funeral orations were delivered in all languages of the strikers." Alar's widow had requested that the burial rites be given by a Catholic priest, but the priests, choosing to remain loyal to the master class, refused to do so. Instead, IWW organizers administered the last rites before a multiethnic gathering in the cemetery. The newspaper went on to document that "the vast and imposing funeral was headed by a large banner carried by four women, upon which was inscribed: MURDERED BY OLIVER GUNMEN."[4] Unbelievably, no one ever served jail time for Alar's shooting. Instead, IWW organizers Sam Scarlett and Carlo Tresca were both charged with criminal libel for carrying the confrontational banner.[5]

Ireland was neither impressed nor moved by Alar's well-attended

At John Alar's funeral procession, mourners carried a deliberately provocative banner that accused the Oliver of outright murder. Although no one was convicted of shooting Alar, those carrying the banner were later arrested for voicing their opposition. Thousands poured into the streets of Virginia and followed the procession to Calvary Cemetery. Courtesy of the Iron Range Research Center, Minnesota Discovery Center.

funeral. In fact, he viewed the solidarity of the strikers coalescing as an ominous sign. "The authorities in Virginia told the strikers Monday that they could not carry red banners or obnoxious signs in the funeral procession Sunday," he wrote. The IWW's banner of protest must have seemed like a defiant slap in the face to mining management. That strikers were able to assert their civil rights in such a brazen way was a definite problem for Ireland, as he complained: "the police at Virginia walked along side of the funeral and made no attempt to take the banner away." Ireland believed that the company police, the same ones who had shot John Alar, ought to be able to enforce law and order if the St. Louis County sheriff was not going to do so: "if the city police and sheriffs do not feel that they can handle the situation they ought to call on the Mining Company's police for aid."[6] Many, including mining company bosses, expected the shooting to dampen the strikers' resolve, but

Carlo Tresca delivered a fiery speech and led mourners in an oath of solidarity at John Alar's graveside. The back of Tresca's head and raised arm can be seen slightly above the crowd in the left–center portion of the image. Photograph by George R. Dawson. Courtesy of the Iron Range Research Center, Minnesota Discovery Center.

the opposite turned out to be true. The IWW appropriately and deftly turned John Alar into a martyr, a labor hero, and his funeral was not just a memorial to the slain striker—it became a rousing call to action with mourners taking a graveside oath to honor his death with further commitment to the strike. Alar's tragic death did not occasion a decline in strike activities; instead, it bolstered tension between the Wobblies' increasingly impassioned membership and a staunchly entrenched mining oligarchy, setting the two bitter rivals on a collision course in an escalating conflict.

A "Law-and-Order" Proclamation from St. Paul

With the death of John Alar it became clear, in no uncertain terms, that the Mesabi Iron Range was in the midst of a labor war. While corporate gun thugs ran rampant, the streets of Range towns were filled with parades of idled and irritated striking workers. IWW members feared for their lives and local law enforcement was reticent to do anything for fear of offending one side or the other. Ireland and other mining managers were flummoxed by how to deal with the IWW's organizing successes and the inability of company tactics to dissuade agitation. "Just arresting these fellows and letting them out on bail does no good," Ireland complained, "in fact the last agitator arrested made a speech in which he thanked the officers for arresting him as he said he did not have money enough to employ a press agent and this free advertising was exactly what he wanted."[7]

The strike also began to severely bite into company profits during a World War I–era mining boom. By late June it was reported that two thousand men had left the Mesabi Range. Ireland expressed concern over the large number of workers abandoning the Hibbing mine districts for other locations. Even if the strike were broken in the near future, company managers were beginning to fear a complete collapse of the workforce.[8] As Ireland was indicating, time was of the essence. The strike had to be broken, and in the hopes of preserving the mines' experienced workforce, post haste.

After John Alar's shooting, Ireland was of the opinion that mining companies had restrained themselves so far. Indicating that there was perhaps a tipping point coming, he and other mine managers sought advocates and allies in high places. Along with C. H. Munger, who was a manager and board member associated with a number of independent mines, Ireland sought counsel with Governor Burnquist. Top item on Ireland's agenda was an insistence that Sheriff Meining become more forcible in his interactions with striking workers, and that Meining find a way to arrest the IWW's leadership and detain them at a place "where they can stir up no more trouble for a while."[9] Having arrived at a desperate crossroads, the mining companies had few options left to deal with the Wobblies' surging influence. Company officials hoped to enlist the governor to act as a political thug for their financial interests. Burnquist was more than willing to oblige, and on June 29, Ireland and Munger arrived for a meeting at Minnesota's state capitol. Burnquist's actions and the consequences that sprang from them would change the course of the strike considerably. Events that took place during the next two months would also alter how Minnesota and the United States would deal with organized labor, immigrants, political discontent, and basic civil rights for many years to come.

Less than a day after Ireland's meeting with the governor and Sheriff

At the time of the strike, Minnesota's Republican Governor Joseph A. A. Burnquist was in his mid- to late thirties and was an accomplished politician, having already served in the state legislature and as Minnesota's lieutenant governor. Courtesy of the George Grantham Bain Collection, Library of Congress Prints and Photographs Division.

Meining, Minnesota's highest elected official sent a telegram to the sheriff, a proclamation issued on June 30, 1916, from St. Paul, that read:

> John Meining, Esq.
> Arrest forthwith and take before magistrate, preferably in Duluth, all persons who have participated and are participating in riots in your county and make complaints against them.
>
> Prevent further breaches of the peace, riots and unlawful assemblies.
>
> Use all your powers, including the summoning of posse, for the preservation of life and property.
>
> The Violation of law in Saint Louis County must be stopped at once.[10]

There was, in fact, a good chance that Meining was still in St. Paul on the heels of his June 29 meeting with Ireland and the governor when the telegram was supposedly sent to him in Duluth. The governor reached out to another northern Minnesota official on June 30, but this call went to Hibbing Mayor Victor Power. Burnquist was likely attempting to gain compliance or drum up support for his missive from the Range's leading progressive. But while Power was taking calls from the governor's office, he was also engaged in substantive discussions with IWW leaders. Power's journal recorded the call, but also noted that "I.W.W. leaders called" the same day.[11] The Wobblies, like many in Minnesota, recognized the significance of the governor's proclamation and were probably attempting to gauge Power's reaction to the governor's inflammatory decree.

While Burnquist's proclamation was a provocative and shameless bit of political theater, rhetorically it was also a savvy application of mass communication. The statement did not pull on any heartstrings, nor was it particularly steeped in legal truths; it came, however, from the pen of the state's governor, which gave the missive great authority. As an elected position, the office of governor held great significance during the strike. Because the proclamation to arrest and take the IWW "rioters" before local magistrates held such credibility, it seemingly had the approval of all those people who had voted Governor Burnquist into office. In essence, the governor used his power as the executive of the state of Minnesota to signal that the public was fed up with the alleged lawlessness of the strike—this was a powerful message to strikers and to those who would execute the edict.

The political theater that surrounded Burnquist's proclamation and his allegiances to the mining companies might merely be dismissed as supposition, but Ireland actually documented the meeting's attendees, occurrence, and topics, creating a record of the wholesale jettisoning of democracy and justice on the Range. In a June 30, handwritten letter to his handlers in Hanna's Cleveland offices, Ireland gloated:

> We held a meeting in the Wolvin Bldg on afternoon of 28th at which Messers. Olcott, McGonagle, House, Frank Adams, Billings, Sutes, Munger and I were present and it was decided that since the Oliver I.M.C. had presented their views on the strike situation to the Governor it was time for the Independents to back it up and the Governor was in a receptive mood.
>
> [We advised] that the Governor should come out with a *very* strong proclamation declaring that law and order *must* be enforced and the Sheriff would have the full power of the state to enforce it and if he could not then the Governor would send the militia to the Range and do it for him.
>
> The Governor said that he had almost made up his mind to these

very things and after going over the matter with the Sheriff it looked as if he was going to get busy right away.

McGonagle tells me that the Governor will probably do these things if he can get started *before* some newspaper gets hold of it, but if the politicians find out what he has in mind it won't be done until he has to do it. Therefore we are keeping very quiet about this in hopes that he will act soon. The Governor was glad to see Sutes and I representing the Independents and if he would only do the things that he acts as if he wanted to do, the strike would be over in 24 hours.

Frank Adams said today that the Governor told Sabenious this afternoon that he had given orders to the Sheriff to arrest all strike leaders and bring them to Duluth and keep them off the range and that if the Sheriff don't do it he will appoint another sheriff.

I am curious to see if he will do this or not.

Please do not let this get out because if it gets out the Governor will back water I know. He means well but is very near election and everyone has an axe to grind.[12]

The fix was in and, consequently, the supposed "riotous and fear"–inciting IWW organizers whom Ireland backhandedly complimented for their ability to strike peacefully "with hands in their pockets," were about to have their basic human rights trampled. Minnesota's governor acted solely in the interests of the Oliver Iron Mining Company and a handful of additional independent operators. One needs look no further for proof than to the text and tone of the governor's June 30 proclamation, which was taken almost entirely from the attitudes, interests, opinions, and even direct words expressed by mining company officials during their meeting. Thus, Minnesota's highest elected public official had publicly ordered the sheriff of Minnesota's third-most-populated county to do the bidding of multi-million-dollar corporations. It seemed that the mining company managers' wish to deport and incarcerate the IWW's strike leadership would finally come true. Furthermore, the governor had promised in private to send in the publicly funded state militia to solve the mining companies' labor problems. Perhaps just as corrupt and immoral, Burnquist did all of this under the cloak of secrecy in the hopes that neither his fellow politicians nor the media would catch on and jeopardize his chances for reelection. Ireland could not have been more pleased with the newly formed alliance and he praised the governor's "decided, strong character." With the enforcement of law and order having passed into Burnquist's hands, Ireland was certain that the strike was headed for a quick resolution.[13]

In a triumphant late-night telegram to Hanna Company officials in Ohio on July 1, composed of fragmented sentences and thoughts, Ireland proclaimed: "Governor issued proclamation ordering sheriff arrest all persons who have or are participating in riots or unlawful assemblies and chief police Duluth says wont [sic] allow agitating in Duluth. County Attorney says will back sheriff up and maximum penalty five years Stillwater [State Prison]." Ireland was certain to inform the company officials that the governor's missive "will kill strike and don't believe any danger of strike on docks."[14] Similar in tone, corporate-influenced newspapers across the state heralded Burnquist's farcical telegram. The *Duluth News-Tribune*, which Ireland insisted was a "slut" earlier in the strike, proclaimed on its front page, "MINNESOTA'S YOUNG EXECUTIVE DIRECTS ARREST OF AGITATORS," and went on to say that "Hibbing and Virginia hear that Deputy Sheriffs will today be disarming every striker—George Andreytchine, one of I.W.W. ringleaders locked up—mob forms at Kinney, but John A. Keyes, lawyer of Duluth, and Carlo Tresca warn it against violence."[15]

Mining company management finally had what it wanted: a means to rid the iron ranges of the IWW. With Burnquist advocating the arrest and deportation of the IWW leadership, others began to follow suit. The same issue of the *Duluth News-Tribune* that ran a banner headline about Burnquist's declaration also noted that "citizens and mining men of Virginia have asked Brown McDonald, immigration officer at Duluth, to come to Virginia and investigate the aliens. More than 90 per cent of strikers are not citizens and the plan Virginia people have in mind is to deport strikers."[16] Yet, even though the mining companies had the state immigration officers, not to mention the governor, in their pockets, they were still anxious to gain control of the Range's immigrant workforce. Even after the governor's proclamation, Ireland, somewhat bewildered and taken by innuendo, wrote that "one of the worst features [of the strike] is that the Italian agitator, Tresco [sic], and his lieutenants are spreading the rumor among the Italians that they are the officials of a society similar to the 'Black Hand' and that they have a secret organization equal to none and that if the Italians work they will get them even if it takes seven years."[17]

Echoing further strains of paranoia, Ireland also wrote that the Austrians and Germans were out to get the mining companies' workers. With a sense of finely crafted suspicion, Ireland surmised that secret "Austrian Associations" were attempting to strong-arm Range workers into supporting strikes by denying scabbing members benefits. If such was the case, Ireland surmised, there were certainly grounds for Germany, Austria's World War I ally, to be responsible for the clandestine threats.[18] Ironically, it was Ireland, the mining companies, and Burnquist who were actually perpetrating most of the cloak-and-dagger chicanery on the Range. The so-called secret immigrant societies were no secret to anyone, with the possible exception of mine bosses, and the solidarity formed in these societies had nothing to do with the Kaiser or the imperial war occurring in Europe. Rather, fraternal and benevolent societies existed because of the unequal distribution of wealth across the iron ranges and these immigrant organizations—born of class struggle—would not extend benefits to workers scabbing while a strike was in effect.

Even after the governor's edict, the IWW was unwilling to concede that strike efforts were flagging. The Wobblies fought on. What mining company managers needed was an incident that would put the governor's plan into action. Such an incident was rather cryptically alluded to in company correspondence. The same day as the governor's proclamation, Ireland wrote to Hanna headquarters advising, "I enclose herewith three sheets giving a lot of words, and if you receive any telegrams from me with foreign words in them you can pick these words out of this code."[19] In another letter discussing strikers' efforts to disrupt transportation, Ireland seemingly predicted, again, that an event of great importance was in the offing regarding the strike situation: "this morning the strikers stopped the trolley cars loaded with men going to work and they made the men get off the cars, but I think that the next day or two will make a difference."[20] Sadly, Ireland's prognostication was eerily prophetic and an incident that changed the entire course of the strike occurred just two days later—with deadly consequences.

Frame-up at the Mosonovich Boardinghouse

The brutal truth behind the governor's proclamation was that it provided mining company thugs with a reason, and official sanctioning, to use violence in fulfilling the aims of company objectives. Where a citizens' group had failed, mining bosses were betting that the communiqué from Minnesota's highest elected official would achieve their intended outcome: a mass deportation of IWW organizers. What was missing was an incident to precipitate action. IWW organizers had been arrested, put on trial, and imprisoned before, but mostly at the behest of local and municipal governments. Well versed in the ways of law and order, organizers such as Carlo Tresca and Sam Scarlett tended to surround themselves with striking workers while nestled within the boundaries of local municipalities. The governor's proclamation, however, likely emboldened the mining companies' private army and pressured an embattled Sheriff Meining into forcing an action to justify it.

This action came on July 3 when a group of mine guards busted into the boardinghouse of strike-supporting Montenegrin immigrants Melitza and Filip Mosonovich.[21] The company thugs, acting as deputy sheriffs, were supposedly executing a search-and-arrest warrant for an illegal liquor operation in the Mosonovich's home within the municipal limits of Biwabik. According to sources partial to the IWW, the intruders entered the home without a valid search or arrest warrant. The primary officer in the raid was Nick Dillon, a reported former bouncer at a house of ill fame with a bad reputation among strikers as a first-rate company thug. Dillon, along with John Myron, Mike Shubiski, and two or three other officers, notified Melitza that they had come to take her husband, Filip, and a boarder, Joe Hercigonovich, to jail. Melitza balked, stating that only Biwabik's village marshall, "Old Man" O'Hara, had the right to remove the inhabitants from their home. Dillon, almost certainly emboldened by the governor's proclamation, refused to take no for an answer. What ensued was chaotic and deadly.[22] According to Melitza's own words:

Dillon was standing near door to bedroom and I went to bedroom to get Filip's shoes and Nick he says, "Ope," and I says, "What ope means, I am going to get shoes for my husband." Then Nick Dillon he got a hold of me and threw me into the bedroom onto my baby. If [my older] boy had not happened to be there I would have [landed on and] killed the baby. I spit blood for three days after. I told Nick to get out of the house and chased him out. I went outside after him and one of those fellas with him hit me over the head with club. Then all the fellows in the house started to hit Filip and the boarders with the clubs. Nick he started to shoot from the yard.[23]

What transpired next is even more difficult to reconstruct, but evidently an all-out brawl erupted between the officers and the boardinghouse inhabitants. Guns were drawn, and in the escalating scrape, one of the deputy sheriffs, John Myron, and a bystander, John Ladvalla, were shot dead. A boarder in the Mosonovich house was also shot twice through the thigh. The Mosonoviches and their boarders, Joe Hercigonovich, John Orlandich, and Joe Nikich, all swore that they did not have guns. The only people known to have been carrying firearms were the company men. During the subsequent trial it was reported that "one of the guards by the name of Schubisky, when testifying before Judge Smallwood, admitted that he fired several shots and that he fired them in the house, but no bullets or bullet holes were to be found in the house."[24]

It never became clear who actually killed John Myron or anyone else, but as he was reportedly beating Orlandich while standing in a doorway, he was shot three times in the back. Although the IWW and *International Socialist Review* blamed Shubiski, who admitted to firing his gun more than once, five immigrant inhabitants of the boardinghouse were arrested and charged with the first-degree murder of John Myron. Ladvalla, a supporter of the strike, was struck by a stray bullet as he had stopped to gawk at the chaos occurring in the house. No one was arrested for his shooting.[25]

What happened next defied logic, but in a strange law-and-order alchemy catalyzed by Governor Burnquist's proclamation, IWW strike leaders were also arrested for John Myron's murder. The *International Socialist Review* remarked: "seven organizers for the I.W.W. stationed at distant points on the Range, were arrested without warrant, refused a

From left to right: Joe Hercigonovich, Joe Orlandich, Melitza Mosonovich, Filip Mosonovich, and Joe Nickich—inhabitants of the Mosonovich boardinghouse during their fall 1916 trials in Duluth for the shooting of John Myron in Biwabik, Minnesota. Courtesy of the Walter P. Reuther Library, Archives of Labor and Urban Affairs, Wayne State University.

hearing, placed on a special train, taken to Duluth seventy miles distant, and lodged in the county jail charged with murder in the first degree . . . under a peculiar Minnesota statute these organizers are charged as principals in the murder of the deputy sheriff on the ground that speeches made by them induced the killing."[26]

IWW organizers were arrested up and down the Mesabi Range as a massive sweep commenced to drive the Wobblies from the ranges. Local organizers such as the Stark brothers were arrested, while in Virginia, seven national organizers including Scarlett and Tresca were taken into custody. As the *International Socialist Review* concluded, "the basis for holding Tresca, Scarlett, Schmidt, Ahlgren and Wassaman is that they told the men in their speeches what their legal rights were in the defense of their home." The IWW organizers' instruction to keep strikers' hands in their pockets unless in fear for life or home mattered not and "this advice that is attributed to have been given to the strikers forms the prosecutor's inference that a conspiracy existed to resist mine guards and that this advice was the important influence that induced the Montenegrin strikers to resist Nick Dillon's detachment of mine guards."[27]

Tresca's Travails

For Carlo Tresca, life and work prior to the Mosonovich affair were somewhat business as usual. He had been arrested, imprisoned, and had feared for his life on numerous occasions, both in his native Italy and in the United States. According to his own recollections, however, the twenty-four hours between July 3 and July 4, 1916, were a day like none other, leading him to write from a St. Louis County jail cell in Duluth: "it was about 10 o'clock in the morning . . . and I could tell myself that one day of my life was completed. T'was a crowded day indeed."[28]

July 3 started with Tresca and two companions taking a grocery delivery truck to Grand Rapids, Minnesota, county seat of Itasca County, in an attempt to bail IWW organizer George Andreytchine out of jail. Andreytchine had been attempting to fan the flames of discontent in the Itasca County mines and was arrested by a deputy sheriff. Tresca was under the impression that he could use money to entice Itasca County officials to let Andreytchine go. According to his autobiography, Tresca felt he was making headway in the attempt to extract Andreytchine from the bonds of Itasca County until he began to sense an overwhelming "lurking danger" that he might be arrested. As he was seated in the district attorney's office having a "nice . . . polite chat," his premonition seemed to come true as the county sheriff busted through the office door. According to Tresca, he entered "in shirtsleeves with a belt of cartridges around his belly with one gun on his hip ferocious looking, with two husky deputy sheriffs at his heels. The man was red in the face, and without introduction began to shout, 'You goddam agitator, what did you come here for?'" (229).

Tresca, the proudly self-proclaimed intercontinental agitator, predictably did little to relieve the tension as the sheriff had a deputy pat him down to look for guns and ammunition. Tresca had none, which seemed to raise the sheriff's ire even more. After the search, the district attorney asked the sheriff for a sidebar in another room and when the two re-appeared it seemed that Tresca was free to go. He bid the formerly cour-teous district attorney a good-natured good-bye, to which the district attorney responded, "get the hell out of here you S.O.B." Taken aback, Tresca was about to respond when "he felt the muzzle of the sheriff's gun at [his] back" and the sheriff began to shout, "Get out, get out!" (230).

Tresca and his two acquaintances got back in the little grocery truck and headed east for Hibbing, where a number of gatherings in support of the strike were scheduled for that evening. As they were leaving town, the intrepid trio noticed that they had company. Looking out the side of the truck, Tresca noted that a car containing the sheriff and another car were in pursuit. After driving another block or more, Tresca observed that three more cars had joined the unfriendly motorcade. Seeing that the men were armed with rifles, Tresca advised the driver of the truck to keep going without delay and that the sheriff was probably just giv-ing the grocery truck an escort to the county line (230–32).

Upon reaching the small mining location of "Mishaevaka," the three travelers were confronted with "two columns of men, some armed with rifles," flanking both sides of the main street. One of Tresca's traveling com-panions leaned over to him and stated, "this is a lynching party for you." Tresca got out of the truck and walked behind it as a way of taking the heat off his two traveling partners. The gauntlet of men began to shout as he walked in back of the car, "DAMNED AGITATOR—SUCKER—DAMN FOREIGNER, GET THE HELL OUT OF HERE!" Tresca noticed that behind the angry mob was a group of strikers offering en-couragement, and more important, protection. The three men in the little Italian grocery truck made it out of Itasca County with their lives, but not before the Itasca County sheriff warned them, "Remember forever that this place is not fit for you. When you come again I will kill you! Go and keep going!" (231–32).

Tresca's trip to Itasca County was harrowing, but his day quickly went from bad to worse. As he arrived back in Hibbing, he heard of the melee at the Mosonovich home and sensed trouble in the air. He went to Hibbing strike headquarters, the Finnish Workers Hall, and noticed that the building was "deserted, closed and dark" (233). It did not take the veteran organizer long to put two and two together, and knowing of the governor's proclamation, he feared the worst. As an article in the *International Socialist Review* about the Mosonovich ordeal concluded, "picketing was absolutely suppressed, and Finnish socialists were thrown out of their own halls and refused the right of lawful assembly."[29] The governor-inspired roundup was under way.

Tresca then made his way to strike headquarters in Virginia and found conditions on the streets, in the businesses, and at the Socialist Opera House much the same. Martial law had come to the Mesabi Range. Finding the city almost deserted, Tresca headed to the small home of Italian immigrant strikers where he was staying. He felt safe in this home as there were a number of his fellow countrymen armed with rifles ready to protect their anarchist Fellow Worker. Upon arriving at the home, Tresca inquired about fellow organizer Frank Little, who had a predisposition for getting himself into harrowing situations—sadly, only a year and one month later, Little was found hanging from a noose under a railroad bridge in Butte, Montana, lynched by vigilantes for his union organizing and opposition to World War I. Tresca's housemates notified him that Little had gone to his downtown Virginia hotel room for the night and was refusing to look for more secure lodgings. Tresca and his Italian bodyguards left to go speak with Little in the hopes of convincing him to relocate. The Italian organizer, so adept at moving audiences, was unable to convince Little to seek new lodgings, as Little cited the want of a good night's sleep as a reason to stay put. Tresca parted ways with his Italian bodyguards, asking only fellow IWW organizer James Gilday to stay on. He then rented a room in the same hotel with Little.[30]

At about four o'clock on the morning of July 4, Tresca's situation worsened. He heard a loud banging on his door, the shuffling of feet, and whispers. He rose and went to the door, stepped onto a chair, and peeked through the doorway's glass transom at a large group of men in the hallway outside his room. The mob of men in plain clothes, accompanied by one suited deputy sheriff, announced that they had come to arrest him. He inquired about an arrest warrant, to which someone in the mob replied, "We don't need no warrants for fellows like you." He was not willing to open the door to the mob, but a female hotel staff member pleaded with him to give up and come out of the room. Speaking through the door, Tresca quipped, "Well, Madame, I never fail with ladies. If you tell me who is there, and tell me the truth, I will open the door."[31] She assured him that there were lawmen present. Slowly, Tresca opened the door, facing the waiting mob of around twenty men.

They took him to the city jail where Little and Sam Scarlett were already imprisoned. Tresca saw Little, who was in a strangely good mood, sarcastically quipping, "You see they did spoil my good sleep, those rascals." The IWW organizers remained in the holding cells for a short time before being escorted by armed guards to a waiting train that consisted of an engine and one railcar. Inside the car, Tresca spied four men, "three of them handcuffed to each other by the wrists, while the fourth was lying on a bench badly wounded in the legs. All of them were without coats; their shirts were badly torn and bespattered with blood; the head of one was all bandaged."[32]

Initially, the train car carrying Tresca, Little, Scarlett, Gilday, and the four unknown passengers was silent—the armed guards, who outnumbered the strikers two to one, did not allow any talking. They assured the agitators that they would not see Virginia again. As the train rolled through the northern Minnesota hinterland toward Duluth, the order of silence began to lift and Tresca found out that the bloodied and bandaged riders were, in fact, the men from the Mosonovich home. Realizing that the car was exclusively carrying passengers charged with murder, Tresca recalled, "as to Little, Gilday, Scarlett and myself, we also were charged with murder as accessories before the fact . . . this is why we were in the car. We were being accused of a murder that took place in our absence in a different town. We were being attached artificially to the murder case in order to eliminate us from the strike picture."[33]

Before concluding commentary on the plot to railroad the IWW organizers from the Iron Range, it is important to acknowledge that there is no documentary evidence to implicate Governor Burnquist, Sheriff Meining, or the mining companies in a premeditated order to shoot up the Mosonovich home. It is possible that the events in the Chicago Mining Location were the sad outcome of a liquor raid gone horribly wrong.

Carlo Tresca (*far left*), Sam Scarlett (*center*), and Joe Schmidt appear in the
St. Louis County jail in Duluth during the fall of 1916. Of the organizers
rounded up and deported from the Range after the shootings at the Mosonovich
boardinghouse, only Tresca, Scarlett, and Frank Little were bound over for
trial and faced first-degree murder charges. Courtesy of the Walter P. Reuther
Library, Archives of Labor and Urban Affairs, Wayne State University.

Even if the violence that day was unintended, Governor Burnquist's
June 30 proclamation provided company gun thugs with a motive and
the motivation to use physical force against striking workers. In all like-
lihood, it was only a matter of time before an event like this happened.
Burnquist's telegram to Meining made the violent deportation of IWW
organizers almost a certainty. His proclamation gave company managers
and their hired thugs the opportunity to provoke a confrontation that
would ensure the arrest of pivotal IWW leaders.

While much of the strike leadership was detained in a Duluth jail, charged with first-degree murder via a manufactured conspiracy, strikers found a way to survive the ravages of a stacked sociopolitical deck. Never mind that the real conspiracy on the ranges was between mining companies and Minnesota's governor. The strike leaders and the Mosonoviches and their boarders were in serious trouble—each charged with a capital offense. An article in the *International Socialist Review* stated it best when summing up the situation: "placing the strike leaders on trial for murder was simply an effort to eliminate their influence and activities in the strike. It is a repetition of the old story of all the great industrial conflicts in this country, namely the prostitution of public authority to the whims, caprices and desires of 'big business.'"[34] At this point, the looming question for the strikers was whether they could salvage their efforts in the midst of great repression, an emboldened band of company thugs, and the loss of their union's most dynamic organizers.

The Struggle to Keep the Fire Lit

The governor's proclamation and the melee at the Mosonovich boarding-house had an immediate effect on the strike as it jailed some of the IWW's most talented organizers and simultaneously demonstrated the power of the mining companies to influence people in high places. Now in the hands of St. Louis County's judicial system, trials for Tresca, the other IWW organizers, and the Mosonoviches began on July 21. The *International Socialist Review* reported:

> When the preliminary hearing of the strike leaders commenced before Judge Smallwood on July 21, 1916, the striking miners gave testimonial to the confidence that they had in their leaders and expressed the sentiment and spirit of the men on strike. The striking miners crowded the court room, corridors and halls of the municipal court at Duluth, and when the men under arrest, led by Carlo Tresca, entered the court room, the men started a demonstration which lasted until the army of court bailiffs cleared the court room.[35]

While they were in jail, the IWW's political prisoners refused to lose their sense of humor. To pass the good deal of time they had on their hands, they resorted to writing letters and song lyrics. One such song, published in the Finnish-language newspaper *Sosialisti*, is titled "The

Iron Miners: (Written in Jail)" and is sung to the tune of "It's a Long Way to Tipperary":

> John Allar died of Mine Guard guns
> The Steel Trust had engaged.
> At Gilbert, wives and children
> Of the Miners were outraged.
> No mine guards were arrested,
> Yet the law is claimed to be
> The mightiest conception of a big democracy.
>
> —Chorus
>
> It's the wrong way to treat the Miners,
> It's the wrong way to go.
> It's the wrong way to best the Miners,
> As the Steel Trust soon will know.
> God help those dirty Mine Guards,
> The Miner's won't forget.
> It's the wrong way to treat the Miners,
> And the guards will know that yet.
>
> —End chorus
>
> Get busy, was the order to
> The lackeys of the Trust,
> Jail all the Organizers,
> And the strike will surely bust.
> Trump up a charge, a strong one,
> That will kill all sympathy,
> So murder was the frame-up,
> And one of the first degree.

While Duluth was humming with the intrigue of murder trials for political prisoners, momentum was lost on the Range as the IWW's rank and file was left to contemplate the jailing of well-known and highly regarded members. Tresca and the other prisoners were engulfed in ominous circumstances—strangers caught in a gridlocked legal system, their lives hanging in the balance. As the initial proceedings ended,

Lapel button featuring the three IWW organizers charged with murder in the Mosonovich boardinghouse shootings. The buttons were sold as a fund-raising item for the defense of the men who were lodged in Duluth's St. Louis County jail while awaiting their trials. The pins were sold for ten cents each at Wobbly gatherings and at a meeting in Eveleth's Urania Hall. Elizabeth Gurley Flynn commented that the buttons should be worn by "everybody in sympathy with the innocent men behind bars." Courtesy of the Labadie Archives, University of Michigan Library.

however, several of the IWW organizers were released from custody. Others were bound over to face a St. Louis County grand jury. As one IWW publication commented, "on July 28 four of these [organizers] were dismissed, namely: Little, Gilday, Stark and Russell. The five others, Tresca, Scarlett, Schmidt, Ahlgren and Wessman were bound over to the Grand Jury for the August term of Court to answer the charge of actual participation in murder."[36] While the release of the four IWW organizers was indeed a small victory, the success of the strike seemed to hinge on re-firing the passion of the IWW's rank and file, raising funds for a protracted strike, and bringing in new and equally talented organizers.

In an attempt to rescue the strike, Bill Haywood sent the IWW's most celebrated orator to the Minnesota ranges. Elizabeth Gurley Flynn stepped off a train and onto the violence-riddled Mesabi Range in mid-July. Almost immediately she captivated the IWW's rank and file as well as the local press. Traveling in a bread truck, Gurley Flynn covered the entire length of the Mesabi Range delivering passionate speeches in defense of striking workers and the political prisoners held in Duluth. She was welcomed by some, and reviled by others—her mission was to rescue the 1916 strike and it was going to be a difficult one. She had visited the Mesabi Range before, acting as an organizer for the Western Federation of Miners during the 1907 strike. During that strike she found love and married fellow organizer J. A. Jones, though the two later parted ways. Minnesota was familiar territory for Gurley Flynn. But her task and travels amid the long distances and violent exchanges of the 1916 strike wore on her greatly, as she later recounted:

> All that summer the strike dragged out a dogged existence. We raced up and down the Range from one end to the other in an old bakery truck driven by a couple of young Italian strikers, who often forgot we were not bread and bounced us unmercifully over the unpaved rocky roads. The deputies came to know the truck and took pot shots at us, so we had to stop using it, much to our relief. There were about 14 towns from one end [of the Mesabi Range] to the other, which we covered. Several times the strikers marched the length of the Range, holding meetings in each town. On one occasion some towns shut off the drinking water while we were there.[37]

Equally distressing was the situation of her fellow organizers who were locked up in Duluth. Gurley Flynn was most concerned with the condition of Carlo Tresca. By 1916, she and the Italian anarchist had developed an affinity for each other and were actively engaged in a romantic relationship. She was worried that, at best, Tresca would remain behind bars for a long time, and at worst, he would be executed for capital murder. She visited him in the St. Louis County jail often. Tresca, in turn, expressed concern over her safety, and feared that the violence and lawlessness of company thugs and deputy sheriffs would not be confined to the IWW's male organizers. After Gurley Flynn left the Range on a fund-raising tour, Tresca wrote mutual friend Mary Heaton Vorse from his jail cell in Duluth: "I am very glad she is out. I feel now very much relefe [sic]. When she was here I can't sleep. My poor girl! Cheer her up, Mary dearest, please!"[38]

Despite Tresca's concerns for her safety, Gurley Flynn's tough demeanor, dynamic oratory, and amiable public persona insulated her from the worst of the strike's assaults. She was just twenty-five at the time; her youth and obvious middle-class trimmings juxtaposed those of the other IWW organizers, while transfixing mixed-class and mixed-gender audiences as she delivered blistering and impassioned oratory against the Mesabi Range's industrial backdrop. Often seen donning long-flowing dresses with neatly pressed white shirts, her jet black hair wrapped in a tight bun under a fancy hat, she made no bones about being an outsider who supported an oppressed working class. Although born and formally educated in the United States with a decidedly middle-class upbringing, she was a staunch champion of working-class immigrants. There was no reason for her to care about the plight of the Range's immigrant working-class families, but she did—passionately. Such zealous oratory from someone who had no immediate class connection with immigrant workers meant something to the outside world and her fiery advocacy of immigrant laborers made it palatable for others of the same class background to share her sentiments.

The local press picked up on this distinction. While she looked the part of a middle-class "lady," her tone and tenor while speaking was anything but middle-class. It was inflammatory. It was impassioned. It was revolutionary. It was powerful. Mary Heaton Vorse commented on Flynn's orations: "when Elizabeth spoke, the excitement of the strikers became a visible thing. She stood up there, young, with her Irish blue eyes, her face magnolia white, her cloud of black hair . . . it was though a spurt of flame had gone through the audience, something stirring and powerful, a feeling which made the liberation of people possible."[39]

While area newspapers of the progressive and corporate-influenced press maligned the IWW's "foreign" agitators such as Tresca and Schmidt, Gurley Flynn was greeted with acceptance, even enthusiasm, by some English-language publications. The Strikers' News picked up on this conversion, announcing in one article that "Elizabeth Gurley Flynn Makes Good Impression," and continuing: "one newspaper man on the Iron Range has decided that all the I.W.W. organizers are not bloodthirsty savages and dehorned devils since hearing Elizabeth Gurley Flynn speak."[40] It was Gurley Flynn's speaking style, her middle-class ethos,

One of the IWW's most gifted organizers, Elizabeth Gurley Flynn made an impeccable impression on many during her stay in northern Minnesota during the 1916 strike. She split her time organizing with sojourns across the country attempting to rally funds for the defense of the union's imprisoned organizers in Duluth. Courtesy of the George Grantham Bain Collection, Library of Congress Prints and Photographs Division.

and her well-appointed fashion sense that captivated middle-class audiences along with the IWW's already sympathetic working-class membership. This middle-class audience was the equality-seeking, literate, and personally wealthy demographic that the IWW sought to tap for monetary help. Funds were needed to keep the strike afloat, but also to wage a legal defense for embattled and imprisoned organizers. Gurley Flynn's blistering rhetoric on the Mesabi Range was an attempt to fire up striking workers during a wearied labor conflict, but it was also an attempt to broadcast the plight of striking workers to an expanded, monied, and hopefully sympathetic middle class.

As the strike ground down in the hot, humid days of midsummer, money became *the* primary concern. In the same manner that Elizabeth

Gurley Flynn was dispatched to the Range in an attempt to resuscitate the strike, the IWW attempted to produce media offerings as fund-raising tools that would bring the events of the strike nationwide exposure. During this time, the IWW commissioned a rhetorical work aimed at an altogether different audience, which sought to elicit support for the flagging efforts surrounding the strike. Titled *The Startling Story of the Minnesota Miners' Strike on the Mesaba Range 1916*, this pamphlet was published by the Minnesota Iron Range Strikers' Defense Committee in New York City. In the sixteen-page narrative of strike events, the IWW sought to make a final argument for the moral imperative and eventual success of the strike. Targeted at an audience that lived away from the Minnesota ranges, the thin, portable "story" was designed with a dual purpose in mind—to raise strike funds and to get the IWW's jailed organizers out of lockup.[41]

Victor Power and the Progressive Pushback

If imprisonments and funding issues were not enough, making matters worse for the IWW was the oppositional attitude of progressive politicians such as Victor Power. A self-proclaimed advocate and friend of the working class, Power's relationship with organized labor did not extend to sympathy for the IWW. While mining company propaganda was pointed and critical of the IWW and its rank and file, Power's skilled oratory, adept rhetorical strategies, and keen political acumen were like a well-positioned punch in the face of Wobbly organizing efforts. Power saw the deportation of the IWW's organizers as a chance to swing the Range's workers away from the IWW and toward the American Federation of Labor (AFL). As a champion of the AFL, Power began a campaign to convince audiences of the potential efficacy of an AFL alignment with striking workers, possibly through the United Mine Workers of America (UMWA) union. With the IWW's organizers mostly out of the way, and with the notable exception of Gurley Flynn, Power and the Range's other progressive mayors attempted to arbitrate the strike and swing a triumphant blow for progressive, reformist ideology.

Newspapers covered their efforts and touted Power's credibility while condemning the IWW's alleged violence. The Hibbing mayor's personal scrapbooks and journals give a chronicle of the progressive-sanctioned

Range Strike Committee and their efforts to end the strike. Power took center stage at the committee's gatherings, and newspaper articles recounted his efforts at these "peace meetings," which were called with the intention of, according to Power, "bringing mining companies and strikers together for a compromise so the men would get back to work."[42] Amid the chaos and violence of the strike, Power seemed to be doing the work of a saint, but his work concealed a more pointed purpose. In his position as Hibbing's mayor, he had gained real political clout and he used this cachet to bring the AFL's state convention to Hibbing. Coincidentally, the convention occurred in the midst of the most intense days of the strike. The state convention began on July 16 with Power addressing the gathering the next day. He used the convention platform to announce his advocacy for the AFL and stated that his main reason for inviting the convention to Hibbing was so that people on the Range could see the "State Federation of Labor's standing, character and power" and that it "was the proper body to organize the workers in the range country."[43] In short, Power hoped to instill the AFL as the representative of Range workers, and a strike administered by the IWW was at odds with the mayor's ideological principles.

In Power, the IWW had a skilled rhetorical adversary. With a much-vaunted college education, legal degree, and a lawyer's gift of gab, Power thrilled at the state labor convention by delivering blistering attacks against mining company greed *and* the ineptitude of the IWW. Referring to the Minnesota State Federation of Labor as a "respectable organization," Power dissected the shortcomings of the IWW by highlighting the character of the AFL-linked state labor federation. A newspaper article in Power's scrapbook emphasized the oratory delivered to the labor organization, "'You,' said Mayor Power to the convention, 'are a respectable organization, you have prestige and you alone as an organization can do real good for the workingmen's cause.' Mr. Power urged that the American Federation of Labor take steps to organize the workmen of the mines and his recommendation will be considered at a special session of the convention this afternoon." Power's advocacy of the AFL went beyond speeches from the bully pulpit. Tucked into the pages of his journal between July 20 and July 21 was a business card that read "W. R. Fairley, International Organizer, U.M.W. of A., Pratt City, Alabama. Washington D.C. Address—Stag Hotel, 9th Street, N.W."[44] It seems that Power had moved beyond hosting AFL state conventions and had become an agent provocateur for the AFL's largest mining industry union—the UMWA. This association was unwelcome news for the IWW's flagging efforts during the 1916 strike. It meant that opposition to the IWW was now coming from three sides: mining companies, progressives, and the largest and most powerful mining union in the United States, the UMWA.

Tracing Power's trajectory of allegiances during the strike is difficult. He was a self-styled champion of the working class who, in the early days of the strike, reluctantly allowed the IWW to organize in Hibbing. While he publicly attacked the Wobblies during the state labor convention, he simultaneously attended the trials of Tresca and others in Duluth, received calls from IWW organizer Joseph Ettor, and held personal meetings with Elizabeth Gurley Flynn. In public he was a harsh and vocal critic of the Wobblies and openly advocated for the AFL, while secretly contacting a UMWA organizer to facilitate that union's organization of the Range's mines, yet also still meeting secretly with members of the IWW.[45]

Power's active political maneuverings did not go unnoticed by mining company management. As he was launching attacks against company profit making, mining bosses were busy devising a way to thwart his authority. Their plan, devised in early August, included leveraging company influence over Hibbing's banks, which were instructed to refuse payment on the Power administration's expenditures. According to one bank official, Hibbing was in debt to the tune of more than a million dollars, but a newspaper report traced the scrutiny of Hibbing's finances back to a dispute between Power and Oliver Iron Mining Company executive W. J. West.[46] Just as the Oliver and Independents had grown tired of dealing with the IWW, they had also tired of Power's political maneuverings. The Steel Trust pushed back against the progressive politician and was moving to shut off Hibbing's finances as a way to discipline Power's government, claiming he had mismanaged municipal funds while steering the city into vast amounts of debt. Power was in the political fight of his life during the 1916 strike. During this time, his strong rhetorical skills temporarily checkmated the financial

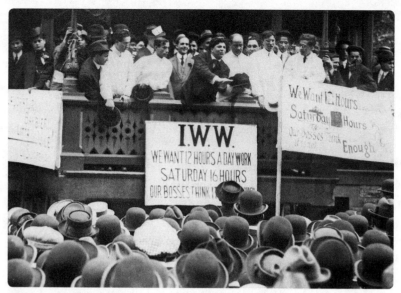

IWW organizer Joseph Ettor (center with hands together) addresses a crowd during the 1913 New York City Barbers' Strike. Ettor arrived on the Range with Elizabeth Gurley Flynn after his fellow organizers had been arrested in conjunction with the Mosonovich boardinghouse shootings. An Italian immigrant, Ettor had a reputation as a feisty but affable organizer and was informally known as "Smiling Joe." Courtesy of the George Grantham Bain Collection, Library of Congress Prints and Photographs Division.

wizardry of the Steel Trust, but the Steel Trust would eventually wear down his political capital. He straddled political death for some time, but remained Hibbing's mayor for nine years, attempted a run at a U.S. congressional seat (but lost), and then retired from politics. He was, however, always a beloved figure on the Iron Range. It is a testament to his rhetorical savvy and political acumen that among the social spaces named for mining company bosses—such as Olcott Park in Virginia, Greenway high school, and the company town of Coleraine, named after Oliver manager Thomas F. Cole—there is a Vic Power Park in Hibbing.

As Power was playing politics on the Range, perhaps attempting to salvage the vestiges of the 1916 strike for later organizing activity partial to the UMWA, the last gasps of IWW organization were occurring. Late July found the federal Department of Labor conducting an assessment of the strike, but even this investigation was not without intrigue, and Power was caught in the middle of it all. The Department of Labor's investigators were H. Davies and W. R. Fairley—the same W. R. Fairley who had left his UMWA organizer's card with Power a few weeks earlier. Although outwardly tasked with an impartial evaluation, Fairley likely met with Power to assess conditions for a restructuring of the strike, and it seemed that Power was more than happy to aid his efforts.[47]

On Friday morning, July 28, Power met officially with the federal investigators in his office, but also held more informal court with them at his lake home and farm later that same day.[48] The intentions of the federal investigation into the strike were not really fooling anyone. IWW leaders knew it was political maneuvering, while Power saw it as a chance to court Fairley and the UMWA. The mining companies, however, were suspicious of the investigation from the very start. As one company-influenced newspaper reported, "[Federal Government] Report Misrepresents Strike to Help I.W.W.—Duluth Officials Assert Falsity of Statements in Document of Industrial Relations Commission— Allegations Absurd."[49] With the government report having little, if any, effect on the strike, the IWW was wandering in the proverbial wilderness and looking for a way out.

The Flames Flare Out

The imprisonment of its members, closing of labor halls, thwarting of sympathy strikes on Duluth and Superior docks, and the railroading of prominent organizers were all obstacles the IWW had overcome throughout the summer of 1916. Elizabeth Gurley Flynn had stepped in admirably in an attempt to resuscitate the strike, but in many ways she was attempting to fan the flames of discontent in an already ashed-over landscape. For months, Minnesota's iron ranges had been on fire with the passion and power of a defining clash between organized labor and capital, but in the dog days of August the flames had dwindled and were about to extinguish. The jailings and legal defense funds for Tresca, Schmidt, and others, competition with progressives for working-class allegiances, and infighting between Bill Haywood and organizers in the field all coalesced to make August a bad month for IWW organizing efforts in northern Minnesota.

Through a very organized network of spies, the mining companies were able to keep tabs on the IWW's management of the strike. Thanks to their efforts, mine managers found out that the IWW was being very discretionary about funding a strikers' benefit account. These funds, typically bolstered by additional assessments or voluntary giving by union members, worked to sustain not only the pocketbooks of striking workers, but also the resolve of families affected by the strike. Strike benefits for prolonged labor–management confrontations demonstrated to strikers that the union could take care of workers and their families just as well as the mining companies. It appeared from the work of labor spies that the IWW was either reticent to devote funds to the dwindling labor actions on the Iron Range or was struggling to catch up in collecting assessments for the strike. Ireland surmised that the promised strikers' benefit funds were in fact only a bluff meant to bring the mining companies to the bargaining table. He was hopeful that strikers would make serious requests for the funds and that these requests would "explode the bubble, for the I.W.W. leaders do not want to distribute any strike funds . . . and their excuse now is that they cannot distribute strike funds until all the underground mines on the Mesaba are closed."[50]

The simple fact was that the IWW had not closed down all the mines on the Mesabi, and had barely penetrated mines on the Vermilion and Cuyuna ranges. Although the strike had been in effect since early June, the *Strikers' News* only began reporting of labor activity on the Cuyuna and Vermilion in mid-August and early September, respectively. A Friday, August 18 article proclaimed, "WHOLE CUYUNA RANGE IS NOW TIED UP" and reported that "the miners of Ironton, Crosby and Woodrow are idle . . . 700 of them have thus far joined the I.W.W., and it is said that they are coming in faster every day." By this time, however, mining company officials were well versed in quelling strike activity, a fact that was made clearly apparent in the press. The same article reported that "John Perich, Austrian organizer who was sent to Crosby from the Mesaba Range, has been arrested, together with four other strikers."[51] By September 1, the strike had spread to the Vermilion Range, but action was confined to one mine in Winton. "On Monday, August 8th, a delegate representing 330 miners of Winton . . . appeared before the Central Strike Committee in Virginia to request that organizers be sent to that section," reported the *Strikers' News*. IWW leadership sent John Pancner, a roving organizer, and Charles Jacobson, president of the Virginia branch, to found a membership branch.[52] The Vermilion Range's lone Metal Mine Workers branch was late to the party, because on September 22, the strike on the ranges was officially called off.

The *Strikers' News* heralded the official proclamation from the Central Strike Committee in Virginia:

> In rebellion against intolerable conditions we came out on strike, entirely unorganized, without funds, experience or even acquaintance with one another. We were compelled to rely on the labor movement throughout the country for relief to provide bread for our wives and babies. Hundreds of our ranks as well as our organizers and speakers were arrested, and the latter group are now in jail facing a charge of murder . . . we have fought all summer and have grappled with the mighty octopus the Steel Trust with all the power we possessed. But we feel it would be unwise to prolong our battle through the terrible cold of a Minnesota winter.[53]

At this point, the difficult process of picking up the pieces became a reality. A defense fund for the jailed organizers began in earnest and was headquartered in Virginia. James Gilday was in charge of the operations and Elizabeth Gurley Flynn began a whirlwind speaking tour throughout Itasca County in hopes of raising money. Her efforts then carried her to the Twin Cities, Chicago, and Omaha.[54]

While Gurley Flynn roamed the countryside in support of the strikers' defense fund, it was actually a group of Italian immigrant anarchists, and not the IWW, who came to Carlo Tresca's aid. Acute infighting had been occurring among IWW leaders regarding the disposition of the jailed Fellow Workers, and organizers such as Joe Ettor had left the organization, claiming that Haywood had centralized the union too much. Gurley Flynn was also on the outs with Haywood because he refused money for the defense fund and, in doing so, for her partner, Tresca. In the long run, the aid was unnecessary because the trials against Tresca, the other organizers, and the Mosonoviches came to a quick but contentious conclusion. In December 1916, Tresca and the other defendants reached plea deals with the St. Louis County prosecutor. The deals specified that Tresca, his fellow organizers, and Melitza Mosonovich and Orlandich would be set free, while the other persons arrested in the boardinghouse would plead guilty to first-degree manslaughter and serve one year of a three-year sentence. The Italian anarchist was a free man, but the acrimony between Tresca, Gurley Flynn, and Haywood would occasion Tresca's leaving the IWW, never to return.[55]

The IWW tried to put a militant face on the ending of strike activities, but the disappointment of the 1916 strike was unavoidable. In addition to local and state repression of the IWW, both the strike and the union lost momentum in September owing in part to the nascent era of "Red" investigations and subversion charges related to the onset of the United States' involvement in World War I.[56] In this way, the IWW's confrontation with American capitalism, the Steel Trust, and the Range's Independent mine operators came at an especially difficult and dangerous time for labor unions. Revolutionary organizations and their members were especially ripe for scrutiny as the rhetoric for involvement in the "war to end all wars" began to crescendo. As a theoretically worldwide organization, committed to the solidarity of *all* workers, the IWW's stance on militarism included a harsh critique of war as a profit-making endeavor sponsored by nations, corporations, and bosses to further exploit the working class. In order to combat such proletarian narratives, Loyalty Leagues and pro-industry citizens' groups organized to support capitalism, militarism, nationalism, and to defend against so-called anti-American sentiment.[57] The repressive walls of a nation that would soon find itself at war were closing in, and the strike, the IWW, and its members became casualties of capitalist warfare.

In a final analysis of the 1916 strike, it would be naive to find the bloodshed of the labor conflict the fault of the mining companies only. Yet, for all the misleading, company-sponsored rhetoric that charged the IWW with intimidation, rioting, and violence, it must be pointed out that the Wobblies never once officially called for the use of institutionalized violence during the conflict. In personal correspondences, mine company manager James D. Ireland even admitted that the IWW advised its members to avoid provoking confrontation. It is evident, however, that when the IWW staged a march or protest, the mining companies did nothing to alleviate tensions. Instead, their hired guns elevated the friction between the two sides, and in many instances, actively provoked violence. Like prior strikes that occurred in the Lake Superior basin, the 1916 Minnesota Iron Ore Strike ultimately died at the hands of mining company bosses. Defiant to the end, the IWW brought an end to strike activities by declaring, "with the calling off of the Mesabi Range Iron Ore Miners Strike in the various range towns, and similar action on the Vermilion and Cuyuna Ranges, IWW leaders here today described their defeat as a temporary truce with the mine operators."[58]

CONCLUSION

Rising from the Ashes

IN A FINAL RENDERING OF THE LABOR CONFLICT THAT ENVELOPED Minnesota's iron ranges in 1916, the epic battle between organized labor and the Steel Trust and Independents had been, at best, a stalemate for the IWW, and at worst, from the mining companies' perspective, a loss for organized labor. What followed, however, was the IWW's darkest hour. Mired in the U.S. government's well-orchestrated repression of the World War I era, and losing converts to the successful 1917 October Revolution in Russia and the international communist movement, the Wobblies' efforts at organizing workers were undermined by the dual pressures of a like-minded group that espoused working-class interests *and* the tyranny of a governmental campaign to persecute and prosecute the IWW out of the United States.

In Minnesota, the campaign to curtail the IWW's influence on the iron ranges was rooted in an increasing vigilantism. Sheriff Meining, having secured his position as St. Louis County's lead law-enforcement officer during the assault on the IWW organizers' civil liberties during the strike, took up the cause of ridding the ranges of the Wobblies. He enlisted the support of spies, some of whom were local townsfolk, to keep tabs on IWW activities. One letter dated June 19, 1917, from a labor spy in Aurora detailed such surveillance:

> Am mailing you a copy of circular which was distributed Sunday night. Am trying to locate parties responsible. Have good idea where they came from but no proof. There is a bunch of I.W.W.s holding meetings in the woods. If I locate them I have authority to arrest. My instructions were to look after Company's property only. Have been requested

by officials of other mines to look over their locations occasionally and on finding agitators to arrest them. If I were to pick a number of reliable men, would it not be advisable to deputize them, to be called on in emergency. There was some talk, last night, of calling a strike. Doubt if majority of miners will agree to it.[1]

Wobblies were under strict scrutiny on the Range, and perhaps with good reason, because after calling off the 1916 strike in September, the union turned its remaining resources on the ranges to organizing northern Minnesota's "Timber Beasts" or lumberjacks. In many respects, the 1916 strike never died, it simply moved north into Minnesota's lumber and paper mills, forests, and isolated logging camps. In many ways, the 1917 Minnesota Timber Strike was a continuation of the mine workers' strike, but in a different industry. The two strikes, both administered by the IWW, shared much in common: the timber strike's early headquarters were located in the Socialist Opera House in Virginia; a key lumber strike organizer, Charles Jacobson, was secretary-treasurer of the Metal Mine Workers No. 490 branch in Virginia during the labor conflict a year before; about two thousand of Virginia's 1916 strike population were still itching for a fight and refocused their efforts on the area's lumber barons such as Frederick Weyerhauser; and perhaps most important, the strike began with a work stoppage at the Virginia and Rainy Lake Lumber Company, a Weyerhaeuser subsidiary. By January 1917, the strike had spread throughout the Northland from Virginia to Bemidji to International Falls, along the Canadian border.[2]

Another similarity between the two strikes was the harsh exploitation of workers. Mine workers had very difficult lives, this much was certain, but lumberjacks may have had it even worse. Working in subzero, deadly conditions for less pay than mine workers, while often living in squalor in isolated lumber camps, made the Timber Beasts ripe candidates for overtures from the IWW. After Virginia's millworkers ignored Bill Haywood's advice not to strike, the Virginia and Rainy Lake Lumber Company's massive mills were shut down in late December 1916. To help spread the strike, the IWW's Agricultural Workers Organization in Minneapolis sent in organizers to work among the region's timber workers. More organizational help was obtained from local branches in Bemidji, Virginia, Duluth, and the small logging camp town of Gemmell, which was located between Bemidji and International Falls. By January 1917, the IWW was calling out workers from scores of isolated mining camps and a mass exodus from the woods followed.[3]

On January 3, 1917, the IWW's official newspaper, *Industrial Worker*, documented the spread and initial success of the strike, proclaiming a "Monster Revolt of Northern Minnesota Lumberworkers"; another headline three days later in *Solidarity* highlighted the fact that Minnesota was undergoing yet another labor revolt when it somewhat triumphantly proclaimed "Minnesota Strike Bound Again." According to the IWW's press, the strike in Minnesota's north woods had more than a thousand participants, which was in addition to the seven hundred to one thousand men striking in Virginia's mills. Lumberjacks were striking for a twenty-five-cent increase in pay and better camp conditions. While the strike was picking up steam in the frozen north woods, managers were attempting to suppress the revolt. The tactics used to combat the lumber strike were eerily similar to what had occurred during the iron-ore strike. Mass arrests of workers—up to seventy at a time—importation of company gun thugs, and the plotted deportation of organizers occurred in earnest in towns such as Bemidji, International Falls, and Gemmell. By mid-February, however, the lumber strike had been called off, with the IWW declaring victory, while logging bosses took the fight into the political arena in the spring and summer.[4]

The political maneuvering of industrial bosses and their cronies in Minnesota's elected offices is perhaps the most sinister legacy of the 1916 strike and the closely associated 1917 strike. On April 13, 1917, Minnesota's legislature, no doubt stirred by IWW labor actions in the previous months, passed an act against criminal syndicalism, which defined the offense in general terms as "a doctrine that advocates crime, sabotage, violence, or other unlawful methods of terrorism as a means of accomplishing industrial or political reform."[5] Repression and violence against the IWW and its members soon followed. On June 23, Elizabeth Gurley Flynn and nine other organizers were arrested in Duluth for violation of the state's ban on "unpatriotic agitation," while four Wobblies were arrested near Bemidji on July 21, accused of burning down the Crookston Lumber Company's No. 1 Mill. The arrested men claimed that the mill owners burned the building down for insurance money. Within days, three of the four men were released, while one was retained for "displaying literature advocating sabotage." Days later, three union members were arrested in a Bemidji IWW hall. This was only the beginning of Bemidji's offensive against the Wobblies.[6]

On July 25, "a crowd of 200 of the leading citizens of Bemidji, led by Mayor Charles W. Vandersluis, rose enmasse [sic] and cleaned the city of the lawless element." According to the unflinchingly nationalistic and pro-corporate *Bemidji Daily Pioneer*, twenty-one people were rounded up at Bemidji IWW headquarters and marched through town to city hall, while "a dray load of their furniture, signs and germ-breeding literature" was pulled behind. Along the way to city hall, four more "I.W.W.s" were added to the group of twenty-one. The corralled Wobblies were then forced to march under an American flag along their way to the city's depot and "stood at the gaze of a thousand aroused Americans who held them and all that they stood for in contempt, and three lusty cheers were given for Old Glory." Just before the train left, Bemidji IWW secretary Jess Dunning was instructed by the mayor to "remember this is an unhealthy town for I.W.W.s" Soon after the deportees were shipped out on an afternoon train to Ebro, a small whistle-stop thirty miles west of Bemidji, the crowd turned its attention to businesses and other supporters of the Wobblies, visiting three locations in town. At one location, Morris Kaplan's store, Mayor Vandersluis instructed the owner to "have nothing more to do with I.W.W. affairs . . . no more speeches, no more meetings and be white." The crowd then hoisted a new American flag over his building. Bemidji was just one of the most extreme cases of repression against the union and the rampant nationalism that accompanied the World War I era and subsequent years of the first Red Scare. In August, Duluth's IWW hall was raided and all the organization's records were burned.[7]

Then, on September 30, in almost a natural succession of repression, Jess Dunning, who apparently ignored the mayor's July instructions, was arrested in Bemidji and charged with criminal syndicalism. The expectation was that Dunning presented some threat to state or national

The aftermath of a raid on the IWW headquarters in New York City, 1919. After the strike, Wobbly offices across the United States were raided in an effort to curtail the union's influence. On September 8, 1917, more than a hundred soldiers raided IWW headquarters in Duluth and burned the organization's records. Courtesy of the Labadie Archives, University of Michigan Library.

security, but according to a 1920 *Columbia Law Review* article on criminal syndicalism, the basis of the indictment was "a set of posters two inches' square bearing such legends as 'Beware Good Pay or Bum Work: The IWW Never Forget: Sabotage' 'Industrial Unionism: Abolition of the Wage System: Join the IWW for Industrial Freedom' 'The IWW are Coming: Join the One Big Union' stuck on various buildings by the defendant. No evidence was offered but the posters themselves."[8] This, apparently, constituted a serious crime against the people of Minnesota and Dunning was sentenced to serve two years in the penitentiary. Dunning's arrest and indictment for criminal syndicalism was significant on a state and national level because he was the first person in the United States to be sentenced using this novel and authoritarian World

War I–era legislation. A number of states had comparable laws on the books and Idaho had a similar criminal syndicalist measure, but Minnesota was first to employ the repressive law to silence First Amendment rights.[9] As more states passed similar legislation, the practice gained acceptance as a way to control and incarcerate a number of dissident groups—immigrants suspected of un-American behavior, critics of the United States' involvement in World War I, and anarchists, communists, and socialists in general—while providing a method to prevent union members from calling strikes against unfair labor practices during the war. Many state laws on supposed subversive behavior, such as Minnesota's, were tried on appeal and upheld—setting a comprehensive and oppressive legal precedent. Additionally, these laws acted in concert with the federal government's Espionage Act of 1917 (and the later 1918 amendments to the act to form the Espionage and Sedition Acts of 1917–18) to almost completely stifle any criticism of U.S. involvement in the Great War.

While the campaign to discredit, harass, surveil, and jail the IWW in Minnesota went on unabated, the push to crush the Wobblies went national as well. In 1917, with the United States having entered the raging war in Europe, the campaign to rid the IWW and other war dissenters from representing industrial workers was on as the federal government began prosecuting, jailing, and even deporting members of the IWW in earnest. The most infamous of these actions was known as the IWW 166 Trials, which decimated the IWW's ranks. Of the original 166 defendants, "ninety-three men were sentenced after the I.W.W. trial at Chicago, on August 30, 1918, to a total of 788 years imprisonment and to pay a fine of $2,788,000." A political prisoner, incarcerated at Leavenworth Penitentiary in Kansas, documented this abuse of human rights. Addressing a typed letter to President Woodrow Wilson, the prisoner chronicled the repression meted out against the IWW: "Since the early part of 1917 the I.W.W. has been subjected to a persecution without parallel. Headquarters, offices and even homes of members, were raided; our letter-files, records, and office equipment seized, and members arrested by the hundreds." Equally insidious was the federal government's attempts to stymie an effective defense against prosecution during the trials. As the prisoner argued, "our defense was hampered

An "Industrial Freedom Certificate" issued to Gilbert, Minnesota's Metal Mine Workers' Industrial Union # 800, circa 1918. The IWW began issuing these certificates as part of a defense fund drive for members arrested and charged with antisyndicalist and antisedition laws during World War I and the following Red Scare era. Courtesy of the Immigration History Research Center, University of Minnesota.

by raids on our union offices. The Post Office Department stopped our papers; thousands of letters, many of them registered, dealing solely with our legal defense, were seized; hundreds of letters were delivered six months to a year after mailing. Furthermore, during the Chicago trial many of our witnesses were intimidated by detectives and Army Intelligence Department officers."[10]

The IWW, headed by Bill Haywood (who was himself a defendant in the 166 Trial) and Vincent St. John, attempted to immediately organize a defense fund for the imperiled Fellow Workers by soliciting fifty-dollar bonds from IWW locals and, in return, giving the locals a handsomely printed, embossed, and officially sealed "Industrial Freedom Certificate." Other efforts to form workers' defense funds came after the conclusion of the trials from unaffiliated organizations partial to radical unionism. After her detachment from the IWW, Elizabeth Gurley Flynn headed one such organization known as the Workers' Defense Union, which was headquartered in New York City. In 1919, with her rhetorical flair intact, Gurley Flynn and the Workers' Defense Union distributed letters seeking donations and solidarity from other radical working-class groups:

> Dear Comrades: We have decided that this first May Day after the last five years of blood and tears should not only be a celebration of the rising tide of proletarian dictatorship in Europe, but a nation-wide protest against the imprisoning and imprisonment of Socialists, I.W.W.'s and all other champions of labor and liberty.
>
> There are nearly two thousand political prisoners in the United States to-day. Many of them are well-known and well-loved, others are obscure and almost forgotten. We must speak and act at once and in a determined manner for all those who pay with their freedom for their devotion to their class.[11]

The mass trials of Wobblies were just one such way to curb the IWW's influence. The federal government also began deporting Wobblies from the United States. Defense funds were begun for these people as well. In a letter to Gurley Flynn, Caroline A. Lowe, an attorney in Chicago, wrote to members and friends of organized labor on March 19, 1919, of "twenty-one men imprisoned on Ellis Island [who] are awaiting deportation. Scores, if maybe hundreds more are being arrested, held for a farcical hearing before prejudiced Government [immigration] inspectors, and condemned to life-long exile from the United States." She went on to state that "these men are being deported solely because of membership and activity in a labor union—the Industrial Workers of the World."[12]

Iron Range locals and Finnish immigrant working-class organizations gave willingly to these defense fund efforts. As seen in the Industrial Freedom certificate, the Gilbert Branch of the Metal and Machinery Workers Industrial Union No. 800 provided fifty dollars to the "Defense of Class War Prisoners" who had been "indicted by the United States Government." Finnish immigrant organizations affiliated with the IWW gave to the Workers' Defense Union efforts of Gurley Flynn as the "Finnish Branch of the IWW" and the "Metal and Machinery Workers Industrial Union, No. 300, Finnish Branch," proudly were listed as supporters of the cause.[13] In spite of these efforts, the harsh repression of the IWW continued, somewhat unabated, even after the Red Scare era of the 1920s. Minnesota's Finnish immigrant population, however, remained bulwarks of the movement, as evidenced by their continual publication of *Industrialisti*, the popular Finnish-language newspaper of the IWW in Duluth, which did not cease publication until the 1970s. Moreover, the IWW has been undergoing a resurgence and continues to organize service industry workers in present-day Minneapolis. The Minnesota IWW branches have even resurrected the Work People's College, now headquartered in Minneapolis. This contemporary rekindling of the flames of discontent demonstrates that even after such harsh repression, IWW sentiment and collective labor action rose from the ashes of the 1916 strike.

Equally significant was the reorganization and resurgence of union and political sentiment on the iron ranges after the 1916 strike. As the labor spy's summer 1917 letter to Sheriff Meining indicated, the IWW had to take to the woods for meetings, but the penchant for collective, class-conscious action survived. The movement had gone underground, but within a generation and with new status as political actors, the children of 1916's immigrant striking population had gained a political voice. The descendants of 1916's strikers had moved away from the IWW's ideology of revolutionary industrial unionism and industrial sabotage, received the vote, and became vested political actors who reappeared from underground movements to become politically active members of a renewed and vigorous labor movement that blossomed after the Red Scare subsided in the mid-1920s. As Iron Range historian Pamela A. Brunfelt has written, "by the 1920s the people of the Iron Range had begun to assert some control over their communities. Many of the immigrants had educated themselves about the American political system, completed the naturalization process, and were poised to become fully engaged in the political process." In the efforts to build such a political identity, interethnic rivalries, which were a subject of great attention while organizing the 1916 strike, seemed to mostly fade into the once-divided social landscape. The children of immigrant workers became full-fledged Americans, married interethnically, and were enfranchised with the vote and a political voice. Many of these Americans found a home in Minnesota's Farmer-Labor Party, which was merged into the Democratic Party in 1944 to form the state's unique Democratic-Farmer-Labor Party (DFL).[14]

By the Great Depression, the vestige of 1916's radical organized labor movement—now rumored to be Communist-influenced—was the Steel Workers Organizing Committee (SWOC). Over the years, this group had made significant inroads into the corporately secured, labor spy-laden iron ranges. Once again, the ranges' contested workscapes became the locations where many Iron Range workers actively supported and joined the SWOC, which would later become the United Steel Workers of America (USW or Steelworkers) in 1942. The Steelworkers formed after a number of unions representing the extractive industries merged to become a founding member of the progressively intentioned Congress of Industrial Organizations (CIO). The CIO would later merge with the American Federation of Labor in 1955. Much of the CIO's revolutionary ideology was abandoned in the 1950s during the McCarthy period, but the radical beginnings of the industrial union were forged in early labor struggles such as those waged in 1916. Today, the USW is the largest industrial union in North America with more than eight hundred thousand members. As the USW Web site acknowledges, "The seeds of this great union were planted in the late 1800s by our fathers and mothers, our grandparents, our great-grandparents and so on. They were seeds of commitment, solidarity and a common interest to fight for better conditions for working men and women everywhere."[15]

Although the IWW had been rebuffed in its attempts to organize the Minnesota Iron Range, the legacy of the 1916 strike paved the way for future union efforts in northern Minnesota. Sam Swanson, the former Wobbly and seasonal wanderer in search of employment, finally set down roots and took up work as a labor organizer with the Steelworkers in the Minnesota iron mines. He too recognized the importance of past labor struggles in the push to organize Minnesota's mines during the Depression:

> On the part of the immigrant mine workers, most of whom had emigrated from Europe to this area of America seeking peace and freedom from oppression and who could not cope with the language of their adopted country, the lack of trade union knowledge and practice was one of the pitfalls of organizational attempts through the early years of industry. But the first-generation Americans, sons of fathers who worked in the mines, were instilled with the backbone and determination of

their fathers, and they were the sparks which ignited the Iron Range in 1937 when they formed the first local union of the C.I.O. in Ely, today's [1960s] Local 1664, United Steel Workers of America.[16]

The ties between the early struggles to organize the ranges and the Depression era's successful drives to unionize were many, but one tangible link existed in particular—the Finn hall as a cultural space of discontent. As Swanson recalled, "in the spring [of 1937], the first open meeting of miners interested in the Congress of Industrial Organizations was held in the old Ely Workers' Hall," which was formerly a Finn hall. In another case on the Cuyuna Range, people from the South Slavic Federation borrowed the local Finnish Workers' Hall to plan for their own Croatian Miners' Orchestra Hall.[17]

One of the SWOC's most influential and gifted organizers was Matti Halberg, the son of a Finnish immigrant striker who was blacklisted by the mining companies after a strike on the Mesabi Iron Range in the first decade of the twentieth century. Halberg's family had been supporters of the IWW, but shifted allegiances to the communist movement sometime after the Bolshevik Revolution in Russia. After his organizing experiences on the iron ranges, and his participation with the SWOC in the 1937 Little Steel Strike in Youngstown, Ohio, Halberg Americanized his name to Gus Hall. He went on to become general secretary of the Communist Party-USA in 1959. Hall's class consciousness and eventual rise in the ranks of the CP-USA can be directly attributed to his family's active participation in the labor struggles of Minnesota's iron ranges during the early twentieth century.[18]

South Slavic ethnicity would also play a major role in Range and Minnesota politics in the coming years. Strongly associated with Minnesota's DFL was the state's first (and only) governor with South Slavic heritage, Rudolf Perpich. "Rudy" Perpich, born in Hibbing and the son of Croatian immigrants, reportedly did not learn English until age fourteen and served terms as Minnesota's thirty-fourth and thirty-sixth governor.[19] The children of South Slavic immigrants did not just rise in state politics. Minnesota's Eighth Congressional District, which included the iron ranges and Duluth, was represented by the descendants of Slovenian immigrants, both from Chisholm, for more than sixty years.

John Blatnik, who represented the Eighth District from 1947 to 1974, and James Oberstar, who served the same district from 1975 until 2011, were dedicated friends to organized labor and drew almost unflinching support from the USW. Oberstar's father was even reportedly the first card-carrying member of the Steelworkers on the iron ranges.[20] Likewise, Minnesota's first female senator to the U.S. Congress, DFLer Amy Klobuchar, has Slovenian heritage on her father's side. Jim Klobuchar's grandparents were from Slovenia and his father was a mine worker from Ely.[21]

Early labor struggles of the twentieth century made a meaningful impact on the people and places of the iron ranges, and the impression of that working-class identity endures. To this day, northern Minnesota is a stubbornly consistent bastion of union sentiment in a nation that is increasingly dispassionate regarding organized labor and this powerful connection with working-class identity and culture can be traced back to the struggles of the 1916 strike. Virginia's USWs' Local No. 1938 is an exceptional example. Representing Virginia's iron ore workers since the Depression, the USW local remains an active participant in the struggle for economic justice. And, only blocks away from USW Local No. 1938's headquarters is the former Virginia Socialist Opera House, which was, up until the 2010s, home to another union, the Carpenters and Joiners Local 606, and a cooperative credit union. Unbeknownst to many is the central role this grand edifice played in one of the region's most significant confrontations between labor and management. The building is nothing less than a national landmark and deserves to be treated as such. The opera house's grand interior was gutted in the late 1950s, however. A retrospective article printed in the *Mesabi Daily News* on January 30, 1958, recounted the transformation of the onetime cultural center for the voices of discontent during the 1916 strike:

> Remodeling Plans for Old Opera House Will Leave Only Memories of Range's Colorful Cultural Center of Yesterday. The city's Socialist Opera House [is] being renovated as a retail and office building by its owners, the local chapter of the United Brotherhood of Carpenters and Joiners, which had bought it in 1955 for $125,000 . . . the gilt has worn away and once-gleaming white boxes and balcony sections are dis-

colored . . . up in the rafters, above the stage rigging, is lashed a wooden boat which once sailed a water-tank in the stage floor.

The legacy of Virginia's Socialist Opera House illustrates that labor history has a story of its own on Minnesota's iron ranges. As Wobbly folk musician, historian, poet, and raconteur U. Utah Phillips termed it, "the Long Memory is the most radical idea in America. It is the loss of long memory which deprives our people of the connective flow of thoughts and events that clarifies our vision, not of where we're going, but where we want to go."[22] In essence, long memory restores events like the 1916 strike to public consciousness so that we can collect the stories and preserve the memories of those who struggled and sacrificed to make our lives better today. Although recollections of the 1916 strike and the repression, arrests, and deaths of striking workers are a distant memory, the ranges' working-class ethos has maintained a strong connection with those who fought and died during this epic clash between labor and management. The memorialization of the 1916 strike through regional labor activism is essentially a localized endeavor, however. The struggle to give a more comprehensive voice to workers, strikers, organizers, and their families is ongoing.

The fight for dignity, justice, and solidarity that occurred in 1916 is essentially the same struggle we encounter today. The parties involved may have changed, but the struggle remains the same. Immigrant rights, workplace democracy, social justice, and the rehumanization of workers in a global, transnationally situated economy concern contemporary populations in the same way they did mine workers in 1916 Minnesota. As George Santayana's well-worn expression might echo, the more we as a society believe that we have escaped the injustices of our past, the more we are condemned to repeat those transgressions in the future.[23] This book is a recollection of such an exploitative past, but holds promise that the lessons and struggles of such a past can help to empower those working today to positively change and shape the future into a more democratic and equitable landscape.

ACKNOWLEDGMENTS

THIS BOOK HAS A LONG ARC. I STARTED THE RESEARCH FOR THIS BOOK as an undergraduate at Minnesota State University–Mankato in 2003. My passion for telling the stories of the working-class heroes who came before us began there, and I would like to thank Drs. Erwin "Ernie" Grieshaber and Charles Piehl for their guidance and encouragement. I went to Mankato a bit bereft and barren (ideologically), but left with a clear path of where I had been and where I wanted to go. It was truly a gift.

Along the way, and after Mankato, there have been many people, professors, and colleagues to thank, and I do so now, but I would also like to mention a few specifically. The book before you comes out of my dissertation work at Michigan Tech and the hard work of my committee is greatly appreciated. I thank Dr. Carol MacLennan, who has been essential in my development as a scholar and person. I would also like to thank and sing the praises of Drs. Robert Johnson and Beth Flynn (no relation to Elizabeth Gurley Flynn, as I found out when I applied to what became Tech's Rhetoric, Theory, and Culture program). Bob and Beth were incredible mentors and teachers for what was, in many ways, a new world of study. I will always appreciate Bob's keen critical perspectives, passion for helping students, and distaste for "The Man." A huge thank you to Beth's intense eye for editing; grammar was never my "thing" and Beth wielded an incredible proofer's pen. I also thank Dr. Fred Quivik for his guidance and additions to my PhD dissertation.

I thank a great colleague and friend, Dr. Saku Pinta. His knowledge and passion for Wobbly history is unparalleled on either side of the border.

Archives are so important to the work historians do, and I want to stress my appreciation and admiration for those who care for and preserve our collective past. Research for this book encompassed an international sweep that included facilities in Minnesota, Canada, and Finland. I thank the Minnesota Discovery Center's archivist Christopher Welter and curator Allyse Freeman. Similarly, I would like to thank University of Minnesota–Duluth's Northeast Minnesota Historical Center Collections and especially archivist Patricia Maus and archives assistant Mags David, as well as the folks who assisted me at the University of Minnesota's Immigration History Research Center, with special thanks to Daniel Necas. Many thanks also go to the numerous folks who retrieved and copied materials for me at the Minnesota Historical Society. Finally, a great thank you to the wonderful people at the Siirtolaisuusinstituutti (Institute of Migration) in Turku, Finland, and especially then director Dr. Ismo Soderling, Dr. Auvo Kostiainen, and archivist Jarno Heinilä, wonderful hosts and ambassadors for the institute, Turku, and Finland. I also thank Dr. Aaron Goings, Fulbright Scholar, and his charming wife, Jess Sheinbaum, for hosting my wife Brooke and me while on our Finnish odyssey.

I thank the University of Minnesota Press for its interest in my work and Minnesota's iron ranges. I especially thank Kristian Tvedten: I am not sure if there is a better or more conscientious editor out there. I enjoyed working with him immensely and have appreciated every edit, image, and thought that he has put into the manuscript. Special thanks as well to editor extraordinaire David Thorstad. The staff at the University of Minnesota Press is phenomenal, from the advisory staff and editors to the marketing department to the design team. Thank you to all who were involved in the process of bringing this manuscript from words on my laptop to a cohesive book. I also thank the manuscript's readers, Drs. Peter Rachleff and Richard Hudelson. Their comments and suggestions molded a semifocused document into a coherent chronicle of the 1916 strike. I am forever appreciative of their critical eyes.

Above all, I thank my family. I dedicated this book to my Grandma Viena and explain why in the Preface, but I thank her here for being an inspiration on many levels—longevity being just one. I have always been proud of being the son and grandson of "Rangers," and this perspective has had a profound effect on my worldview and scholarship. Speaking of being a son, I would like to thank my parents, Art "Urho" and Edie Kaunonen. I would wager a good sum of money that when I was in my midtwenties they never thought I would someday have a PhD (and probably deservedly so), but they stuck by me through many moves and nonsensical situations. Their support has been way above the call of duty for parents, and I have appreciated every instance of their encouragement and patience.

My children are the best. Every time I look in their eyes or hear their voices, my faith in humanity is restored. A great philosopher—I believe it was Whitney Houston—once said: "I believe the children are our future, teach them well and let them lead the way." Whitney was right. If you have kids, give them a hug. Last, but of course not least, I thank "Ashley" Brooke Boulton. Every once in a while, a transcending force peeks into a person's life: never ignore it. Her quiet and wonderfully quirky yet immensely strong character has made me an infinitely better human being. And, after all, isn't that what it's all about—just humans being?

NOTES

Preface

1. Thompson, *The Essential E. P. Thompson*, 481–89.

Introduction

1. United Nations, "The Universal Declaration of Human Rights."
2. Byrkit, "The Bisbee Deportation" and "The Bisbee Deportation of 1917."
3. United Food and Commercial Workers Union 324, "Frank Little: A Murder in Butte," and Stead, "Introduction."
4. Haynes, "Revolt of the 'Timber Beasts,'" 299. Thanks to Dr. Saku Pinta for bringing this quotation to my attention.

1. A Place Hard as Iron

1. Lamppa, *Minnesota's Iron Country*.
2. Ibid.
3. Cronon, *Nature's Metropolis*, 8.
4. Bullard, "Personal Correspondence," 204.
5. Ibid.
6. Ibid.
7. M. S. Hawkings to Mr. Pentecost Mitchell, "Living Conditions 2, 1908–1919." Most often the classification of unskilled laborer included immigrants.
8. Swanson, "Organizing the Steel Workers Union on the Range."
9. John C. Greenway to William J. Olcott, "Business Correspondence."
10. Ibid.
11. Ibid.
12. Ibid.
13. Oliver Iron Mining Company to W. J. Trescott, surface foreman, "Business Correspondence, Canisteo Mine, 1908–1918," and Dr. N. D. Kean to Dr. W. H. Magie, "Business Correspondence, Canisteo Mine, 1908–1918."
14. M. S. Hawkings to Mr. Pentecost Mitchell, general manager OIMC, Duluth, n.d., "Living Conditions 2, 1908-1919."

15. Ibid.

16. City of Eveleth, Municipal Court Records Ledger, "Register of Criminal Actions," September–October 1904 to May–June 1906.

17. Ibid.

18. Ibid. and City of Eveleth, Municipal Records Ledger, "Register of All Persons Committed to the Lockup at Eveleth, Minn., 1909–1915."

19. Oliver Iron Mining Company, "Business Correspondences."

20. Pentecost Mitchell to R. R. Trezona, "Business Correspondence."

21. The term "Austrian" here refers to people coming from the Austro-Hungarian Empire. The use of "Austrian" in this time period referred to several ethnicities administered by the Austrian Empire, including peoples from present-day Hungary, Croatia, the Czech Republic, Montenegro, Romania, Poland, Slovenia, Serbia, Ukraine, Slovakia, and a number of other ethnic minorities. The "Austrians" on the Mesabi Range were primarily Croatian, Slovenian, and Montenegrin. This term and a history of immigrants from the Austro-Hungarian Empire will be covered in depth in chapter 4.

22. J. H. Hearding to Pentecost Mitchell, "Business Correspondence," May 27, 1908.

23. J. H. Hearding to Pentecost Mitchell, "Business Correspondence," June 3, 1908.

24. J. H. Hearding to Pentecost Mitchell, "Business Correspondence," May 20, 1908.

25. Ibid.

26. Oliver Iron Mining Company to Various Breweries, and Various Breweries to Oliver Iron Mining Companies, "Business Correspondences."

27. R. R. Trezona to Pentecost Mitchell, "Business Correspondence," August 11, 1909.

28. Superintendent of Eveleth Schools to Thos. F. Cole, "Personal Correspondence," January 30, 1908.

29. In a somewhat small boomtown industrial city, it seems unlikely that a town father such as the school's superintendent would not know of the house of ill fame in question.

30. Ponikvar, "Oral History."

31. Bullard, "Personal Correspondence," 204.

32. Dragosich Family Papers; Klemencic, "Slovene Settlements in the United States of America"; and for a discussion of Finnish immigrant boarding houses, see Kaunonen, *Finns in Michigan*, and Kaunonen, *Challenge Accepted*.

33. Torma, "Oral History Interview," 26–27.

34. Ibid., 27.

2. The Seasonal Struggle

1. Acuña, *Corridors of Migration*, xiii.

2. Swanson, "Organizing the Steel Workers Union on the Range."

3. Ibid.

4. Ibid. See also Heckman, "The Agricultural Workers Organization"; and Welter, "IWW Surveillance Photos."

5. Unknown songwriter, "The Mysteries of a Hobo's Life," in *I.W.W. Songs to Fan the Flames of Discontent*.

6. Swanson, "Organizing the Steel Workers Union on the Range." Subsequent references are given in the text.

7. E. M. to G. C. S., "Labor: Working Conditions, 1885–1928."

8. Lamppa, *Minnesota's Iron Country*, 193–95.

9. As the Mesabi open-pit mines went deeper, the soft ore became more consolidated so that it was difficult to scoop the ore out with steam shovels. Gopher holers would use pickaxes and shovels to tunnel into the side of an ore deposit, and then used a blasting agent to loosen the material so that it was easier to scoop. Ibid., 184.

10. John C. Greenway to Oliver Mining Company Labor Agent, "Business Correspondence," June 8, 1908.

11. Wenzell, *Cases Argued and Determined in the Supreme Court of Minnesota*, 130–33.

12. John C. Greenway to Oliver Mining Company Labor Agent, "Business Correspondence," March 11, 1907.

13. Ibid.

14. John C. Greenway to George W. Morgan, "Business Correspondence," May 22, 1916.

15. Joseph Mantel to W. H. Johnston, "Personal Correspondence," March 18, 1912.

16. Ibid.

17. Ibid.

18. W. H. Johnston to Oliver Iron Mining Company, "Business Correspondence," March 25, 1912.

19. W. H. Johnston to Oliver Iron Mining Company, "Business Correspondence," March 19, 1912.

20. Swanson, "Sam Swanson Radio Message on Labor Movement in Ely, Minnesota, and Iron Range."

21. Ibid.

22. *Vermilion Iron Journal*, June 23, 1892.

23. John Penguilly to T. F. Cole, "Materials Relating to the Oliver Iron Mining Company," January 20, 1903.

24. Pinola, "Labor and Politics on the Iron Range of Northern Minnesota," 17–20.

25. Pentecost Mitchell to T. F. Cole, "Business Communication," April 15, 1905.

26. Pinola, "Labor and Politics on the Iron Range and Northern Minnesota," 17–20.

27. *Wage Slave*, April 24, 1908.

28. Industrial Workers of the World, *An Economic Interpretation of the Job.*

29. Pinta, "Interview on IWW History."

30. Ibid., and Trautmann, *Why Strikes Are Lost and How to Win.*

31. Pinta, "Interview on IWW History."

32. Karni, "The Founding of the Finnish Socialist Federation," 74, and Pinola, "Labor and Politics on the Iron Range of Northern Minnesota," 20.

33. Pinola, "Labor and Politics on the Iron Range of Northern Minnesota," 20.

34. Ibid., 21–23. See also Karni, "The Founding of the Finnish Socialist Federation," 65–70; *Mesaba Ore*, July 23, 1907; and Western Federation of Miners, *Official Proceedings of the Sixteenth Annual Convention, 1908.*

35. P. F. Chamoream to Charles Trezona, "Business Correspondence," July 24, 1907.

36. Charles Trezona to P. F. Chamberlain, "Business Correspondence," July 24, 1907.

37. Ibid.

38. Dunnell, *Revised Laws, Minnesota, 1905*, 1089.

39. *Labor Review*, October 4, 1907, 8–14.

40. Myllymäki, "Personal Correspondence," 208.

41. Pinola, "Labor and Politics on the Iron Range of Northern Minnesota," 24.

42. Western Federation of Miners, *Official Proceedings of the Sixteenth Annual Convention, 1908*, 257.

43. *Hibbing News Tribune*, "Election Returns 1913."

44. Victor L. Power to J. A. O. Preus, "Government Correspondence," August 1, 1915.

45. Ibid.

46. Power, "Scrapbook."

3. Wobbly Firebrands

1. Dubofsky, *We Shall Be All.*

2. Burgmann, *Revolutionary Industrial Unionism*, 62.

3. Salerno, *Red November, Black November*, 10.

4. Markkanen, "K. A. Suvanto," 7–8.

5. Campbell, "The Cult of Spontaneity," 121.

6. Dubofsky, *We Shall Be All*, 91–93, and Thompson and Murfin, *The I.W.W.*, 6 and 12.

7. Kaunonen, *Finns in Michigan.*

8. Kivisto, "The Decline of the Finnish American Left, 1925–1945," 68.

9. Passi, "Finnish Immigrants and the Radical Response to Industrial America," 12, 121; and Karni, "The Founding of the Finnish Socialist Federation," 65–70.

10. Kostiainen, "The Forging of Finnish-American Communism, 1917–1924," 25, 38, and Pinola, "Labor and Politics on the Iron Range of Northern Minnesota," 25–28.

11. Karni, "The Founding of the Finnish Socialist Federation," 82.

12. Pinola, "Labor and Politics on the Iron Range of Northern Minnesota," 26–28.

13. Passi, "Finnish Immigrants and the Radical Response to Industrial America," 16, and Ollila, "From Socialism to Industrial Unionism," 159.

14. Avrich, *The Modern School Movement.*

15. Ibid., and Altenbaugh, *Education for Struggle.*

16. Altenbaugh, *Education for Struggle,* 99.

17. Ollila, "The Work People's College," 105–6. Subsequent references are given in the text.

18. Kaunonen, *Challenge Accepted,* 189.

19. Kostiainen, "Tie Vapauteen," 230.

20. Rein, *Nuoriso, Oppi ja Tyo (Youth, Learning and Labor),* 118.

21. Ibid., 119.

22. Ibid., 123.

23. Industrial Workers of the World, *What Is the I.W.W. Preamble?,* 11–12.

24. Karni, *For the Common Good,* 12–13.

25. Torma, "Oral History Interview," 26–27. Subsequent references are given in the text.

26. Hannula, *An Album of Finnish Halls,* 24.

27. Ibid.

28. Karni and Olilla, *For the Common Good,* 82. See also Hoglund, *Finnish Immigrants in America, 1880–1920,* 98.

29. Kostiainen, "The Forging of Finnish-American Communism, 1917–1924," 36–37.

30. Roe, "Virginia, Minnesota's Socialist Opera," 38–39.

31. Ibid., 38, 41.

32. Ibid., 38–40.

33. Nelson-Walkama, "Oral History Interview," July 20, 2006.

34. *Wage Slave,* May 22, 1908.

35. *Työmies,* December 1910.

36. Industrial Workers of the World, *I.W.W. Songs,* 38.

4. From Strikebreakers to Solidarity

1. Deaux, "Social Identity."

2. Ibid. Reference to the IWW added by the author to highlight connections between Deaux's theory and IWW's history of organizing immigrant workers.

3. For a discussion of the intersection between identity and politics, see Gerring, "Ideology," 957.

4. Parker, "Five Theses on Identity Politics," 53.

5. Puotinen, "Early Labor Organizations in the Copper Country," 136–40.

6. Karni, "The Founding of the Finnish Socialist Federation, 65–74; Pinola, "Labor and Politics on the Iron Range of Northern Minnesota," 20–23; and *Mesaba Ore* (Hibbing, Minnesota), July 23, 1907.

7. Table statistics from data compiled and tabulated from collected resources in Richard H. Hudelson Labor History Research Collection S6143, "1907 Strike Folder," Northeast Minnesota Historical Center Collections, University of Minnesota–Duluth.

8. Tracy, "William E. Tracy's Report," 294–95. Subsequent references are given in the text.

9. Official confirmation of the WFM's joining with the AFL can be found in a number of AFL convention proceedings. One such passage in a 1910 convention resolution read, "Whereas, the Western Federation of Miners was granted a charter by the American Federation of Labor in the year 1910, recognizing jurisdiction over men employed in mines, mills, and smelters . . ." (American Federation of Labor, *Report of the Proceedings of the Thirty-sixth Annual Convention of the American Federation of Labor*, 331).

10. Tracy, "William E. Tracy's Report," 299–300 and 304.

11. Kaunonen and Goings, *Community in Conflict*, 144–46.

12. Ibid.

13. Charles Trezona to Thomas F. Cole, "Business Correspondence," July 24, 1907.

14. Karni, "The Founding of the Finnish Socialist Federation," 78. In large numbers, Finnish immigrant mine workers had been jettisoned from the laboring masses at the Oliver's Minnesota mines. Many moved to and founded, or occupied, homesteads in outlying agricultural hamlets such as Toivola, Cherry, Embarrass, and Floodwood. Interestingly, often many of these small rural hamlets composed of Finnish immigrants had three very distinctive, holdover features from experiences with industrial exploitation: a consumers' cooperative store, a social hall, and an auxiliary IWW local. Because the blacklisted mine workers had moved to subsistence agriculture to make a living and were now nonindustrial toilers of the land, they were no longer able to join the IWW. Thus, these former Wobblies had to organize locals as "auxiliaries" and not as industrial union locals. The small, rural IWW auxiliaries and consumers' coops that sprang up in these countryside locations would prove essential to the 1916 strike as they provided foodstuffs and organizational talent during the labor upheaval. For a discussion of Finnish immigrants on the industrial periphery, see Kaunonen, *Finns in Michigan*. Evidence of IWW agricultural auxiliaries can be found in various editions of the Finnish immigrant-produced IWW newspapers *Sosialisti* and *Industrialisti*.

15. Statistics and percentages come from data compiled and tabulated from the James S. Steel Collection, "Nationalities, Statistics, 1909," Minnesota Historical Society, St. Paul, Box 1, Folder 150.

16. "The Austrian" to Charles Trezona, "Worker's Correspondence," January 8, 1908.

17. Kralj, "Balkan Minds," 2–5.

18. Stanoyevich, "The Jugoslavs," 7.

19. Stipanovich, "In Unity Is Strength," 77.

20. Cizmic, *History of the Croatian Fraternal Union of America, 1894–1994*, 114; and Bach and Zubrinic, "Croatian Fraternal Union Founded in 1894 in the USA, Celebrates 120 Years of Existence";

21. Cizmic, *History of the Croatian Fraternal Union of America, 1894–1994*, 121–23.

22. Stipanovich, "In Unity Is Strength," 188–89.

23. Ibid., 160. In regard to Finnish immigrants and their numbers in the SPA: in 1911 there were 9,139 Finns in the SPA and that number peaked at 12,651 in 1913, but after the schism between IWW-linked Finns and SPA-inclined Finns fractured membership, the number of Finns in the SPA had dipped to 8,859 in 1915, but jumped back over 10,000 in 1916. In second place as far as SPA immigrant membership were German immigrants with 5,150 in 1916, followed by "Jews" with 3,048 in the same year. South Slavic members, then, were the fourth-largest language federation in the SPA with 2,112 members in 1916. A detailed membership by year indicates that in 1911 there were 982 members; in 1912, 1,328 members; in 1913, 1,778 members; in 1914, 1,864 members; and by 1916, 2,112 members.

24. Lamppa, *Minnesota's Iron Country*, 209–10.

25. *Superior Telegram*, August 1, 1913.

26. *Superior Telegram*, August 5, 1913.

27. *Superior Telegram*, August 12, 1913.

28. *Superior Telegram*, August 11 and 12, 1913; *International Socialist Review*, "Boats Tied Up," September 1913, 184.

29. In his work, Joseph Stipanovich, a South Slavic immigration historian, argued that Slovenian immigrant socialists "reacted negatively to the anarcho-syndicalist tendencies of the IWW. They and the Serbs preferred to support the more conservative unions such as the United Mine Workers of America and, after its withdrawal from the IWW, the Western Federation of Miners" (Stipanovich, "In Unity Is Strength," 16–17). I would argue that this was not the case, at least for a certain period of time on the Minnesota Iron Range, because after the initial suspicion of IWW organizers began to wane with repeated overtures prior to the 1916 strike, South Slavic strikers became some of the most impassioned and loyal members of organized labor in the Lake Superior basin.

30. Ponikvar, "Oral History."

31. Ibid. Ponikvar stated in the interview that while Chisholm was ethnically nonsegregated, Eveleth's nationalities were more likely to live in distinct, ethnic neighborhoods.

32. *Virginia Daily Enterprise*, June 17, 1916.

33. *Strikers' News*, September 8, 1916. According to the IWW's current online dictionary, www.iww.org/history/dictionary, a scissorbill is "a worker who is not class conscious; a homeguard who is filled with bourgeois ethics and ideals."

34. Ibid., n.d.

35. Ibid.

36. Ibid., August 4, 1916. The other two women arrested were Mrs. Staka

Rajecich and Mrs. Rosna Romau, who were from the Nelson location. These two women, along with their children, were arrested for (according to the *Strikers' News*) "gathering to talk over the action of the mining company refusing to let the strikers get water from the only good well in the neighborhood, which happened to be on Company property."

37. Ibid., n.d.

38. Ibid.

5. The Rhetoric of Revolution

1. Pilacinski, "'We've Been Robbed Long Enough. It's Time to Strike.'"

2. Pinola, "Labor and Politics on the Iron Range of Northern Minnesota," 28–29.

3. Industrial Workers of the World, *The Startling Story of the Minnesota Miners' Strike on the Mesaba Range 1916*, 10–11.

4. State of Minnesota, Department of Labor and Industries, *Fifteenth Biennial Report*, 168, and Lamppa, *Minnesota's Iron Country*, 210–15.

5. Kostiainen, "The Forging of Finnish-American Communism, 1917–1924," 36–37.

6. *Strikers' News*, August 4, 1916.

7. State of Minnesota, Department of Labor and Industries, *Fifteenth Biennial Report*, 168–69.

8. *Strikers' News*, various issues.

9. State of Minnesota, Department of Labor and Industries, *Fifteenth Biennial Report*, 168.

10. *Strikers' News*, August 18, 1916.

11. Ibid.

12. Power, "Scrapbook: Newspaper Clippings."

13. Ibid.

14. Ibid.

15. James D. Ireland to M. A. Hanna & Co., "Strike Situation Correspondence," June 23, 1916.

16. *Duluth Herald*, July 1, 1916.

17. James D. Ireland to M. A. Hanna & Co., "Strike Situation Correspondence," June 23, 1916.

18. Ibid.

19. Ibid.

20. James D. Ireland to Virginia Ore Mining Company, "Personal Correspondence," June 28, 1916.

21. Ibid.

22. *Duluth News-Tribune*, June 6, 1916.

23. *Duluth Herald*, August 16, 1916.

24. Power, "Standard Diary, 1916."

25. Ibid.

26. Ibid.

27. James D. Ireland to M. A. Hanna & Co., "Strike Situation Correspondence," June 23, 1916.

28. James D. Ireland to Howard Hanna Jr., "Personal Correspondence," June 15, 1916.

29. Ibid.

30. Ibid.

31. Ibid.

32. James D. Ireland to M. A. Hanna & Co., "Strike Situation Correspondence," June 16, 1916.

33. Ibid.

34. *Duluth News-Tribune*, June 16, 1916.

35. James D. Ireland to M. A. Hanna & Co., "Strike Situation Correspondence," June 17, 1916.

36. Ibid.

37. Howard M. Hanna Jr. to James D. Ireland, "Personal Correspondence," June 19, 1916.

38. James D. Ireland to M. A. Hanna & Co., "Strike Situation Correspondence," June 24, 1916.

39. *Duluth News-Tribune*, July 1, 1916.

40. James D. Ireland to M. A. Hanna & Co., "Personal Correspondence," July 1, 1916.

41. James D. Ireland to M. A. Hanna & Co., "Strike Situation Correspondence," June 17, 1916.

42. Ibid., June 24, 1916.

43. Ibid., July 1, 1916; and James D. Ireland to M. A. Hanna & Co., "Business Correspondence," July 3, 1916.

44. James D. Ireland to Virginia Ore Mining Company, "Personal Correspondence," June 28, 1916.

6. Flash Point

1. *Strikers' News*, n.d.

2. James D. Ireland to M. A. Hanna & Co., "Strike Situation Correspondence," June 23, 1916.

3. James D. Ireland to M. A. Hanna & Co., "Handwritten Personal Correspondence," n.d.

4. *Strikers' News*, n.d.

5. *Duluth News-Tribune*, July 1, 1916.

6. James D. Ireland to Virginia Ore Mining Company, "Personal Correspondence," June 28, 1916.

7. James D. Ireland to M. A. Hanna & Co., "Personal Correspondence," July 1, 1916.

8. James D. Ireland to Virginia Ore Mining Company, "Personal Correspondence," June 28, 1916.

9. Ibid.

10. *Duluth News-Tribune*, July 1, 1916.

11. Victor L. Power, "Personal Journal Entry," June 30, 1916.

12. James D. Ireland to M. A. Hanna & Co., "Personal Correspondence," June 30, 1916. As the letter is handwritten, some of the forenames and surnames may not be accurately transcribed from the letter.

13. James D. Ireland to M. A. Hanna & Co., "Strike Situation Correspondence," July 1, 1916.

14. James D. Ireland to M. A. Hanna & Co., "Western Union Telegram," July 1, 1916.

15. James D. Ireland to M. A. Hanna & Co., "Strike Situation Correspondence," July 1, 1916.

16. *Duluth News-Tribune*, July 1, 1916.

17. James D. Ireland to M. A. Hanna & Co., "Personal Correspondence," June 30, 1916.

18. Ibid.

19. Ibid.

20. James D. Ireland to M. A. Hanna & Co., "Personal Correspondence," July 1, 1916.

21. This surname is spelled Mesomovich in the *International Socialist Review*, but the name is also written as Masenovich or Masonovich in some publications. This work will use the most commonly used spelling, Mosonovich.

22. Christensen, "Invading Miner's Homes," 161–62.

23. Ibid., 162.

24. Ibid.

25. Ibid., and Lamppa, *Minnesota's Iron Country*, 213–14.

26. West, "The Mesaba Strike," 160.

27. Christensen, "Invading Miner's Homes," 162.

28. Carlo Tresca Papers, "Autobiography," 1879–1943, 238. Subsequent references are given in the text.

29. West, "The Mesaba Strike," 161.

30. Carlo Tresca Papers, 233–35.

31. Ibid., 235.

32. Ibid., 235–36.

33. Ibid., 237. Of note, in his autobiography, Tresca recalled the story he heard of the incident while on the train: "four deputy sheriffs had gone to the house of a striker by the name of Filip Masonovich with a warrant for the arrest of one of the boarders. The men of the law were very rough and they beat up Filip's wife. There were three Montenegrin workers boarding in the house. The fellows were former soldiers who had participated in many a war in the Balkans. They could not allow the deputy sheriffs to continue their dastardly acts. So they dashed against the

four deputy sheriffs, took away their guns, killed one and wounded another. It was a real battle between deputy sheriffs and strikers, and they were all arrested." Tresca's account, written years after the fact and included in early drafts of his autobiography, differed from the account of Melitza Mosonovich, and other strikers' publications. Tresca was seeming to imply that the residents of the Mosonovich home were protecting themselves and got the upper hand on the sheriffs in the fracas, shooting them to save their own lives. He also mistakenly mentions that only one deputy died, and another deputy was wounded, leaving out the fact that while one deputy, Myron, did die, the other "deputy" who was shot was in fact John Ladvalla, a passerby sympathetic to the strike.

34. Christensen, "Invading Miners' Homes," 162.

35. Ibid.

36. Industrial Workers of the World, *The Startling Story of the Minnesota Miners' Strike on the Mesaba Range 1916*, 15.

37. Quoted in Karni, "Elizabeth Gurley Flynn and the Mesabi Strike of 1916," 5.

38. Pernicone, *Carlo Tresca*, 91.

39. Mary Heaton Vorse as quoted in Lammpa, *Minnesota's Iron Country*, 215.

40. Ibid.

41. Industrial Workers of the World, *The Startling Story of the Minnesota Miners' Strike on the Mesaba Range 1916*, 1–2.

42. Victor L. Power Papers, "Scrapbook: Newspaper Clippings," vol. 1.

43. Ibid.

44. Ibid.

45. Ibid.

46. Ibid.

47. Victor L. Power Papers, "Personal Journal Entries."

48. Ibid.

49. *Duluth News-Tribune*, August 2, 1916.

50. James D. Ireland to Virginia Ore Mining Company, "Typed Personal Correspondence," June 28, 1916.

51. *Strikers' News*, August 18, 1916.

52. Ibid., September 1, 1916.

53. Ibid., September 22, 1916.

54. Ibid.

55. Pernicone, *Carlo Tresca*, 91–93. A more substantial discussion of the Tresca–IWW split is contained in this work.

56. Pinola, "Labor and Politics on the Iron Range of Northern Minnesota," 37.

57. "Doings of the Month," *International Socialist Review* (August 1916): 71–72.

58. *Duluth News-Tribune*, September 18, 1916.

Conclusion

1. "Emil" to John R. Meining, "Spy Report," June 19, 1917.

2. Haynes, "Revolt of the 'Timber Beasts,'" 163–66.

3. Ibid.

4. "IWW Yearbook 1917."

5. Ascher and Wolf, "Current Legislation," 233. Idaho was the first state to pass similar criminal syndicalist legislation.

6. *Bemidji Daily Pioneer*, July 26, 1917; and "IWW Yearbook 1917."

7. *Bemidji Daily Pioneer*, July 26, 1917.

8. "IWW Yearbook 1917" and "Criminal Syndicalism," 234–35.

9. Ascher and Wolf, "Current Legislation," 232–35.

10. Leavenworth Prisoners to President Woodrow Wilson, "Personal Communication," March 9, 1919, Elizabeth Gurley Flynn Papers.

11. Elizabeth Gurley Flynn, Secretary of the Workers' Defense Fund, "Letter to Comrades," March 25, 1919, Elizabeth Gurley Flynn Papers.

12. Caroline A. Lowe to Elizabeth Gurley Flynn, "Organizational Communication Letter," March 20, 1919, Elizabeth Gurley Flynn Papers.

13. Elizabeth Gurley Flynn, Secretary of the Workers' Defense Fund, "Letter to Comrades," March 25, 1919.

14. Brunfelt, "Political Culture in Microcosm."

15. United Steel Workers, "Our History."

16. Swanson, "Sam Swanson Radio Message on Labor Movement in Ely, Minnesota, and Iron Range."

17. Brunfelt, "Political Culture in Microcosm," 4.

18. Kaunonen, "Arvo Halberg/Gus Hall."

19. Aamodt, "Perpich, Rudy (1928–1995)."

20. "Blatnik, John Anton"; "Oberstar, James Louis"; and "Ore Boat Renamed after Son of Iron Ore Miner."

21. "U.S. Senator for Minnesota Amy Klobuchar"; and "Amy Klobuchar Ancestry."

22. Phillips, "The Long Memory"

23. Santayana, *The Life of Reason*, 172.

BIBLIOGRAPHY

Periodicals
Ahjo (Duluth, Minnesota)
Bemidji (Minnesota) *Daily Pioneer*
Duluth (Minnesota) *Herald*
Duluth (Minnesota) *News-Tribune*
Hibbing (Minnesota) *Daily Tribune*
Hibbing (Minnesota) *News Tribune*
Industrialisti (Duluth, Minnesota)
Industrial Worker (Spokane, Washington)
International Socialist Review (Chicago)
Labor Review (Minneapolis)
Labor World (Duluth, Minnesota)
Labour/Le Travail (Edmonton, Alberta, Canada)
Mesaba Ore (Hibbing, Minnesota)
Mesabi Daily News (Virginia, Minnesota)
Solidarity (Cleveland, Ohio)
Sosialisti (Duluth, Minnesota)
Star Tribune (Minneapolis)
Strikers' News (Virginia, Minnesota)
Superior (Wisconsin) *Telegram*
The Bemidji (Minnesota) *Daily Pioneer*
Tie Vapauteen (Duluth, Minnesota)
Työmies (Superior, Wisconsin)
Vermilion Iron Journal (Tower, Minnesota)
Virginia (Minnesota) *Daily Enterprise*
Wage Slave (Hancock, Michigan)

Aamodt, Britt. "Perpich, Rudy (1928–1995)." In *MNOpedia*. Accessed at http://www.mnopedia.org/structure/socialist-opera-house-virginia, December 1, 2015.

Acuña, Rodolfo F. *Corridors of Migration: The Odyssey of Mexican Laborers, 1600–1933.* Tucson: University of Arizona Press, 2008.

Alanen, Arnold. "Considering the Ordinary: Vernacular Landscapes in Small Towns and Rural Areas." In *Preserving Cultural Landscapes in America,* ed. Arnold R. Alanen and Robert Z. Melnick, 112–42. Baltimore: Johns Hopkins University Press, 2000.

———. "Early Labor Strife on Minnesota's Mining Frontier, 1882–1906." *Minnesota History* 52:7 (fall 1991): 246–63. St. Paul: Minnesota Historical Society Press.

———. *Morgan Park: Duluth, U.S. Steel, and the Forging of a Company Town.* Minneapolis: University of Minnesota Press, 2007.

Allard, Andrea C. "A War of Words: The *Mesaba Ore* and *Hibbing News* Take on the 'Big Fellows.'" *Minnesota History* (fall 2016): 101–10. St. Paul: Minnesota Historical Society Press.

Altenbaugh, Richard J. *Education for Struggle: The American Labor Colleges of the 1920s and 1930s.* Philadelphia: Temple University Press, 1990.

American Federation of Labor. *Report of the Proceedings of the Thirty-sixth Annual Convention of the American Federation of Labor.* Washington, D.C.: Law Reporter Printing Company, 1916.

"Amy Klobuchar Ancestry." Accessed at http://freepages.genealogy.rootsweb .ancestry.com/~battle/senators/klobuchar.htm, December 1, 2015.

Aristotle. *Rhetoric—Books I-III.* Trans. W. Rhys Roberts. Accessed at http:// classics.mit.edu/Aristotle/rhetoric.html, November 1, 2014.

Ascher, Charles S., and James M. Wolf. "Current Legislation." *Columbia Law Review* 20:2 (1920). New York: Columbia Law Review Association.

"Austrian, The," to Charles Trezona. "Worker's Correspondence," January 8, 1908. Oliver Iron Mining Company Collection, Minnesota Historical Society, St. Paul, Box 2.

Avrich, Paul. *The Modern School Movement: Anarchism and Education in the United States.* Oakland, Calif.: AK Press, 2005.

Bach, Nenad R., and Darko Zubrinic. "Croatian Fraternal Union Founded in 1894 in the USA, Celebrates 120 Years of Existence," March 16, 2014. In *CROWN: Croatian World Network.* Accessed at http://www.croatia.org /crown/articles/10535/1/Croatian-Fraternal-Union-CFU-founded-in -1894-in-the-USA-celebrates-120-years-of-existence.html, January 17, 2016.

Betten, Neil. "Riot, Revolution, Repression in the Iron Range Strike of 1916." *Minnesota History* 41:2 (summer 1968): 82–93. St. Paul: Minnesota Historical Society Press.

———. "Strike on the Mesabi—1907." *Minnesota History* 40:7 (fall 1967): 340–47. St. Paul: Minnesota Historical Society Press.

"The Bisbee Deportation of 1917: A University of Arizona Web Exhibit." Accessed at http://www.library.arizona.edu/exhibits/bisbee/history /overview.html, November 5, 2016.

"Blatnik, John Anton." In *Biographical Directory of the United States Congress.* Accessed at http://bioguide.congress.gov/scripts/biodisplay.pl?index=B000550, December 1, 2015.

Brunfelt, Pamela A. "Political Culture in Microcosm: Minnesota's Iron Range." Accessed at www.minnesotahumanities.org/resources/political%20culture %20in%20microcosm.pdf, November 15, 2014.

Bullard, Polly. "Personal Correspondence." In *Bring Warm Clothes: Letters and Photos from Minnesota's Past,* compiled by Peg Meier. Minneapolis: Star and Tribune Company, 1981.

Burgmann, Verity. *Revolutionary Industrial Unionism: The Industrial Workers of the World in Australia.* Cambridge: Cambridge University Press, 1995.

Burke, Peter. *What Is Cultural History?* 2d ed. Malden, Mass.: Polity Books, 2008.

Butler Brothers and M. A. Hanna Company Records Collection. Iron Range Research Center, Chisholm, Minnesota. Box MSS 158, Folder NE, Lake Superior—General—Labor Lake Superior Situation 1916, 8370.

Byrkit, James. "The Bisbee Deportation." In *American Labor in the Southwest,* ed. James C. Foster, 149–70. Tucson: University of Arizona Press, 1982.

Campbell, J. Peter. "The Cult of Spontaneity: Finnish-Canadian Bushworkers and the Industrial Workers of the World in Northern Ontario, 1919–1934." *Labour/Le Travail* 41 (spring 1998): 117–46.

Carlo Tresca Papers. "Autobiography," 1879–1943 (Microfilm). Italian American Collection, Immigration History Research Center, University of Minnesota.

Chamoream, P. F., to Charles Trezona. "Business Correspondence," July 24, 1907. Materials Relating to the Oliver Iron Mining Company, Minnesota Historical Society, St. Paul.

Chaplin, Ralph. "Solidarity Forever." In *I.W.W. Songs to Fan the Flames of Discontent.* Joe Hill Memorial Edition. Cleveland, Ohio: I.W.W. Publishing Bureau, n.d.

Christensen, Otto. "Invading Miners' Homes." *International Socialist Review* 17 (1916). Chicago: Charles H. Kerr Publishing Co.

City of Eveleth. Municipal Court Records Ledger. "Register of Criminal Actions," September–October 1904 to May–June 1906. Iron Range Research Center, Chisholm, Minnesota, Box 16.

———. Municipal Records Ledger. "Register of All Persons Committed to the Lockup at Eveleth, Minn., 1909–1915." Iron Range Research Center, Chisholm, Minnesota, Box 16.

Cizmic, Ivan. *History of the Croatian Fraternal Union of America, 1894–1994.* Zagreb, Croatia: Golden Marketing, 1994.

Cohen, Michael. "Cartooning Capitalism: Radical Cartooning and the Making of American Popular Radicalism in the Early Twentieth Century." *International Review of Social History* (2007): 35–58. Cambridge: Cambridge University Press.

Cothren, Marion B. "When Strike Breakers Strike: The Demands of the Miners on the Mesaba Range." *The Survey* 36 (April 1916–September 1916). New York: Survey Associates.

"Criminal Syndicalism." *Columbia Law Review* 20:2 (1920). New York: Columbia Law Review Association.

Cronon, William. *Nature's Metropolis: Chicago and the Great West.* Reprint ed. New York: W. W. Norton, 1992.

Dardess, George. "Review, Bringing Comic Books to Class." *College English* 57:2 (February 1995): 214–22. National Council of Teachers of English.

Deaux, Kay. "Social Identity." Accessed at http://www.utexas.edu/courses/stross /ant393b_files/ARTICLES/identity.pdf, November 15, 2014.

DeGenaro, William. *Who Says?: Working-Class Rhetoric, Class Consciousness, and Community.* Pitt Comp Literacy Culture Series. Pittsburgh: University of Pittsburgh Press, 2007.

Detienne, Marcel, and Jean-Pierre Vernant. *Cunning Intelligence in Greek Culture and Society.* Trans. Janet Lloyd. Chicago: University of Chicago Press, 1991.

Dragosich Family Papers. "Croatian Fraternal Union of America." Iron Range Research Center, Chisholm, Minnesota.

Dubofsky, Melvyn. *We Shall Be All: A History of the Industrial Workers of the World.* Champaign: University of Illinois Press, 2000.

Dunnell, Mark B., ed. *Revised Laws, Minnesota, 1905.* St. Paul: State of Minnesota, 1905.

Eleff, Robert M. "The 1916 Minnesota Miners' Strike against U.S. Steel." *Minnesota History* 51:2 (summer 1988): 63–74. St. Paul: Minnesota Historical Society Press.

Elizabeth Gurley Flynn Papers. Italian American Collection. Immigration History Research Center, University of Minnesota, Minneapolis.

E. M. to G. C. S. "Labor: Working Conditions, 1885–1928," February 10, 1885. James S. Steel Collection, Minnesota Historical Society, St. Paul, Box 1, Folder 50.

"Emil" to John R. Meining, "Spy Report," June 19, 1917. Strikes Folder, Richard H. Hudelson Labor History Collection 1880–2006, Northeast Minnesota Historical Collections Center, University of Minnesota Duluth

"Emmi." "IWW:n Marssi" (IWW March). In *Raatajain Lauluja.* Duluth: Workers Socialist Publishing Company, n.d.

Fedo, Michael. *The Lynchings in Duluth.* St. Paul: Minnesota Historical Society Press, 2000.

Feenberg, Andrew. "Democratic Rationalization: Technology, Power, and Freedom." In *Philosophy of Technology: The Technological Condition, An Anthology,* ed. Robert C. Scharff and Val Dusek. Malden, Mass.: Blackwell Publishing, 2003.

———. *Transforming Technology: A Critical Theory Revisited.* Cambridge: Oxford University Press, 2002.

Flynn, Elizabeth Gurley. *Sabotage: The Conscious Withdrawal of the Workers'*

Industrial Efficiency, October 1916. Accessed at http://www.iww.org/culture
/library/sabotage, March 10, 2010.

Foner, Philip S. *History of the Labor Movement in the United States*. Vol. 4, *The
Industrial Workers of the World, 1905–1917*. New York: International Publishers, 1965.

Freire, Paulo. *Pedagogy of the Oppressed*. 30th Anniversary Edition. Trans. Myra
Bergman Ramos. New York: Bloomsbury Academic, 2000.

Gerring, John. "Ideology: A Definitional Analysis." *Political Research Quarterly*
50:4 (1997): 957–94.

Greenway, John C., to George W. Morgan. "Business Correspondence," May 22,
1916. Oliver Iron Mining Company Papers, Correspondence and Miscellaneous Papers, 1901–29, Box 1.

Greenway, John C., to Oliver Mining Company Labor Agent. "Business Correspondence," June 8, 1908. James S. Steel Collection, Minnesota Historical
Society, St. Paul, Box 2, Folder 6.

———. "Business Correspondence," March 11, 1907. James S. Steel Collection,
Minnesota Historical Society, St. Paul, Box 2, Folder 6.

Greenway John C., to William J. Olcott. "Business Correspondence," October 27,
1906. James S. Steel Collection, Minnesota Historical Society, St. Paul, Box 2,
Folder 6.

Hanna, Howard M., Jr., to James D. Ireland, "Personal Correspondence," June 19,
1916. Butler Brothers and M. A. Hanna Company Records Collection, Iron
Range Research Center, Chisholm, Minnesota, Box MSS 158, Folder NE,
Lake Superior—General—Labor Lake Superior Situation 1916, 8370.

Hannula, Reino. *An Album of Finnish Halls: Yesterday and Today*. San Luis
Obispo, Calif.: Finn Heritage, 1991.

Hawkings, M. S., to Mr. Pentecost Mitchell, General Manager OIMC, Duluth,
n.d., "Living Conditions 2, 1908–1919." James S. Steel Collection, Minnesota
Historical Society, St. Paul, Box 1, Folder 140.

Haynes, John E. "Revolt of the 'Timber Beasts': IWW Lumber Strike in Minnesota." In *The North Star State: A Minnesota History Reader*, ed. Anne J. Aby,
285–301. St. Paul: Minnesota Historical Society Press, 2002.

Hearding, J. H., to Pentecost Mitchell. "Business Correspondence," May 20,
1908. James S. Steel Collection, Minnesota Historical Society, St. Paul, Box 1,
Folder 140.

———. "Business Correspondence," June 3, 1908. James S. Steel Collection, Minnesota Historical Society, St. Paul, Box 1, Folder 140.

———. "Business Correspondence," May 27, 1908. James S. Steel Collection,
Minnesota Historical Society, St. Paul, Box 1, Folder 140.

Heckman, Jesse. "The Agricultural Workers Organization." Conference
paper, Kansas City Labor History, University of Missouri—Kansas City,
April 29, 2004. Accessed at http://cas.umkc.edu/labor-ed/documents
/AgrWorkersOrganizationIWW.pdf, September 15, 2016.

Hidy, Ralph W., Muriel E. Hidy, and Roy V. Scott. *The Great Northern Railway: A History*. Cambridge: Harvard Business School Press, 1988. Reprint, Minneapolis: University of Minnesota Press, 2004.

Hill, Joe. "The Good Old Wooden Shoe." In *I.W.W. Songs: To Fan the Flames of Discontent, Joe Hill Memorial Edition*. Cleveland, Ohio: I.W.W. Publishing Bureau, n.d.

Hoglund, A. William. *Finnish Immigrants in America, 1880–1920*. Madison: University of Wisconsin Press, 1960.

Hudelson, Richard, and Carl Ross. *By the Ore Docks: A Working People's History of Duluth*. Minneapolis: University of Minnesota Press, 2006.

Industrial Workers of the World. *An Economic Interpretation of the Job*. Chicago: Department of Education, Agricultural Workers Industrial Union, 1922. Accessed at https://www.marxists.org/history/usa/unions/iww/1922/economic.html, May 1, 2014.

———. "IWW Chronology: 1904–1911." Accessed at www.iww.org, September 2010.

———. *I.W.W. Songs: To Fan the Flames of Discontent, Joe Hill Memorial Edition*. Cleveland, Ohio: I.W.W. Publishing Bureau, n.d.

———. "Solidarity Forever." In *IWW Cultural Icons*. Accessed at http://www.iww.org/history/icons/solidarity_forever, May 1, 2014.

———. *The Startling Story of the Minnesota Miners' Strike on the Mesaba Range 1916*. New York: Minnesota Iron Range Strikers' Defense Committee, 1916.

———. *Teollisuus-Unionismin Opas*. 3d printing. Virginia, Minn.: Quick Print, n.d.

———. *What Is the I.W.W. Preamble? A Dialogue*. 4th printing. Chicago: Department of Education, Agricultural Workers Industrial Union, 1923.

Ireland, James D., to Howard Hanna Jr. "Personal Correspondence," June 15, 1916. Butler Brothers and M. A. Hanna Company Records Collection, Iron Range Research Center, Chisholm, Minnesota, Box MSS 158, Folder NE, Lake Superior—General—Labor Lake Superior Situation 1916, 8370.

Ireland, James D., to M. A. Hanna & Co., "Handwritten Personal Correspondence," n.d. Butler Brothers and M. A. Hanna Company Records Collection, Iron Range Research Center, Chisholm, Minnesota, Box MSS 158, Folder NE, Lake Superior—General—Labor Lake Superior Situation 1916, 8370.

Ireland, James D., to M. A. Hanna & Co. "Strike Situation Correspondence," June 23, 1916. Butler Brothers and M. A. Hanna Company Records Collection, Iron Range Research Center, Chisholm, Minnesota, Box MSS 158, Folder NE, Lake Superior—General—Labor Lake Superior Situation 1916, 8370.

Ireland, James D., to Virginia Ore Mining Company, "Personal Correspondence," June 28, 1916. Butler Brothers and M. A. Hanna Company Records Collection, Iron Range Research Center, Chisholm, Minnesota, Box MSS 158,

Folder NE, Lake Superior—General—Labor Lake Superior Situation 1916, 8370.

"IWW Yearbook 1917." *IWW History Project: Industrial Workers of the World 1905–1935*, 2015. Accessed at http://depts.washington.edu/iww/yearbook1917 .shtml, October 1, 2016.

Johnson, Robert R. *User-Centered Technology: A Rhetorical Theory for Computers and Other Mundane Artifacts*. SUNY Series, Studies in Scientific and Technical Communication. Albany: State University of New York Press, 1998.

Johnston, W. H., to Oliver Iron Mining Company. "Business Correspondence," March 19, 1912. James S. Steel Papers, Minnesota Historical Society, St. Paul, Box 1.

———. "Business Correspondence," March 25, 1912. James S. Steel Papers, Minnesota Historical Society, St. Paul, Box 1.

Karni, Michael. "Elizabeth Gurley Flynn and the Mesabi Strike of 1916." *Range History* 5:4 (1981): 1–6. Chisholm, Minn.: Iron Range Research Center.

———. "The Founding of the Finnish Socialist Federation." In *For the Common Good: Finnish Immigrants and the Radical Response to Industrial America*, ed. Michael G. Karni and Douglas J. Ollila Jr., 65–86. Superior, Wis.: Työmies Society, 1977.

Karni, Michael, and Douglas J. Ollila Jr., eds. *For the Common Good: Finnish Immigrants and the Radical Response to Industrial America*. Superior, Wis.: Työmies Society, 1977.

Kaunonen, Gary. "Arvo Halberg/Gus Hall: The Making of an American Communist." Unpublished senior honors thesis. Minnesota State University-Mankato, 2003.

———. *Challenge Accepted: A Finnish Immigrant Response to Industrial America on Michigan's Copper Country*. East Lansing: Michigan State University Press, 2010.

———. *Finns in Michigan*. Discovering the Peoples of Michigan Series. East Lansing: Michigan State University Press, 2009.

Kaunonen, Gary, and Aaron Goings. *Community in Conflict: A Working-Class History of the 1913–14 Michigan Copper Strike and Italian Hall Tragedy*. East Lansing: Michigan State University Press, 2013.

Kean, Dr. N. D., to Dr. W. H. Magie. "Medical Correspondence, Canisteo Mine, 1908–1918." James S. Steel Collection, Minnesota Historical Society, St. Paul, Box 2, Folder 6.

Kessler-Harris, Alice. *Out to Work: A History of Wage-Earning Women in the United States*. New York: Oxford University Press, 1982.

Kim, Young Yun. "Ideology, Identity, and Intercultural Communication: An Analysis of Differing Academic Conceptions of Cultural Identity." *Journal of Intercultural Communication Research* 36:3 (2007): 237–53.

Kivisto, Peter. "The Decline of the Finnish American Left, 1925–1945." *International*

Migration Review 17:1 (spring 1983). Available at http://www.jstor.org, accessed February 13, 2003.

Klemencic, Matjaz. "Slovene Settlements in the United States of America." Accessed at http://www.theslovenian.com/articles/klemencic4.htm, October 30, 2014.

Kostiainen, Auvo. "The Forging of Finnish-American Communism, 1917–1924: A Study in Ethnic Radicalism." *Turun Yliopiston Julkaisuja, Annales Universitatis Turkuensis.* Series editor Sarja B, Humaniora. Turku, Finland: Turun Yliopisto, 1978.

———. "Tie Vapauteen." In *The Immigrant Labor Press in North America, 1840s–1970s: An Annotated Bibliography: Migrants from Northern Europe,* vol. 1, ed. Dirk Hoerder and Christane Harzig, 230–31. Westport, Conn.: Greenwood Press, 1987.

Kralj, Dejan. "Balkan Minds: Transnational Nationalism and the Transformation of South Slavic Identity in Chicago, 1890–1941." PhD dissertation, Loyola University of Chicago, 2012.

Lamppa, Marvin. *Minnesota's Iron Country: Rich Ore, Rich Lives.* Duluth: Lake Superior Port Cities, 2004.

Lankton, Larry. *Cradle to Grave: Life, Work, and Death at the Lake Superior Copper Mines.* New York: Oxford University Press, 1991.

LaVigne, David. "Rebel Girls: Women in the Mesabi Iron Range Strike of 1916." *Minnesota History* (fall 2016): 90–100. St. Paul: Minnesota Historical Society Press.

Mantel, Joseph, to W. H. Johnston. "Personal Correspondence," March 18, 1912. James Steel Papers, Minnesota Historical Society, St. Paul, Box 1.

Markkanen, Kristiina. "K. A. Suvanto: Political Satirist." *Finnish Americana: A Journal of Finnish American History and Culture* 9 (1992): 6–13, ed. Michael G. Karni. New Brighton, Minn.: Finnish Americana, 1992.

Marx, Karl. *A Contribution to the Critique of Political Economy.* Accessed at Marxists.org, http://www.marxists.org/archive/marx/works/1859/critique -pol-econom, March 16, 2014.

———. *Theses on Feuerbach 1845.* Trans. Cyril Smith. Marx-Engels Internet Archive. Accessed at http://www.marxists.org/archive/marx/works/1845 /theses/theses.htm, March 16, 2014.

McCloud, Scott. *Understanding Comics: The Invisible Art.* New York: Harper Paperbacks, 1994.

"The Mining Strike in Minnesota: From the Miners' Point of View." *The Outlook: A Weekly Newspaper* 113 (May–August 1916). New York: The Outlook Company, 1916.

Minnesota Historical Society. *MNOpedia.* "The Relocation of Hibbing, 1919–1921." Accessed at http://www.mnopedia.org/event/relocation-hibbing -1919–1921, October 14, 2014.

Mitchell, Pentecost, to R. R. Trezona. "Business Correspondence," August 11,

1909. James S. Steel Collection, Minnesota Historical Society, St. Paul, Box 1, Folder 140.

Mitchell, Pentecost, to T. F. Cole. "Business Communication," April 15, 1905, Correspondence and Miscellaneous Papers, 1901–29, Oliver Iron Mining Company Records, Minnesota Historical Society, St. Paul, Box 1, Folder "Community Morals, 1907–10, 1925."

Myllymäki, Victor. "Personal Correspondence." In *Bring Warm Clothes: Letters and Photos from Minnesota's Past*, compiled by Peg Meier. Minneapolis: Star and Tribune Company, 1981.

Nelson-Walkama, Daisy. "Oral History Interview," July 20, 2006. Conducted by Gary Kaunonen. Finnish American Historical Archive, Hancock, Michigan.

"Oberstar, James Louis." In *Biographical Directory of the United States Congress*. Accessed at http://bioguide.congress.gov/scripts/biodisplay.pl?index =O000006, December 1, 2015.

Oliver Iron Mining Company to W. J. Trescott. "Business Correspondence, Canisteo Mine, 1908–1918." James S. Steel Collection, Minnesota Historical Society, St. Paul, Box 2, Folder 6.

———. "Business Correspondences." Correspondence and Miscellaneous Papers, 1901–29, Oliver Iron Mining Company Records, Minnesota Historical Society, St. Paul, Box 1, Folder "Community Morals, 1907–10, 1925."

Ollila, Douglas J., Jr. "Ethnic Radicalism and the 1916 Mesabi Strike." *Range History* 3:4 (1978): 1–4, 10. Chisholm, Minn.: Iron Range Research Center.

———. "From Socialism to Industrial Unionism." In *The Finnish Experience in the Western Great Lakes Region*. Turku, Finland: Institute for Migration, 1975.

———. "A Time of Glory: Finnish-American Radical Industrial Unionism, 1914–1917." In *Publications of the Institute of History, University of Turku*, no. 9, ed. Vilho Niitemaa, 31–53. Vaasa, Finland: Vaasan Kirjapaino OY, 1977.

———. "The Work People's College: Immigrant Education for Adjustment and Solidarity." In *For the Common Good: Finnish Immigrants and the Radical Response to Industrial America*, ed. Michael G. Karni and Douglas J. Ollila Jr., 87–118. Superior, Wis.: Työmies Society, 1977.

Oppenheimer, Moses. "Direct Action and Sabotage." *New Review* 1:4 (1913).

"Ore Boat Renamed after Son of Iron Ore Miner." In *Minnesota Progressive Project*, May 25, 2011. Accessed at http://mnprogressiveproject.net/?p=9263, December 1, 2015.

Parker, Richard D. "Five Theses on Identity Politics," *Harvard Journal of Law and Public Policy* 29 (2005): 53–59. Accessed at http://www.law.harvard.edu /students/orgs/jlpp/Vol29_No1_Parker.pdf.

Passi, Michael M. "Finnish Immigrants and the Radical Response to Industrial America." In *For the Common Good: Finnish Immigrants and the Radical Response to Industrial America*, ed. Michael G. Karni and Douglas J. Ollila Jr., 9–22. Superior, Wis.: Työmies Society, 1977.

Penguilly, John, to T. F. Cole. "Materials Relating to the Oliver Iron Mining Company," January 20, 1903. Minnesota Historical Society Archives, St. Paul.

Pernicone, Nunzio. *Carlo Tresca: Portrait of a Rebel*. Oakland, Calif.: AK Press, 2010.

Phillips, Duncan. "The Long Memory," 2010. Accessed at http://thelongmemory .com/, October 2, 2016.

Phillips, U. Utah. "Unless You Are Free." On *Fellow Workers*. New York: Righteous Babe Records, 1999.

Pilacinski, Jeff. "'We've Been Robbed Long Enough. It's Time to Strike.': Remember the 1916 Strike on Minnesota's Iron Range," March 30, 2006. *Industrial Workers of the World: A Union for All Workers*, www.iww.org/pt/node/2556, accessed September 15, 2016.

Pinola, Rudolf. "Labor and Politics on the Iron Range of Northern Minnesota." PhD thesis, University of Wisconsin, 1957.

Pinta, Saku. "Interview on IWW History." Conducted by Gary Kaunonen. Thunder Bay, Ontario, Canada, May 1, 2014.

Ponikvar, Veda. "Oral History: Minnesota Radicalism Project." Interview conducted by Carl Ross. Minnesota Historical Society, St. Paul, May 13, 1988.

Pouget, Émile. *Sabotage*. Trans. and Intro. Arturo Giovannitti. Chicago: Charles H. Kerr and Company, 1913.

Power, Victor L. "Personal Journal Entries." Victor L. Power Papers, Minnesota Historical Society, St. Paul, Box 1.

———. "Scrapbook: Newspaper Clippings." Vol. 1. Victor L. Power Papers, Minnesota Historical Society, St. Paul, Box 1.

———. "Standard Diary, 1916." Vol. 2. Victor L. Power Papers, Minnesota Historical Society, St. Paul, Box 1.

Power, Victor L., to J. A. O. Preus. "Government Correspondence," August 1, 1915. Victor L. Power Papers, Minnesota Historical Society, St. Paul, Box 1.

Puotinen, Arthur. "Early Labor Organizations in the Copper Country." In *For the Common Good: Finnish Immigrants and the Radical Response to Industrial America*, ed. Michael G. Karni and Douglas J. Ollila, Jr., 119–66. Superior, Wis.: Työmies Society, 1977.

Rachleff, Peter. "Turning Points in the Labor Movement: Three Key Conflicts." In *Minnesota in a Century of Change: The State and Its People since 1900*, ed. Clifford E. Clark Jr., 195–222. St. Paul: Minnesota Historical Society Press, 1989.

Rein, Wm. *Nuoriso, Oppi ja Tyo (Youth, Learning and Labor)*. Duluth: Workers Socialist Publishing Company, 1929.

Richard H. Hudelson Labor History Collection 1880–2006. Northeast Minnesota Historical Center Collections, Archives and Special Collections, Kathryn A. Martin Library, University of Minnesota–Duluth.

Roberts, Kate. "Socialist Opera House, Virginia." In *MNOpedia*. Accessed at http://www.mnopedia.org/structure/socialist-opera-house-virginia, December 1, 2014.

Roe, James A. "Virginia, Minnesota's Socialist Opera: Showplace of Iron Range Radicalism." *Finnish Americana: A Journal of Finnish American History and Culture* 9 (1992): 36–43. Ed. Michael Karni. New Brighton, Minn.: Finnish Americana.

Ronning, Gerald. "Jack Pine Savages: Discourses of Conquest in the 1916 Mesabi Iron Range Strike." *Labor History* 44:3 (2003): 359–82. New York: Routledge.

Sale, Kirkpatrick. *Rebels against the Future: The Luddites and Their War on the Industrial Revolution.* Cambridge, Mass.: Perseus Publishing, 1996.

Salerno, Salvatore. *Red November, Black November: Culture and Community in the Industrial Workers of the World.* Albany: State University of New York Press, 1989.

Santayana, George. *The Life of Reason: Or the Phases of Human Progress.* "Introduction and Reason in Common Sense, Critical Edition." Ed. Marianne S. Wokeck and Martin A. Coleman. Cambridge: MIT Press, 2011.

Schlereth, Thomas J. *Cultural History and Material Culture: Everyday Life, Landscapes, Museums.* Ann Arbor: UMI Research Press, 1990.

———. "Social History Scholarship and Material Culture Research." In *Material Culture: A Research Guide,* 155–96. Lawrence: University Press of Kansas, 1985.

Selzer, Jack. "Rhetorical Analysis: Understanding How Texts Persuade Readers." In *What Writing Does and How It Does It: An Introduction to Analyzing Texts and Textual Practices,* ed. Charles Bazerman and Paul Pryor, 279–307. London: Routledge, 2003.

Smith, Walker C. *Sabotage: Its History, Philosophy, and Function.* Chicago: I.W.W. Publishing Bureau, n.d.

Stanoyevich, M. S. "The Jugoslavs." In *The Jugoslavs in the United States of America.* New York: International Press, 1921.

State of Minnesota, Department of Labor and Industries. *Fifteenth Biennial Report.* St. Paul: State Printing Office, 1916.

Stead, Arnold. "Introduction." In *Always on Strike: Frank Little and the Western Wobblies.* Chicago: Haymarket Books, 2014.

Stipanovich, Joseph. "In Unity Is Strength: Immigrant Workers and Immigrant Intellectuals in Progressive America: A History of the South Slav Social Democratic Movement, 1900–1918." PhD dissertation, University of Minnesota, 1978.

Streeby, Shelley. *Radical Sensations: World Movements, Violence, and Visual Culture.* Durham, N.C.: Duke University Press, 2013.

Sturken, Marita, and Lisa Cartwright. *Practices of Looking: An Introduction to Visual Culture.* 2d ed. New York: Oxford University Press, 2009.

Superintendent of Eveleth Schools to Thos. F. Cole. "Personal Correspondence,"

January 30, 1908. Oliver Iron Mining Company Papers, Correspondence and Miscellaneous Papers, 1901–29, Minnesota Historical Society, St. Paul, Box 1, Folder "Community Morals, 1907–10, 1925."

Swanson, Samuel. "Organizing the Steel Workers Union on the Range." Speech at the Virginia (Minnesota) Teachers' Institute, September 14, 1968. Samuel Swanson Collection, Minnesota Historical Society, St. Paul.

———. "Sam Swanson Radio Message on Labor Movement in Ely, Minnesota, and Iron Range," n.d. Samuel Swanson Collection, Minnesota Historical Society, St. Paul, Folder P187.

Tate, Ryan Driskell, "Flash in the Pan: Gender and Cross-Class Cooperation in the 1916 Iron Range Strike." Conference Paper, *Retrospection and Respect: The 1913–14 Mining/Labor Strike Symposium of 2014*, Michigan Technological University. Accessed at http://digitalcommons.mtu.edu/copperstrikesymposium /Schedule/Saturday/13/, August 8, 2016.

Theado, C. Kendall. "Narrating a Nation: Second Wave Immigration, Literacy, and the Framing of the American Identity." *JAC: A Journal of Rhetoric, Culture, and Politics* 33:1–2 (2013): 11–39.

Thompson, E. P. *The Essential E. P. Thompson.* Ed. Dorothy Thompson. New York: New Press, 2001.

———. *The Making of the English Working Class.* New York: Vintage Books, 1966.

———. *The Poverty of Theory and Other Essays.* 1st ed. New York: Monthly Review Press, 1978.

Thompson, Fred W., and Patrick Murfin. *The I.W.W.: Its First Seventy Years, 1905–1975.* Chicago: Industrial Workers of the World, 1976.

Torma, Fred. "Oral History Interview." Oral History Collection, Finnish American Historical Archive, Hancock, Michigan.

Tracy, William E. "William E. Tracy's Report." In *Official Proceedings of the Fifteenth Convention of the Western Federation of Miners.* Denver, Colo.: W. H. Kistler Stationery, 1909.

Trautmann, William E. *Why Strikes Are Lost and How to Win.* New Castle, Pa.: I.W.W. Publishing Bureau, 1912. Accessed at http://www.iww.org/nl/history /library/Trautmann/loststrikes, May 1, 2014.

Trezona, Charles, to P. F. Chamberlain. "Business Correspondence," July 24, 1907. Materials Relating to the Oliver Iron Mining Company, Minnesota Historical Society Archives, St. Paul.

Trezona, Charles, to Thomas F. Cole. "Business Correspondence," July 24, 1907. Oliver Mining Company Collection, Minnesota Historical Society, St. Paul.

Trezona, R. R., to Pentecost Mitchell. "Business Correspondence," August 11, 1909. James S. Steel Collection, Minnesota Historical Society, St. Paul, Box 1, Folder 140.

United Food and Commercial Workers Union 324. "Frank Little: A Murder in Butte." Accessed at https://ufcw324.org/frank-little-a-murder-in-butte/, November 5, 2016.

United Nations. "The Universal Declaration of Human Rights." In *Human Rights*. Accessed at http://www.un.org/en/rights/, December 12, 2014.

United Steel Workers. "Our History." In *Our Union*, accessed at http://www.usw.org/union/history, December 8, 2014.

Unknown Songwriter. "The Mysteries of a Hobo's Life." In *I.W.W. Songs to Fan the Flames of Discontent*, Joe Hill Memorial Edition. Cleveland, Ohio: I.W.W. Publishing Bureau, n.d.

"U.S. Senator for Minnesota Amy Klobuchar: Biography." Accessed at https://web.archive.org/web/20070221013430/http://klobuchar.senate.gov/biography.cfm, archived from the original on February 21, 2007, accessed December 1, 2015.

Van Cleef, Eugene. "The Finn in America." *Geographical Review* 6:3 (September 1918). Available at http://www.jstor.org, accessed February 17, 2003.

Walker, David A. *Iron Frontier: The Discovery and Early Development of Minnesota's Three Ranges*. St. Paul: Minnesota Historical Society Press, 1979.

Welter, Christopher. "IWW Surveillance Photos: Historical Note." Industrial Workers of the World Photographic Collection, Iron Range Research Center, Chisholm, Minnesota.

Wenzell, Henry Burleigh. *Cases Argued and Determined in the Supreme Court of Minnesota*. Minnesota Reports, vol. 23. St. Paul: Lawyers Co-operative Publishing Co., 1913.

West, George P. "The Mesaba Strike." *International Socialist Review* 17 (1916). Chicago: Charles H. Kerr Publishing Co.

Western Federation of Miners. *Official Proceedings of the Sixteenth Annual Convention, Western Federation of Miners, July 13 to July 29, 1908*. Denver: W. H. Kistler Stationary Company, 1908.

Winner, Langdon. "Luddism as Epistemology." In *Philosophy of Technology: The Technological Condition, An Anthology*, ed. Robert C. Scharff and Val Dusek. Malden, Mass.: Blackwell Publishing, 2003.

Zinn, Howard. *A People's History of the United States: 1492 to Present*. New York: Harper Perennial Modern Classics, 2005.

Zinn, Howard, and Donald Macedo. *Howard Zinn on Democratic Education*. 1st ed. Boulder, Colo.: Paradigm Publishers, 2008.

INDEX

Alar, John, 170–74, 175
American Federation of Labor (AFL), 2, 9, 54, 63, 77, 114, 155, 157, 195–96, 214, 228n9
Aurora, Minnesota, ix, 1, 23, 113, 136, 139, 158, 205

Bemidji, Minnesota, 11, 43; World War I–era repression in, 206–9. *See also* deportations
Biwabik, Minnesota, 17, 23, 27, 136, 158; Mosonovich boarding house melee, 181–83
Boylan, Michael, 165–66
Brunt Mine lawsuit (1913), 48–51
Burnquist, Joseph A. A., 3, 11, 12, 21, 158, 170, 180; law and order proclamation, 176–79; meeting with mining company officials, 175; role in IWW organizer deportations, 182, 187–88

company (mining) police, 2, 34, 56, 61, 145, 147, 153–54, 156, 159, 161–62, 166, 171
Congress of Industrial Organizations (CIO), 214–15
criminal syndicalist legislation, 13, 207–10, 234n5
Cuyuna Iron Range: description of,

18–19, 20, 47, 122, 139; during 1916 strike, 200, 203, 215

Department of Labor: investigation into 1916 strike, 198–200
deportations: Bemidji, 208–9; Bisbee, 11–12; Frank Little from Superior, 125–26; organizers from 1916 strike, 186–89; of strike leaders in Mesabi Range, 162–64
Duluth, Minnesota, 3, 9, 114, 123–124, 129, 139–40, 148, 157, 162, 169, 176, 178, 199, 207, 208–9, 213, 215; Finnish immigrant radical press in, 85–86; and Iron Range, 20–23, 33, 62; IWW organizer trials in, 182–84, 188, 189, 190, 192, 197; in opposition to Hibbing, 66–67; Work People's College, 79–81
Dunning, Jess, 208–9

Ely, Minnesota, 17, 32, 37, 46, 52, 55, 135, 216; dwindling Western Federation of Miners' membership, 112–13; early Steel Workers Organizing Committee union, 215
Embarrass, Minnesota, ix–xii, 228n14
Espionage and Sedition Acts, 210
Ettor, Joseph, 146, 197–98, 201
Eveleth, Minnesota, 17, 191, 229n31;

early strikes in, 39, 56, 60, 62; early labor organizing in, 111, 113; 1916 strike activity in, 136, 145, 157, 158, 165; social description of city, 22–25; social problems, 29–36

Fayal Location. *See* Eveleth, Minnesota
Finnish immigrants, ix, xi; during early strikes, 12, 55–56, 59, 110, 115, 117, 122–25; Finn Halls, 91–99, 100, 102, 114, 133, 140, 146, 158, 186, 215; Finnish Socialist Federation, 77, 81, 229n23; immigrant population, 36–38, 76–77, 80–81, 131, 142, 148, 213, 228n14; IWW affiliation, 69, 71–73, 76–79, 83–88, 99, 101–2, 103, 114; IWW Defense Fund participation, 212–13; Lapatossu cartoon character, 71–73; during 1907 strike, 63–64, 111–13, 126–27; during 1916 strike, 133–35, 139, 140, 142–43, 158, 172; relationship with other ethnicities, 2, 6, 9, 10, 78, 94–95, 102, 109, 121; socialism in immigrant population, 9, 24–25, 32, 60–61, 77–78, 81–82, 229n23
Flynn, Elizabeth Gurley, 146, 197–98, 199, 207; arrives on Mesabi during 1916 strike, 191–95; defense fund committee member, 211–13; split with IWW, 201–2

Gemmell, Minnesota, 207
Greenway, John C., 26–27, 48, 51–52, 54
gun thugs. *See* company (mining) police

Hagerty, "Father" Thomas J., 74–76
Haywood, William D., 83, 138, 139, 191, 199, 206, 211; fallout over IWW organizer trials, 201–2; introduction to striking population in 1916, 142–44

Hibbing, Minnesota, 8, 23, 27, 33, 55; activity during 1916 strike, 132, 133, 136, 140, 145, 153–55, 179, 185–86; birthplace of Rudy Perpich, 215; early labor organizing in, 56, 60, 63, 77, 94, 111, 113–14; home of Victor Power, 2, 11, 65–67, 159–60, 165, 176, 196–98; industrial site, 18, 25, 44; 1913 mayoral election, 65–66
history as a human right, 3–5, 13, 54, 170, 178, 217

Industrial Workers of the World (IWW), ix, 1, 8, 9; Agricultural Workers Organization, 42–43, 139, 206; contrast with other unions and organizations, 2, 11, 12, 57, 64–65, 67–68, 77–78, 105, 114, 159–60, 195–99; cultural apparatus, 69–73, 99–103, 106–7, 150–52; deportation of members, 3, 11–12, 21, 125–26, 162–64, 170, 183–89, 207–9; falters during 1916 strike, 199–202; history, 57–58, 70, 73–76, 83, 86, 126–27; ideology, 9, 15, 42, 58–59, 69, 79–80, 87–91, 108–9, 110; Metal Mineworkers Industrial Union No. 490, 140, 142, 206; Metal Mineworkers Industrial Union No. 800, 211, 212; mining company against, 153–59, 160–67, 174–78; during 1916 strike, 7, 16, 129–30, 134–36, 137–52, 157–59, 172–74, 180–82, 194; 1913 dockworkers strike organizers, 122–26; repression of, 12–13, 207–12; on trial in 1916, 189–92
International Falls, Minnesota, 206–7
Ireland, James D., 137, 165–66, 180, 200, 202; description of first days of strike, 156–58; and Governor Burnquist, 1916 strike, 174–79; planned use of violence by com-

panies, 160–64; response to Alar's death, 171–73

Italian immigrants, 10; involved in industrial accident, 48; IWW Defense Fund participation, 201–2; leadership during strikes, 9, 59, 111, 117, 138, 184–89, 198; 1907 strike participation, 64, 111, 117; 1913–14 Michigan Copper Strike, 115–16; 1916 strike participation, 134–36, 139, 179–80, 186, 192; population, 37, 51, 112, 113, 118, 130–32; relationship with other ethnicities, 6, 9, 103, 109, 126–28

Little, Frank, 12, 124–25, 139, 186–88, 191

logging, x; as landscape, 70; 1917 Timber Beasts strike, 12, 206–7; Virginia and Rainy Lake Lumber Company and Mill, 206; work in, 41, 44, 116

M. A. Hanna & Co., 48, 90, 156, 161–62, 164, 166, 177, 179, 180

Meining, John, 158, 162, 171, 175–76, 181, 187–88, 205, 213

Mesabi Iron Range, ix; description of, 17–18, 19; industrial area, 10, 21, 23, 37, 41–45, 46, 78, 112, 225n9; 1907 strike, 9, 32, 39, 51, 57–63, 90, 94–95, 103, 111, 115, 117, 122; 1916 strike, 138–41, 143, 148, 156–59, 162, 164, 174–75, 183–84, 186, 191–94, 200, 203; social area, 28, 29–31, 49, 55–56, 77, 98, 113, 215, 224n21

Minot, North Dakota, 42–43

Mosonovich family, 181–84, 185, 187–89, 201–2, 232n21, 233n33

Mountain Iron, Minnesota, 23, 25, 27

North Hibbing, Minnesota. See Hibbing, Minnesota

Oliver Iron Mining Company (OIMC), 1–2, 5, 6, 8, 23, 27, 44, 50, 51; blacklists, 116–17; control of workers, 30–36; disputes with Victor Power, 67, 197–98; during early strikes, 60–63, 78, 111; fear of organized labor, 55; importation of scabs in 1907, 117–18; labor management, 56–57, 90, 129, 131, 137, 228n14; during 1916 strike, 153–54, 156–57, 160–64, 170–73, 177, 178; working conditions, 50–54

Petriella, Teofilo, 9, 59–60, 63, 78, 111, 117

Ponikvar, Veda, 36, 105, 126–27, 229n31

Power, Victor, 2, 11, 65–68, 159–60, 165–66, 176–77, 195–99

proletarian literacy programs, 79–83

sabotage, 89–91

Scarlett, Sam, 139, 158, 163, 172, 181, 183–84, 187–88, 191

Slavic immigrants, 2, 3; disgust with mining companies, 117, 131–32; ethnic organizations, 119–21; ethnic press, 121; heritage in contemporary Minnesota politics, 215–16; immigrant history, 118–19, 229n23, 229n29; during 1916 strike, 133–34, 145, 152; relationship with other ethnicities, 9–10, 103, 122, 126–27, 135; strikebreakers, 6, 63, 109, 111, 114; as union members, 113–14, 115, 127–28, 149, 215

social halls, 8, 10, 60, 63, 69, 94, 99, 100, 102, 103, 114, 134, 199; centers during strikes, 140, 146, 158, 159, 163, 186; Finn, 124, 208; Hibbing Workers', 94, 98–99, 114, 159, 186; Italian, 115–16; IWW, 208; Nashwauk Socialist Finn, 92–93, 94, 97; Palace Finn, 93–94; Socialist

Opera House, 94–98, 133, 140–42, 146, 151–52, 163, 171–72, 186, 206, 216–17; as spaces of cultural discontent, 91–99, 215; Stevenson Location Temperance, 38, 92; Urania, 191; Woodmen, 124; workers', 215, 228n14

social ills, mining communities: alcohol consumption, 30–36, 38, 92; crime listings, 30–31; gambling, 29–30; prostitution, 29–30, 36, 38

socialist politics, 38, 40, 59–60, 63, 76, 79, 133, 151; in Finnish immigrant population, 24–25, 32, 37–38, 60, 77–78, 81–85, 92–98, 111, 114, 172, 186; Socialist Party of America, 74, 77, 98, 120; in South Slavic immigrant population, 119–22, 152, 229n29; in World War I, 210–12

Soudan, Minnesota, 17, 55, 61

Steel Trust. *See* M. A. Hanna & Co.; Oliver Iron Mining Company

Steel Workers Organizing Committee (SWOC), 214

St. James Mine: start of 1916 strike, 1, 139

strike: 1904 Wildcat, 56; 1905 Western Federation of Miners, 56; 1906 Rockland, 110; 1907 Mesabi, 2, 9, 31–32, 33, 35, 39, 51, 57, 59–64, 77–78, 90, 94–95, 103, 111–13, 114, 115, 116–17, 122, 126, 127, 131, 140, 192; 1913 Cuyuna, 122; 1913 Duluth–Superior dockworkers, 12, 122–26; 1913–14 Michigan Copper, 2, 83, 94–95, 115–16, 122, 140, 147; 1917 Timber, 12–13, 206–7

Superior, Wisconsin, 12, 20–21, 122–25, 157, 199

Torma, Fred, 37–38, 92–93

Tower, Minnesota, 17, 46, 61

Tracy, William E., 111–15, 136

Tresca, Carlo, 134, 138, 172, 174, 179; deportation, 184–89; leaves IWW, 201–2, 233n55; Mosonovich boardinghouse melee and, 181, 183; trial and incarceration, 189–92, 193, 197, 232n33

Two Harbors, Minnesota, 20, 123, 124, 157

United Mine Workers of America (UMWA), 2, 195, 229

United States Steel Corporation. *See* Oliver Iron Mining Company

United Steelworkers of America (USW), 214, 216

Vermilion Iron Range, ix, 20, 46, 52, 78, 203; description of, 17; early strike on, 54–55; 1916 strike on, 139, 200–201; prevent labor organizing on, 60–61

vigilante violence, 2, 3, 11–12, 160–63, 186, 206–9

Virginia, Minnesota, ix, 5, 17, 18, 28, 99; John Alar shooting in, 170–74; contemporary Steelworkers Local, 216; and IWW organizer deportations, 183–84, 186–87; location of Socialist Opera House, 94, 95–96, 217; during 1907 strike, 60, 63, 111; during 1916 strike, 133, 136, 139, 140, 143, 151–52, 158, 163, 164, 179, 200–201; and 1917 Timber Beasts strike, 206–7

Virginia Ore Mining Company. *See* M. A. Hanna & Co.

Vorse, Mary Heaton, 192–93

Western Federation of Miners (WFM), 2; administration of 1907 strike, 57–60, 63–64, 111, 117, 192; history of union, 56, 94, 110–11, 140; 1908 organizer's report, 111–14, 136;

1913–14 Michigan Copper Strike administration, 115–16, 122; as part of IWW, 75, 77–78; split with IWW, 114–15, 228n9, 229n29

Wobblies. *See* Industrial Workers of the World

working conditions in mines, 1, 38, 39, 58, 64, 110, 149, 170; 8-hour work day, 52–53; gopher-holer deaths, 48; Milford Mine disaster, 47–48; pit mine, 17–19, 25, 33, 44–46, 48; planned job scarcity, 51; promotions, 51–52; underground, 46–48; Work People's College, 9, 79–85, 98–99, 114, 213

World War I, 3, 13, 16, 85, 156, 166, 175, 180, 186, 202, 205, 208, 210–11

GARY KAUNONEN is an independent labor, immigration, social, and cultural historian and a documentary filmmaker in International Falls, Minnesota. He is author of *Finns in Michigan, Challenge Accepted: A Finnish Immigrant Response to Industrial America in Michigan's Copper Country,* and (with coauthor Aaron Goings) *Community in Conflict: A Working-Class History of the 1913–14 Michigan Copper Strike and the Italian Hall Tragedy.* His documentary *Northern Minnesota's Labor Wars* examines the 1916 and 1917 strikes and their significance to World War I–era political deportations and repression.